KILLER
Princesses

oni
PRESS

KILLER
Princesses

Written by

Gail Simone

Illustrated by

Lea Hernandez

Cover colors by

Laura Martin

Introduction by

Mark Waid

Book design by

Keith Wood

Edited by

James Lucas Jones

Published by

Oni Press, Inc.

Joe Nozemack, publisher

Randal C. Jarrell, Managing Editor

This collects issues 1-3 of the miniseries

KILLER
Princesses

ONI PRESS, INC.
6336 SE Milwaukie Avenue, PMB 30
Portland, OR 97202
USA

www.onipress.com

First edition: November 2004
ISBN 1-929998-31-7

1 3 5 7 9 10 8 6 4 2
PRINTED IN CANADA.

Introduction

"YOU EAT WITH THAT MOUTH?"

GAIL SIMONE HAD E-MAILED ME THE SCRIPT FOR *KILLER PRINCESSES* #1. OFTEN, SHE'LL SEND ME A SCRIPT BEFORE IT GOES TO AN ARTIST IN HOPES I'LL LOOK IT OVER WITH ONLY MINOR DISDAIN AND DRYLY CORRECT HER IN MANNERS OF CRAFT, WHICH AT THIS POINT IN GAIL'S CAREER IS KIND OF LIKE MR. GOODWRENCH GETTING INEXPLICABLY NERVOUS OVER AN OIL CHANGE. IN OTHER WORDS, IT'S CUTE AND ONLY VAGUELY WEARYING TO LISTEN TO GAIL GO ALL WACK-JOB INSECURE OVER HER MANUSCRIPTS GIVEN THAT, EVEN IN FIRST-DRAFT FORM, THEY'RE BETTER THAN 90% OF THE ACTUAL PUBLISHED COMICS I READ THESE DAYS AND I ONLY WISH I'D BEEN THAT GOOD BACK WHEN I WAS THAT NEW.

(TO BE FAIR, IT'S NOT LIKE I FEEL TERRIBLY PUT-UPON BY HER WHIMPERING FOR VALIDATION. IN TURN, I'LL OFTEN SEND HER MY SCRIPTS BEFORE THEY GO TO AN ARTIST IN HOPES SHE'LL TELL ME WHAT AN UNPARALLELED, IMPROPERLY REWARDED GENIUS I AM. THAT'S THE KIND OF DEPTH AND HONESTY OUR FRIENDSHIP IS BASED UPON. I'M A LUCKY MAN.)

AT ANY RATE, I DISTINCTLY REMEMBER (AFTER HAVING READ UP TO THAT POINT ONLY HER SIMPSONS AND MARVEL COMICS SCRIPTS) HOW SURPRISED I WAS BY *KILLER PRINCESSES*--NOT ONLY BECAUSE IT WAS EXTRA-FUNNY BUT BECAUSE IT WAS...IT...I...WELL, YOU'LL FIND A REFERENCE TO CHEWBACCA EARLY ON THAT STILL MAKES ME BLUSH AND WONDER HOW SOMEONE SO SWEET, WHOLESOME AND SOFT-SPOKEN AS SIMONE COULD HAVE CHARACTERS TALKING ABOUT...THAT. KIND. OF STUFF. I ADMIRE GAIL FOR HAVING VERY HEALTHY, VERY MATURE ATTITUDE WHEN IT COMES TO CASUALLY DISCUSSING AND WRITING ABOUT SEX AND BODILY FUNCTIONS. I ADMIRE IT BECAUSE I PERSONALLY FIND IT TO BE AN ALIEN CONCEPT. I PRETEND TO BE A GROWN SOPHISTICATE, BUT TRUTH IS I CAN'T EVEN USE THE WORD "FART" IN CONVERSATION WITHOUT MUTTERING AND CRINGING. IN FACT, I

CRINGED JUST TYPING IT. IMAGINE MY DAWNING HORROR AS I READ ALL
THE KP SCRIPTS AND GRADUALLY DISCOVERED THAT ONE OF MY BEST
FRIENDS--THIS VIRTUOUS, INNOCENT, CLEAN-LIVING, COOKIE-BAKING WIFE,
MOTHER, AND PART-TIME HAIRDRESSER--WAS PERFECTLY CAPABLE OF
WRITING AND EAGER TO WRITE FOR AN AUDIENCE WHOSE SOULS WERE
BLACKER THAN THE SOOT COATING THE ABBATOIRS OF HELL.

"YOU SHOULD GO TO ONI PRESS WITH THIS," I SAID.

SHE WAS AHEAD OF ME.

MORE THAN THAT, SHE'D ALSO ALREADY FOUND A KINDRED SPIRIT IN
ARTIST LEA HERNANDEZ, WHO WAS PERFECTLY AND UNIQUELY SUITED TO
BRINGING THE PRINCESSES TO LIFE ON THE PRINTED PAGE. LEA'S WORK IS
AS BRIGHT AND EXPRESSIVE AS SHE HERSELF IS, AND IT'S A TERRIFIC
COMPLEMENT TO GAIL'S SURPRISINGLY DARK WIT.

I'M GOING ON TOO MUCH. *KILLER PRINCESSES* ISN'T REALLY ALL ABOUT
PERSONAL GROOMING JOKES. IF IT WERE, IT WOULD STILL BE FUNNY, YES,
BUT GAIL AND LEA AREN'T SOPHOMORES AT SEXY COMEDY. (UNLIKE, SAY,
ME.) THERE'S NO POINT IN BEING "EDGY" UNLESS YOU ACTUALLY HAVE, OH,
A STORY TO TELL--AND THEIRS IS GREAT. THE VERY CONCEPT OF THE SERIES
IS WICKEDLY CLEVER, THE PRINCESSES SPORT INDIVIDUAL AND COMPELLING
VOICES AND (AGAIN, THANKS TO LEA) LOOKS, AND THE HIGH ADVENTURE
THEY GET WRAPPED UP IN IS UNEXPECTEDLY POIGNANT. AND HAS GUNS. IT'S
POIGNANT WITH GUNS. THIS IS A MUCH MORE DIFFICULT ACHIEVEMENT THAN
I'M MAKING IT SOUND. BUT IT'S REALLY, REALLY GOOD. YOU'LL SEE. *KILLER
PRINCESSES* IS A TRUE GEM OF A COMIC.

BUT DON'T LET YOUR MOM SEE YOU READING IT, OR SHE'LL SEND YOU
TO YOUR ROOM.

Mark Waid

PURE OF SOUL
OCTOBER 2003

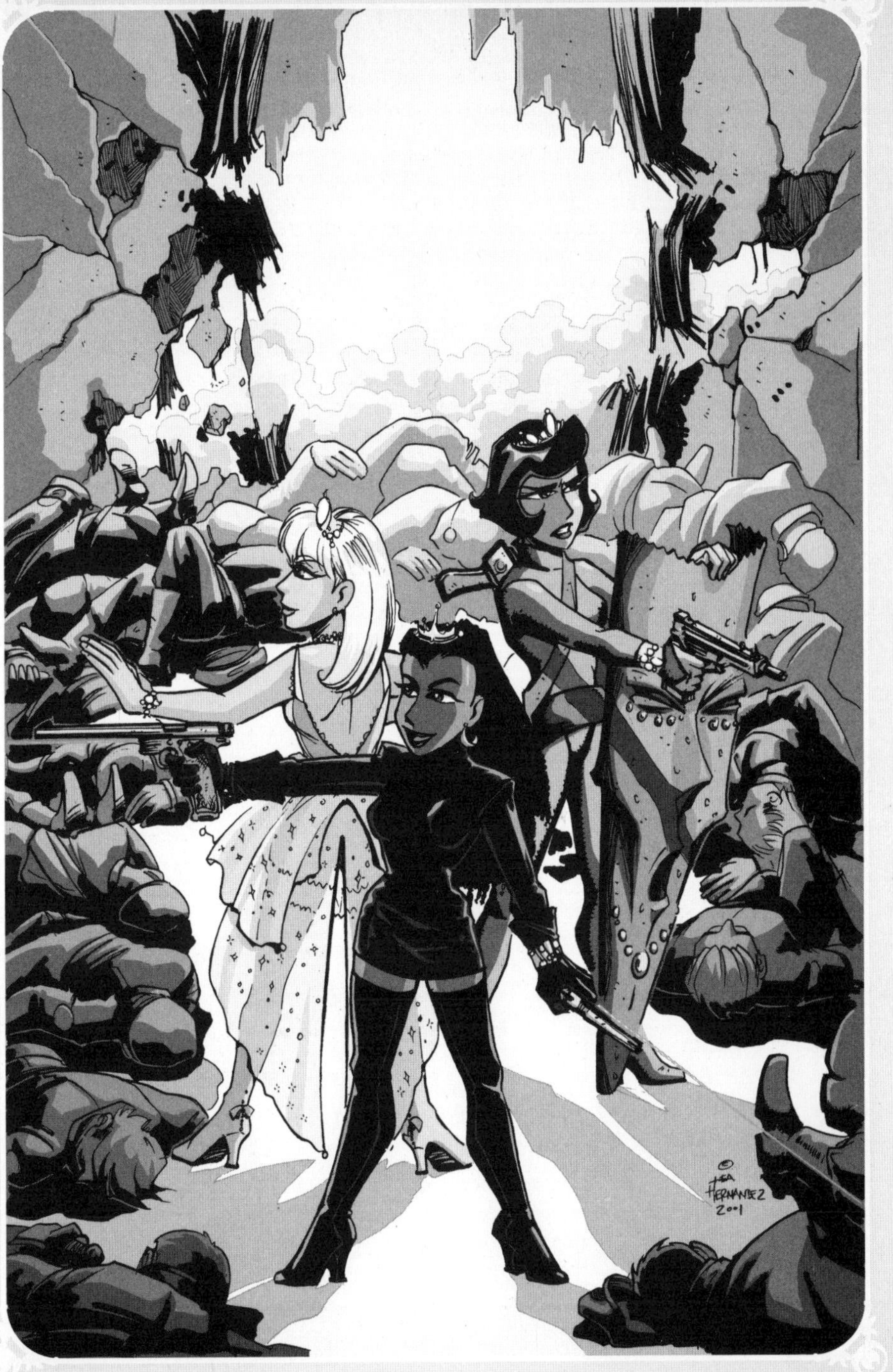
© LEA HERNANDEZ 2001

Chapter 1

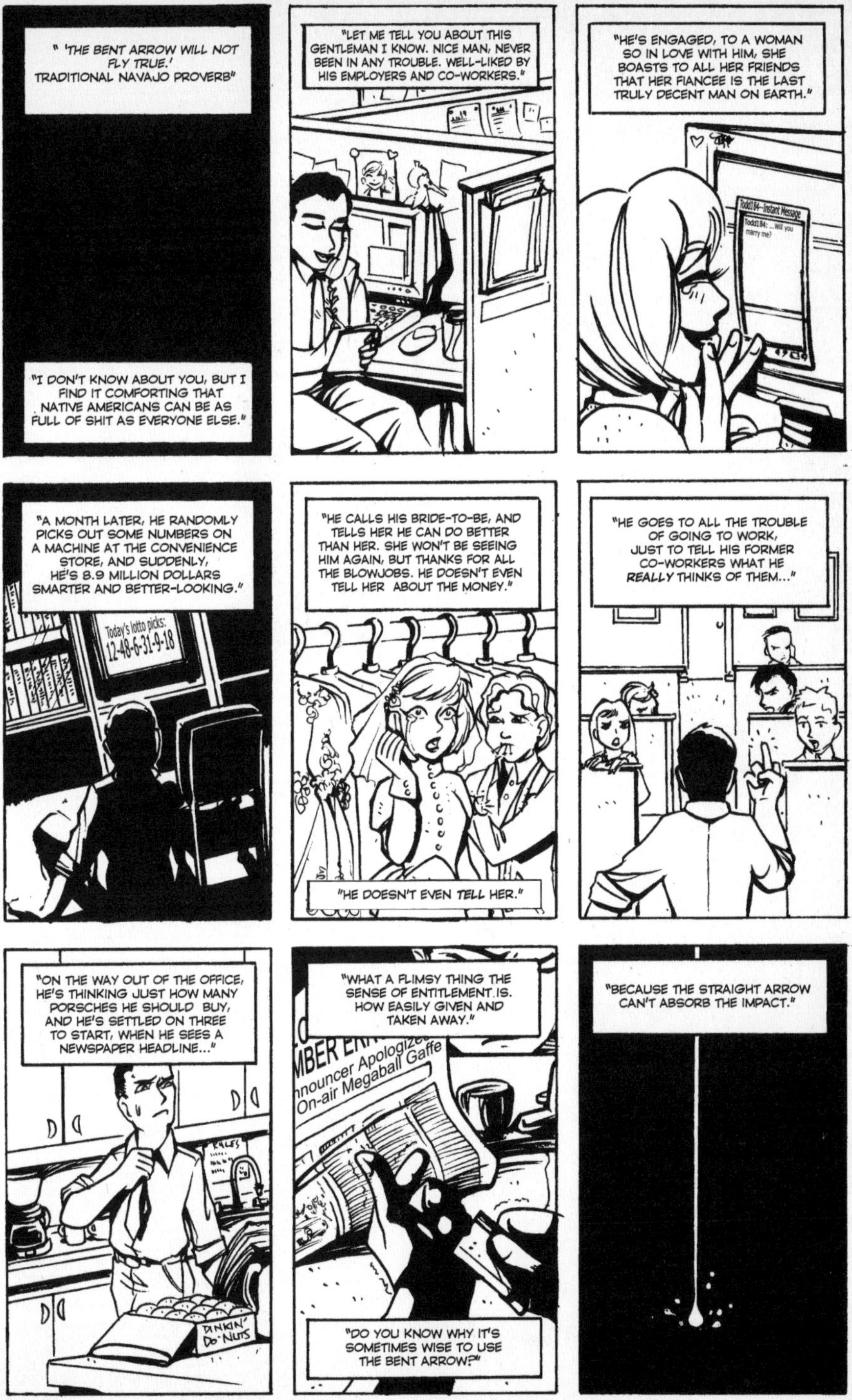
" 'THE BENT ARROW WILL NOT FLY TRUE.' TRADITIONAL NAVAJO PROVERB"
"I DON'T KNOW ABOUT YOU, BUT I FIND IT COMFORTING THAT NATIVE AMERICANS CAN BE AS FULL OF SHIT AS EVERYONE ELSE."
"LET ME TELL YOU ABOUT THIS GENTLEMAN I KNOW. NICE MAN, NEVER BEEN IN ANY TROUBLE. WELL-LIKED BY HIS EMPLOYERS AND CO-WORKERS."
"HE'S ENGAGED, TO A WOMAN SO IN LOVE WITH HIM, SHE BOASTS TO ALL HER FRIENDS THAT HER FIANCEE IS THE LAST TRULY DECENT MAN ON EARTH."
Todd184--Instant Message
Todd184: ...Will you marry me?
"A MONTH LATER, HE RANDOMLY PICKS OUT SOME NUMBERS ON A MACHINE AT THE CONVENIENCE STORE, AND SUDDENLY, HE'S 8.9 MILLION DOLLARS SMARTER AND BETTER-LOOKING."
Today's lotto picks:
12-48-6-31-9-18
"HE CALLS HIS BRIDE-TO-BE, AND TELLS HER HE CAN DO BETTER THAN HER. SHE WON'T BE SEEING HIM AGAIN, BUT THANKS FOR ALL THE BLOWJOBS. HE DOESN'T EVEN TELL HER ABOUT THE MONEY."
"HE DOESN'T EVEN TELL HER."
"HE GOES TO ALL THE TROUBLE OF GOING TO WORK, JUST TO TELL HIS FORMER CO-WORKERS WHAT HE REALLY THINKS OF THEM..."
"ON THE WAY OUT OF THE OFFICE, HE'S THINKING JUST HOW MANY PORSCHES HE SHOULD BUY, AND HE'S SETTLED ON THREE TO START, WHEN HE SEES A NEWSPAPER HEADLINE..."
DINKIN' DO-NUTS
"WHAT A FLIMSY THING THE SENSE OF ENTITLEMENT IS. HOW EASILY GIVEN AND TAKEN AWAY."
MBER ERR
nnouncer Apologizes
On-air Megaball Gaffe
"DO YOU KNOW WHY IT'S SOMETIMES WISE TO USE THE BENT ARROW?"
"BECAUSE THE STRAIGHT ARROW CAN'T ABSORB THE IMPACT."

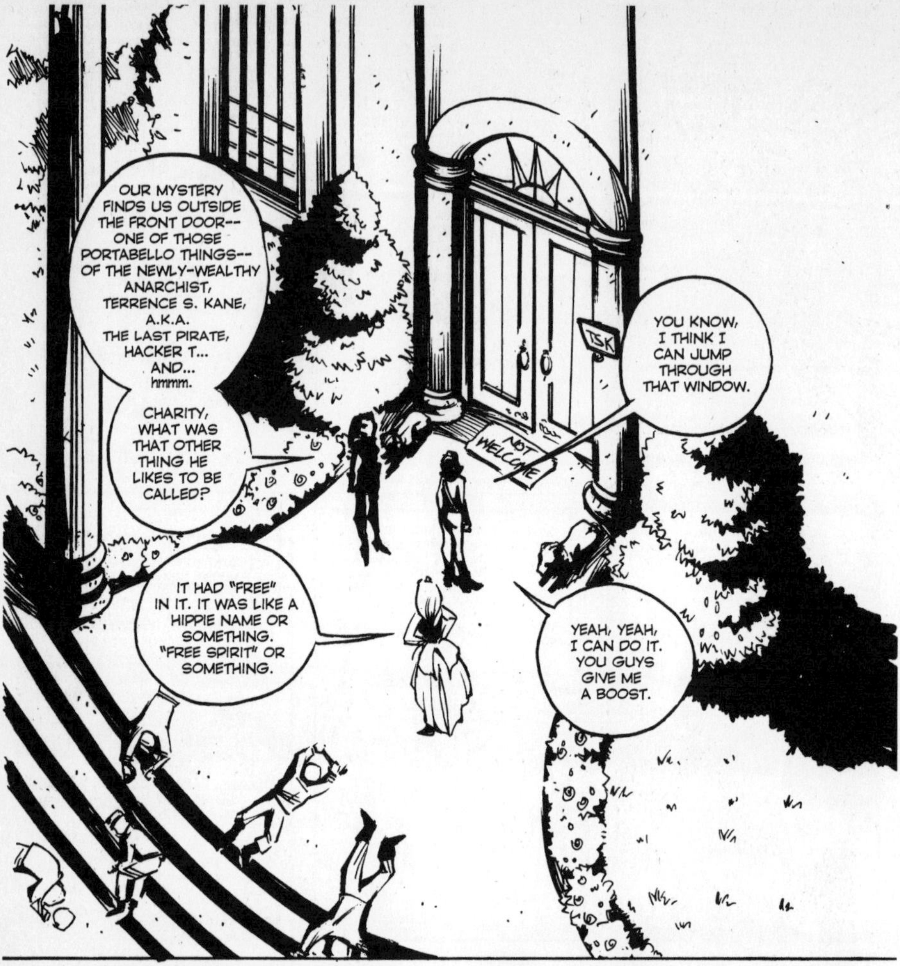
OUR MYSTERY FINDS US OUTSIDE THE FRONT DOOR-- ONE OF THOSE PORTABELLO THINGS-- OF THE NEWLY-WEALTHY ANARCHIST, TERRENCE S. KANE, A.K.A. THE LAST PIRATE, HACKER T... AND... hmmm.
CHARITY, WHAT WAS THAT OTHER THING HE LIKES TO BE CALLED?
TSK
NOT WELCOME
YOU KNOW, I THINK I CAN JUMP THROUGH THAT WINDOW.
IT HAD "FREE" IN IT. IT WAS LIKE A HIPPIE NAME OR SOMETHING. "FREE SPIRIT" OR SOMETHING.
YEAH, YEAH, I CAN DO IT. YOU GUYS GIVE ME A BOOST.

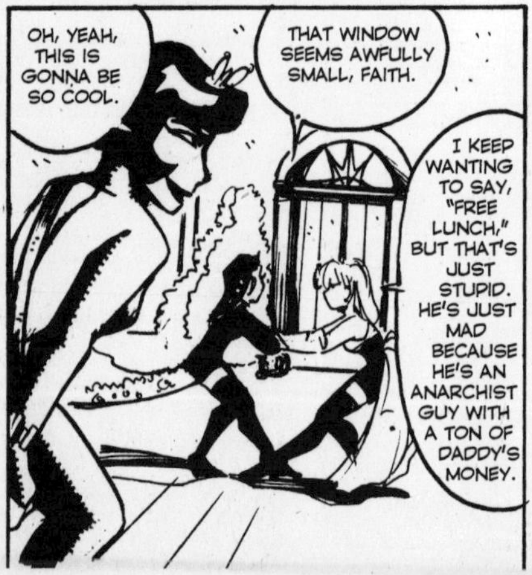
OH, YEAH, THIS IS GONNA BE SO COOL.
THAT WINDOW SEEMS AWFULLY SMALL, FAITH.
I KEEP WANTING TO SAY, "FREE LUNCH," BUT THAT'S JUST STUPID. HE'S JUST MAD BECAUSE HE'S AN ANARCHIST GUY WITH A TON OF DADDY'S MONEY.

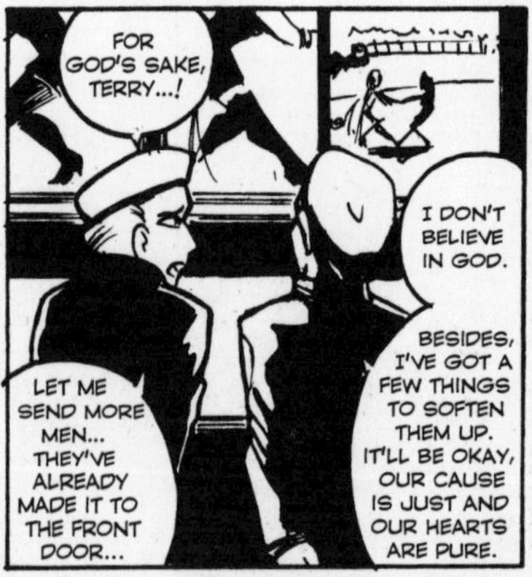
FOR GOD'S SAKE, TERRY...!
I DON'T BELIEVE IN GOD.
LET ME SEND MORE MEN... THEY'VE ALREADY MADE IT TO THE FRONT DOOR...
BESIDES, I'VE GOT A FEW THINGS TO SOFTEN THEM UP. IT'LL BE OKAY, OUR CAUSE IS JUST AND OUR HEARTS ARE PURE.

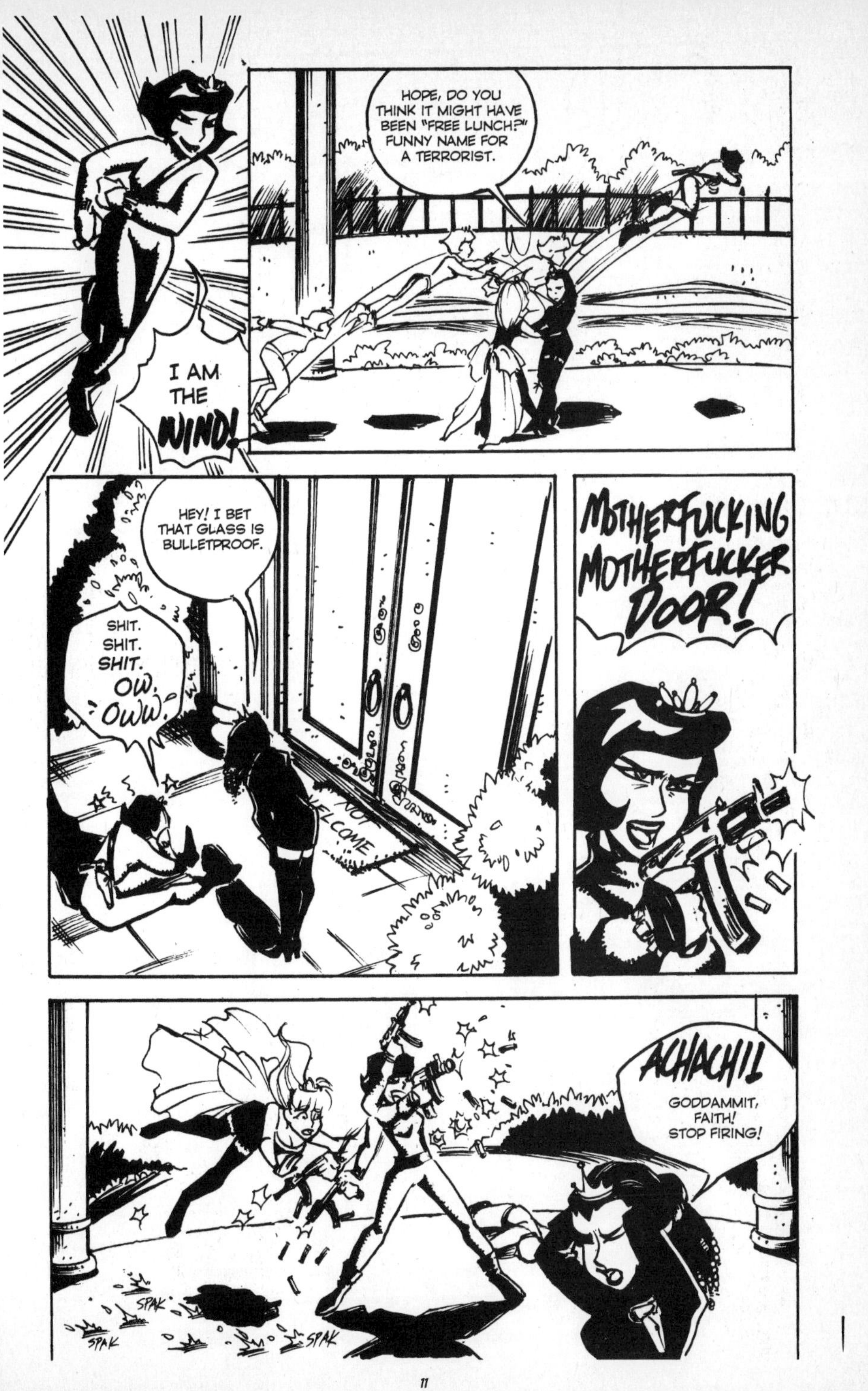
I AM THE WIND!
HOPE, DO YOU THINK IT MIGHT HAVE BEEN "FREE LUNCH?" FUNNY NAME FOR A TERRORIST.
HEY! I BET THAT GLASS IS BULLETPROOF.
SHIT. SHIT. SHIT. OW. OWW.
NOT WELCOME
MOTHERFUCKING MOTHERFUCKER DOOR!
ACHACHI!
GODDAMMIT, FAITH! STOP FIRING!
SPAK
SPAK
SPAK

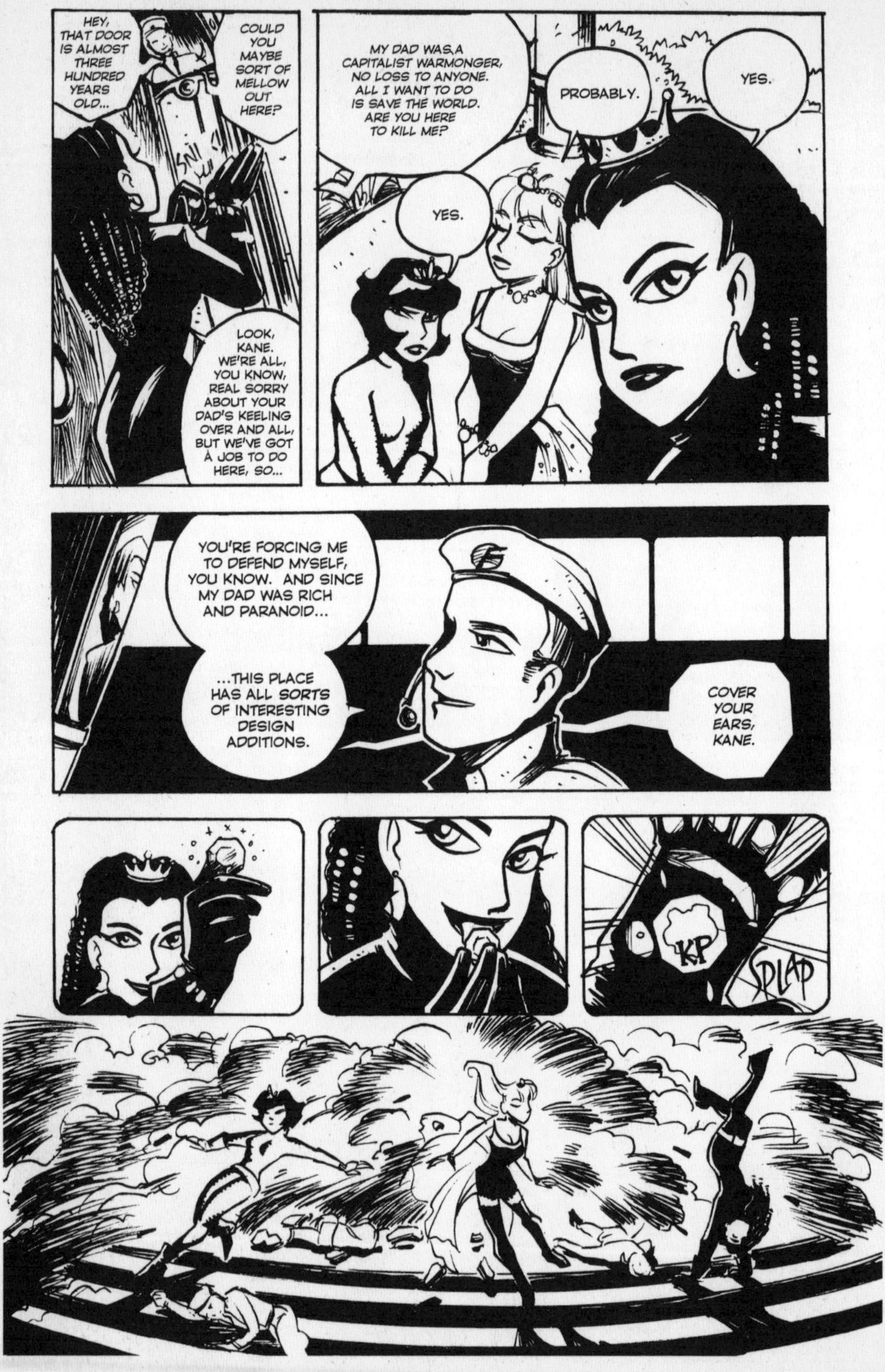
HEY, THAT DOOR IS ALMOST THREE HUNDRED YEARS OLD...
COULD YOU MAYBE SORT OF MELLOW OUT HERE?
LOOK, KANE. WE'RE ALL, YOU KNOW, REAL SORRY ABOUT YOUR DAD'S KEELING OVER AND ALL, BUT WE'VE GOT A JOB TO DO HERE, SO...
MY DAD WAS A CAPITALIST WARMONGER, NO LOSS TO ANYONE. ALL I WANT TO DO IS SAVE THE WORLD. ARE YOU HERE TO KILL ME?
PROBABLY.
YES.
YES.
YOU'RE FORCING ME TO DEFEND MYSELF, YOU KNOW. AND SINCE MY DAD WAS RICH AND PARANOID...
...THIS PLACE HAS ALL SORTS OF INTERESTING DESIGN ADDITIONS.
COVER YOUR EARS, KANE.
KP
SPLAP

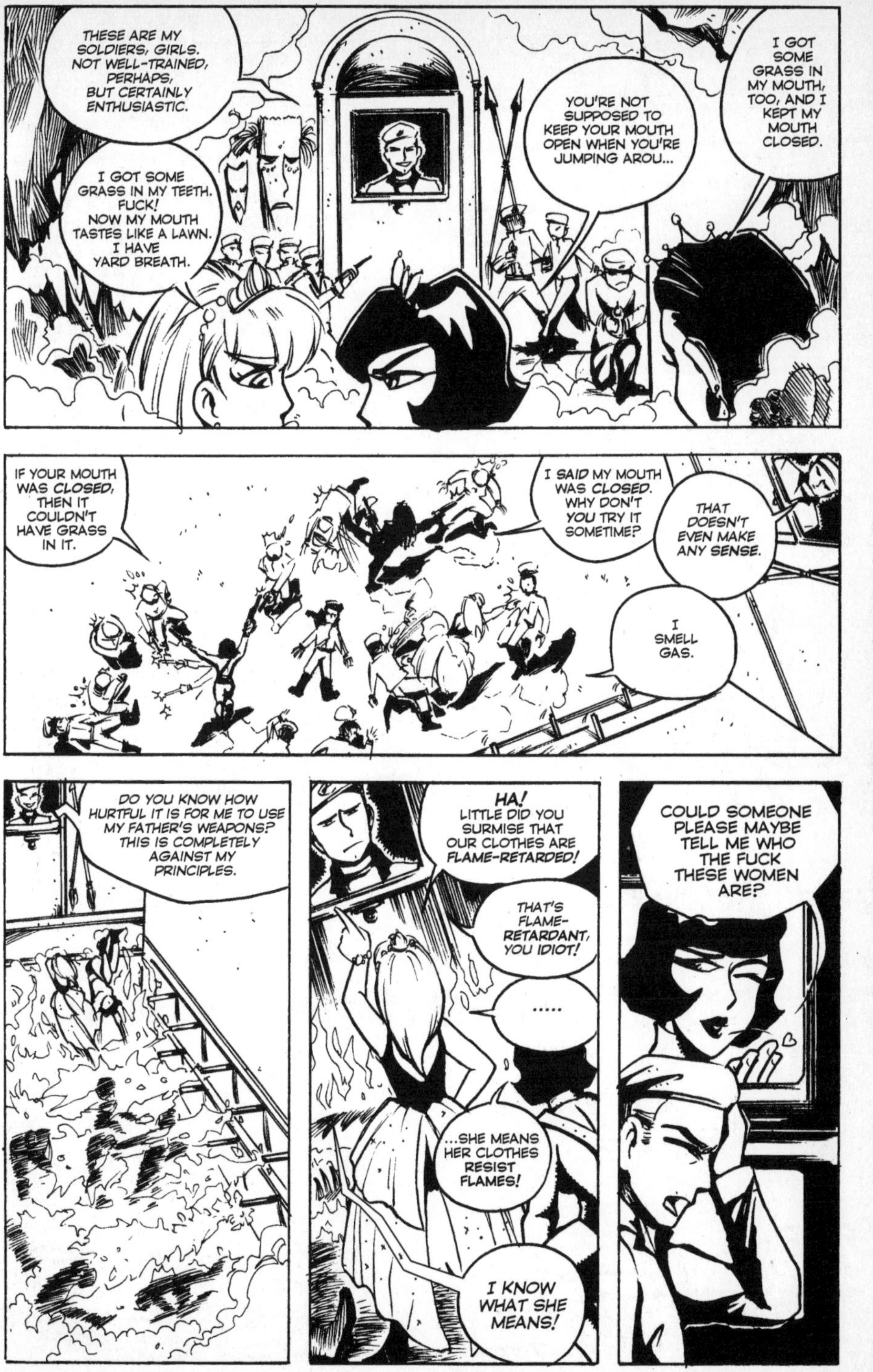
THESE ARE MY SOLDIERS, GIRLS. NOT WELL-TRAINED, PERHAPS, BUT CERTAINLY ENTHUSIASTIC.
I GOT SOME GRASS IN MY TEETH. FUCK! NOW MY MOUTH TASTES LIKE A LAWN. I HAVE YARD BREATH.
YOU'RE NOT SUPPOSED TO KEEP YOUR MOUTH OPEN WHEN YOU'RE JUMPING AROU...
I GOT SOME GRASS IN MY MOUTH, TOO, AND I KEPT MY MOUTH CLOSED.
IF YOUR MOUTH WAS CLOSED, THEN IT COULDN'T HAVE GRASS IN IT.
I SAID MY MOUTH WAS CLOSED. WHY DON'T YOU TRY IT SOMETIME?
THAT DOESN'T EVEN MAKE ANY SENSE.
I SMELL GAS.
DO YOU KNOW HOW HURTFUL IT IS FOR ME TO USE MY FATHER'S WEAPONS? THIS IS COMPLETELY AGAINST MY PRINCIPLES.
HA! LITTLE DID YOU SURMISE THAT OUR CLOTHES ARE FLAME-RETARDED!
THAT'S FLAME-RETARDANT, YOU IDIOT!
.....
...SHE MEANS HER CLOTHES RESIST FLAMES!
I KNOW WHAT SHE MEANS!
COULD SOMEONE PLEASE MAYBE TELL ME WHO THE FUCK THESE WOMEN ARE?

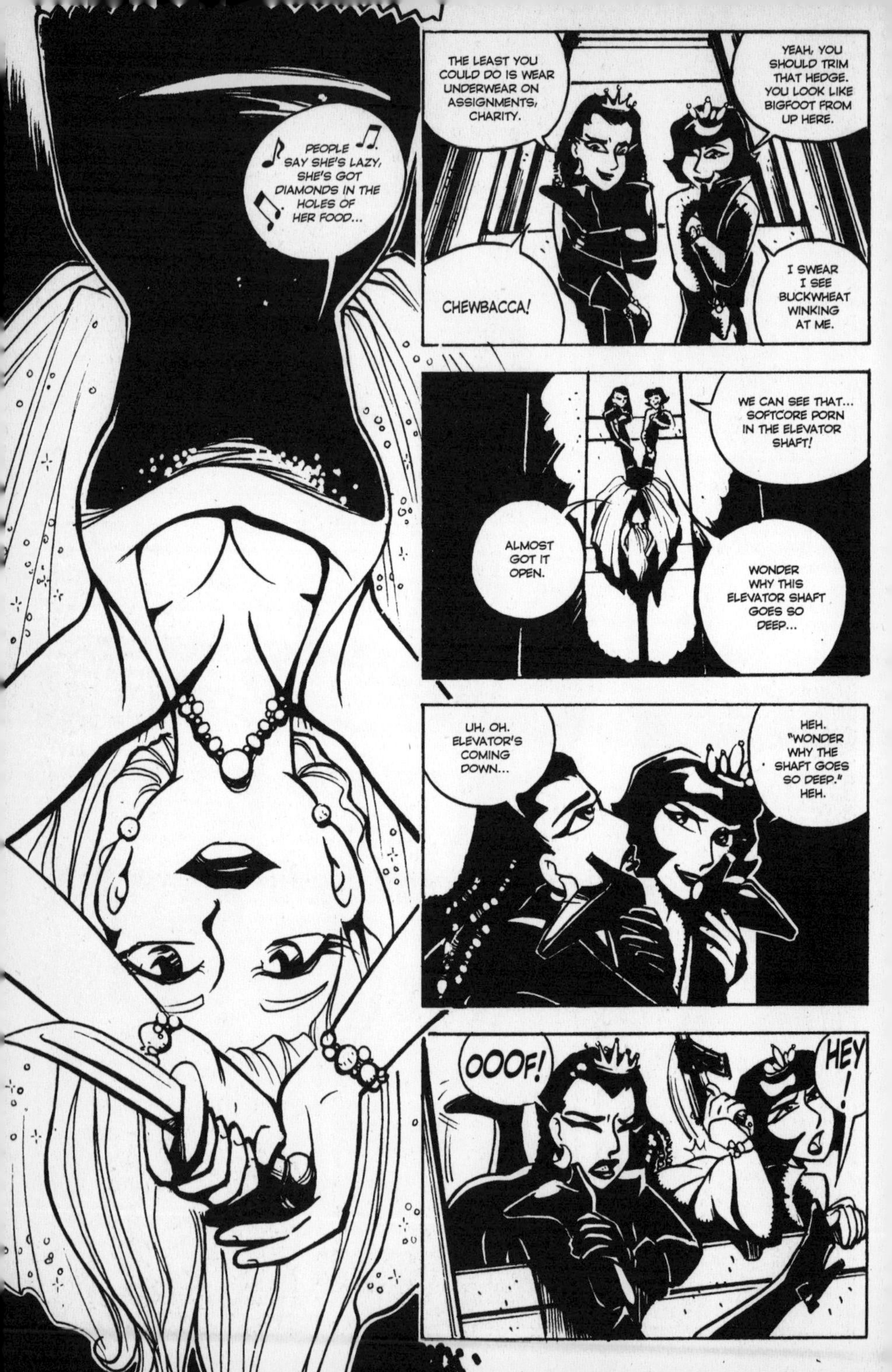
PEOPLE SAY SHE'S LAZY, SHE'S GOT DIAMONDS IN THE HOLES OF HER FOOD...
THE LEAST YOU COULD DO IS WEAR UNDERWEAR ON ASSIGNMENTS, CHARITY.
YEAH, YOU SHOULD TRIM THAT HEDGE. YOU LOOK LIKE BIGFOOT FROM UP HERE.
CHEWBACCA!
I SWEAR I SEE BUCKWHEAT WINKING AT ME.
WE CAN SEE THAT... SOFTCORE PORN IN THE ELEVATOR SHAFT!
ALMOST GOT IT OPEN.
WONDER WHY THIS ELEVATOR SHAFT GOES SO DEEP...
UH, OH. ELEVATOR'S COMING DOWN...
HEH. "WONDER WHY THE SHAFT GOES SO DEEP." HEH.
OOOF!
HEY!

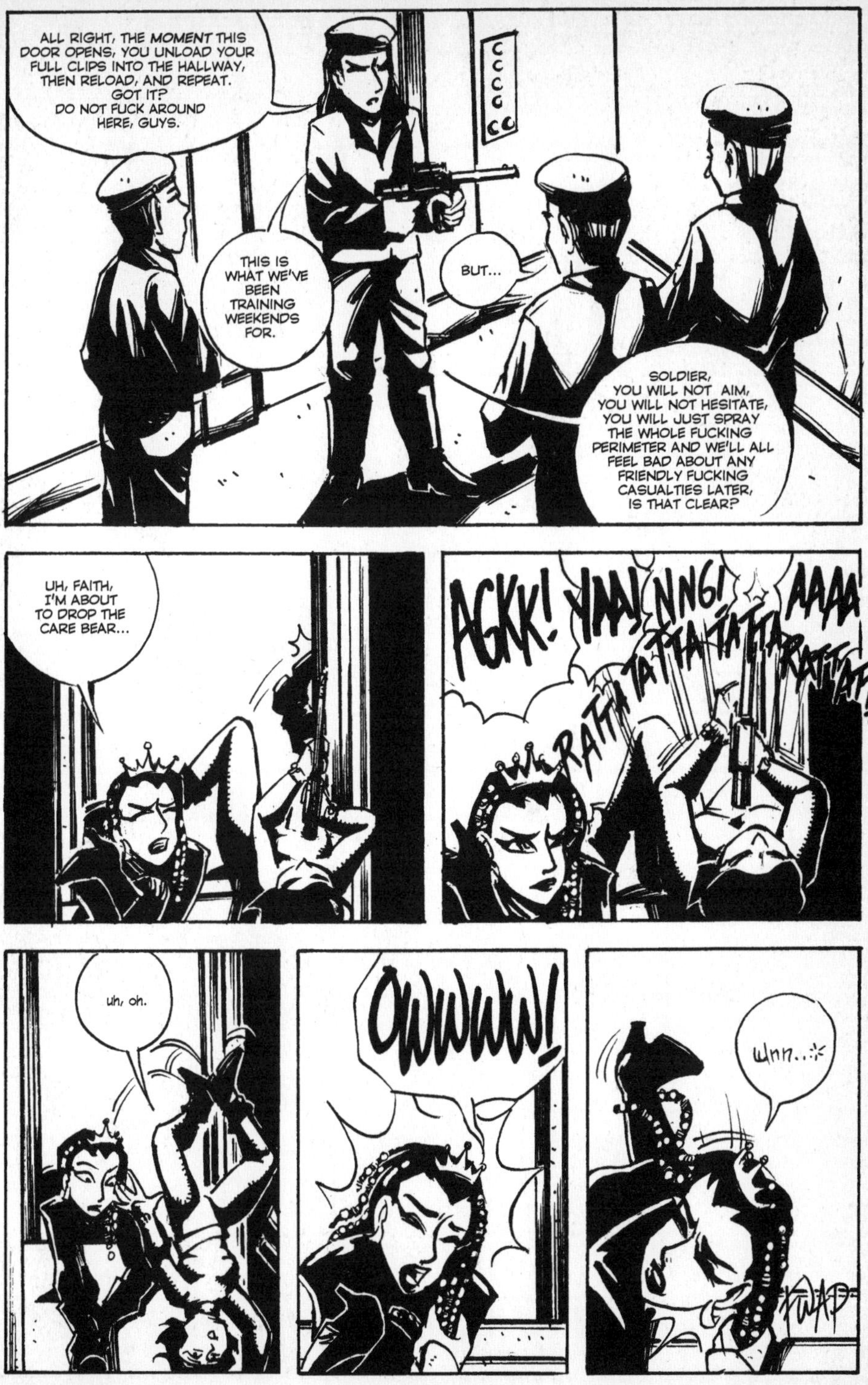
ALL RIGHT, THE MOMENT THIS DOOR OPENS, YOU UNLOAD YOUR FULL CLIPS INTO THE HALLWAY, THEN RELOAD, AND REPEAT. GOT IT? DO NOT FUCK AROUND HERE, GUYS.
THIS IS WHAT WE'VE BEEN TRAINING WEEKENDS FOR.
BUT...
SOLDIER, YOU WILL NOT AIM, YOU WILL NOT HESITATE, YOU WILL JUST SPRAY THE WHOLE FUCKING PERIMETER AND WE'LL ALL FEEL BAD ABOUT ANY FRIENDLY FUCKING CASUALTIES LATER, IS THAT CLEAR?
UH, FAITH, I'M ABOUT TO DROP THE CARE BEAR...
AGKK! YAA! NNG! AAAA
RATTA TATTA TATTA RATTATTA
uh, oh.
OWWWW!
unn...
FWAP

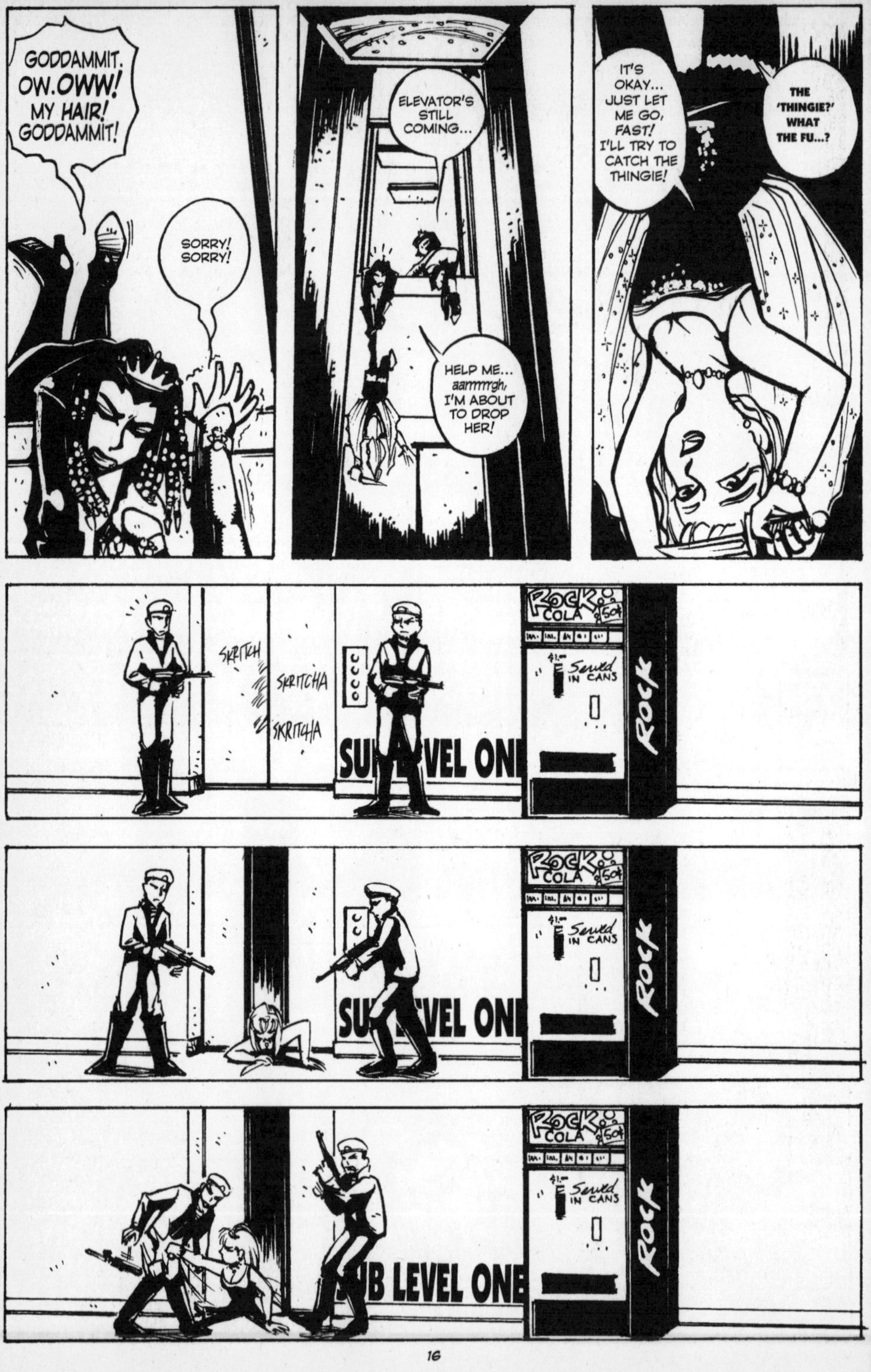
GODDAMMIT. OW.OWW! MY HAIR! GODDAMMIT!
SORRY! SORRY!
ELEVATOR'S STILL COMING...
HELP ME... aarrrrrgh, I'M ABOUT TO DROP HER!
IT'S OKAY... JUST LET ME GO, FAST! I'LL TRY TO CATCH THE THINGIE!
THE 'THINGIE?' WHAT THE FU...?
SKRITCH
SKRITCHA
SKRITCHA
ROCK COLA 50¢
$1.00 Served IN CANS
ROCK
SUB LEVEL ONE

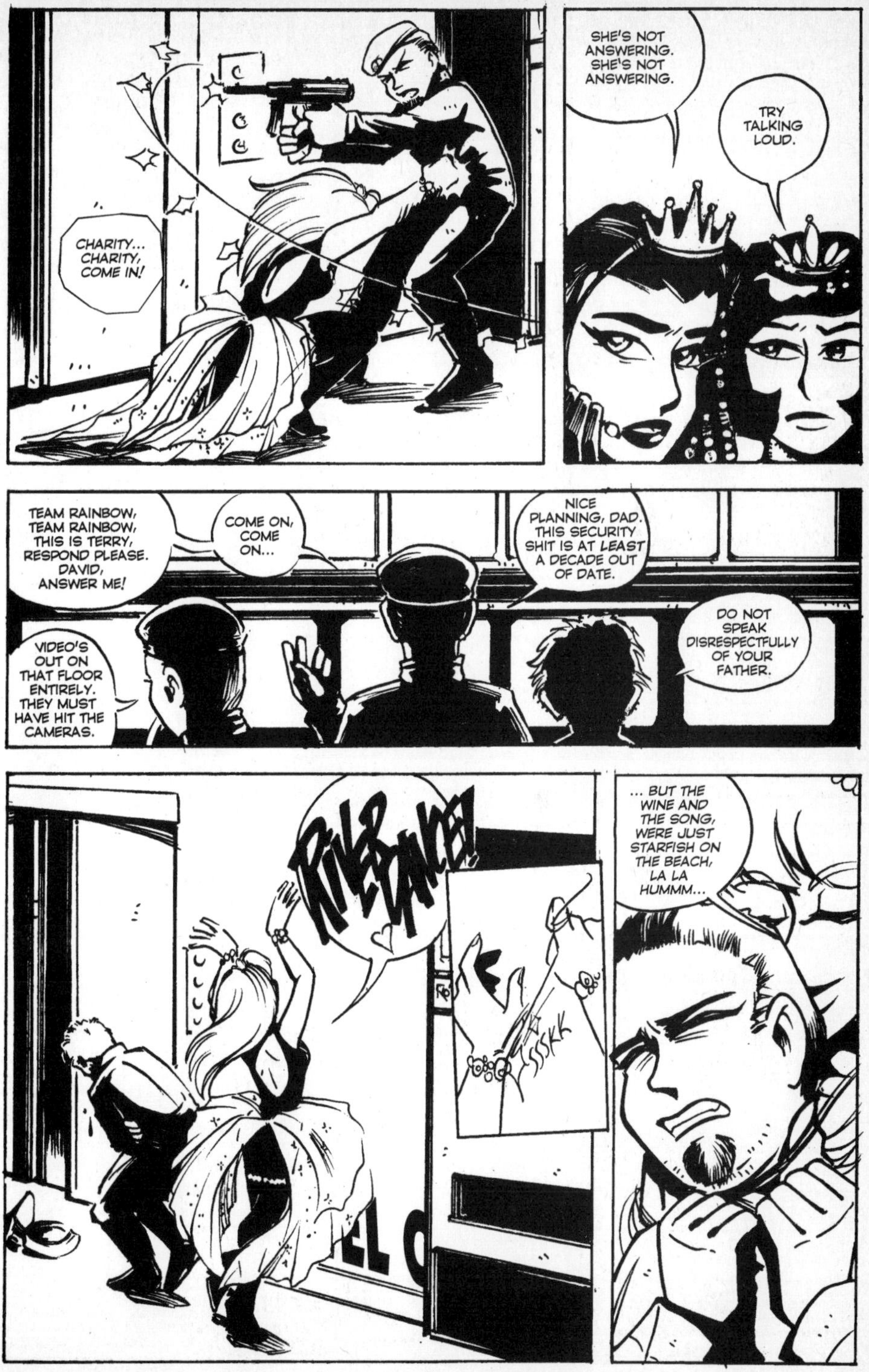
CHARITY... CHARITY, COME IN!
SHE'S NOT ANSWERING. SHE'S NOT ANSWERING.
TRY TALKING LOUD.
TEAM RAINBOW, TEAM RAINBOW, THIS IS TERRY, RESPOND PLEASE. DAVID, ANSWER ME!
COME ON, COME ON...
NICE PLANNING, DAD. THIS SECURITY SHIT IS AT *LEAST* A DECADE OUT OF DATE.
VIDEO'S OUT ON THAT FLOOR ENTIRELY. THEY MUST HAVE HIT THE CAMERAS.
DO NOT SPEAK DISRESPECTFULLY OF YOUR FATHER.
RIVERDANCE!
... BUT THE WINE AND THE SONG, WERE JUST STARFISH ON THE BEACH, LA LA HUMMM...

bzzzzzztt bzzzzzztt KOCK

...IF SHE WAS DEAD! DUH!

'M OKAY, GUYS. I'M CHECKING THE SCANNER THING.

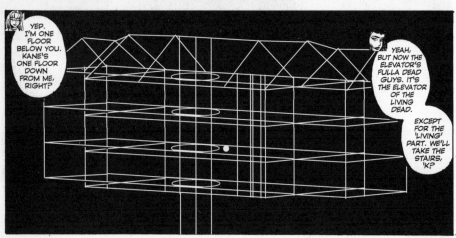

YEP. I'M ONE FLOOR BELOW YOU. KANE'S ONE FLOOR DOWN FROM ME, RIGHT?

YEAH, BUT NOW THE ELEVATOR'S FULLA DEAD GUYS. IT'S THE ELEVATOR OF THE LIVING DEAD.

EXCEPT FOR THE 'LIVING' PART. WE'LL TAKE THE STAIRS, 'K?

MASTER CHEN. YOU HAVE ALWAYS BEEN A FRIEND TO MY FATHER.

NOW I RESPECTFULLY ASK YOU TO HELP ME HERE.

PLEASE.

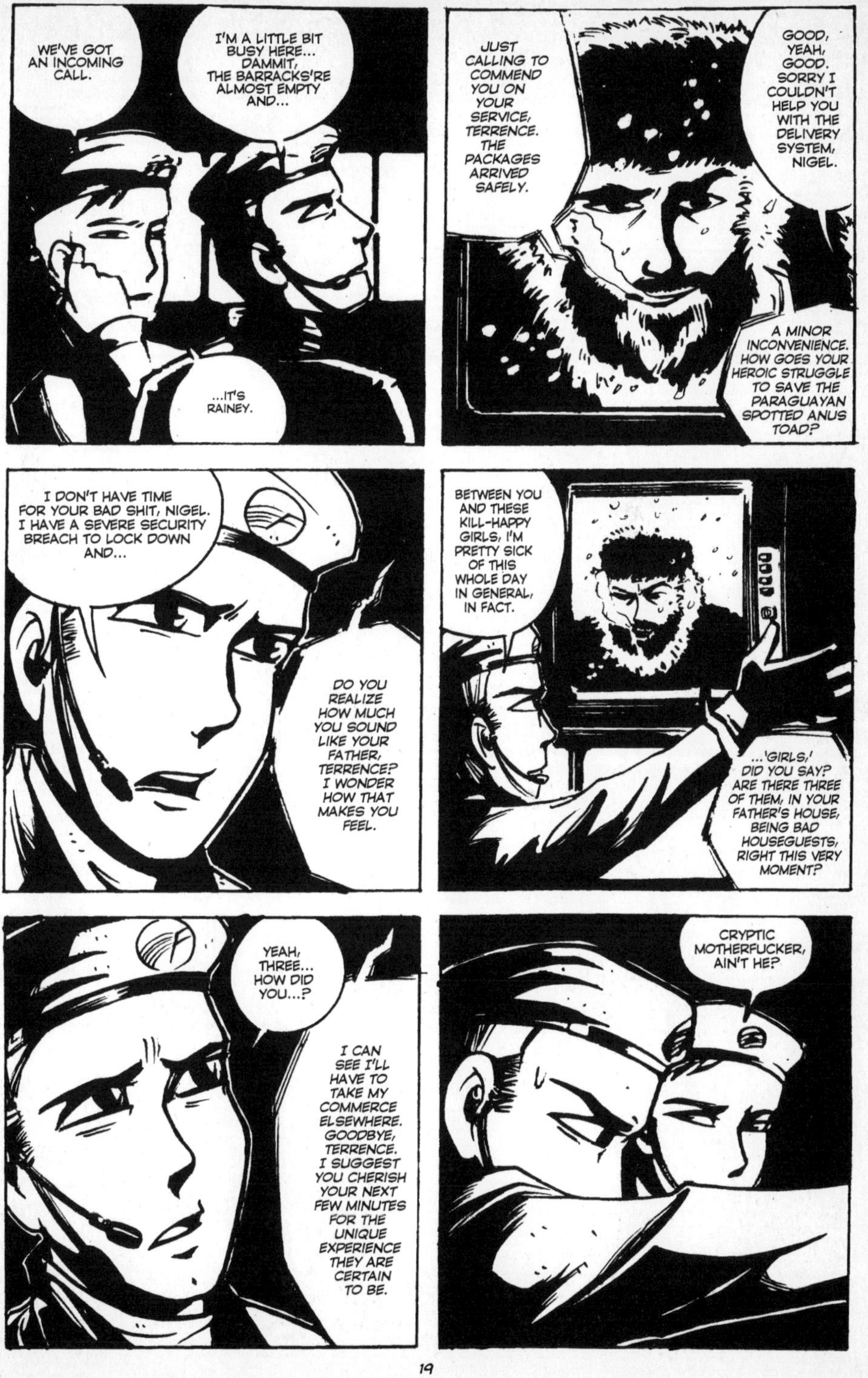
WE'VE GOT AN INCOMING CALL.
I'M A LITTLE BIT BUSY HERE... DAMMIT, THE BARRACKS'RE ALMOST EMPTY AND...
...IT'S RAINEY.
JUST CALLING TO COMMEND YOU ON YOUR SERVICE, TERRENCE. THE PACKAGES ARRIVED SAFELY.
GOOD, YEAH, GOOD. SORRY I COULDN'T HELP YOU WITH THE DELIVERY SYSTEM, NIGEL.
A MINOR INCONVENIENCE. HOW GOES YOUR HEROIC STRUGGLE TO SAVE THE PARAGUAYAN SPOTTED ANUS TOAD?
I DON'T HAVE TIME FOR YOUR BAD SHIT, NIGEL. I HAVE A SEVERE SECURITY BREACH TO LOCK DOWN AND...
DO YOU REALIZE HOW MUCH YOU SOUND LIKE YOUR FATHER, TERRENCE? I WONDER HOW THAT MAKES YOU FEEL.
BETWEEN YOU AND THESE KILL-HAPPY GIRLS, I'M PRETTY SICK OF THIS WHOLE DAY IN GENERAL, IN FACT.
...'GIRLS,' DID YOU SAY? ARE THERE THREE OF THEM, IN YOUR FATHER'S HOUSE, BEING BAD HOUSEGUESTS, RIGHT THIS VERY MOMENT?
YEAH, THREE... HOW DID YOU...?
I CAN SEE I'LL HAVE TO TAKE MY COMMERCE ELSEWHERE. GOODBYE, TERRENCE. I SUGGEST YOU CHERISH YOUR NEXT FEW MINUTES FOR THE UNIQUE EXPERIENCE THEY ARE CERTAIN TO BE.
CRYPTIC MOTHERFUCKER, AIN'T HE?

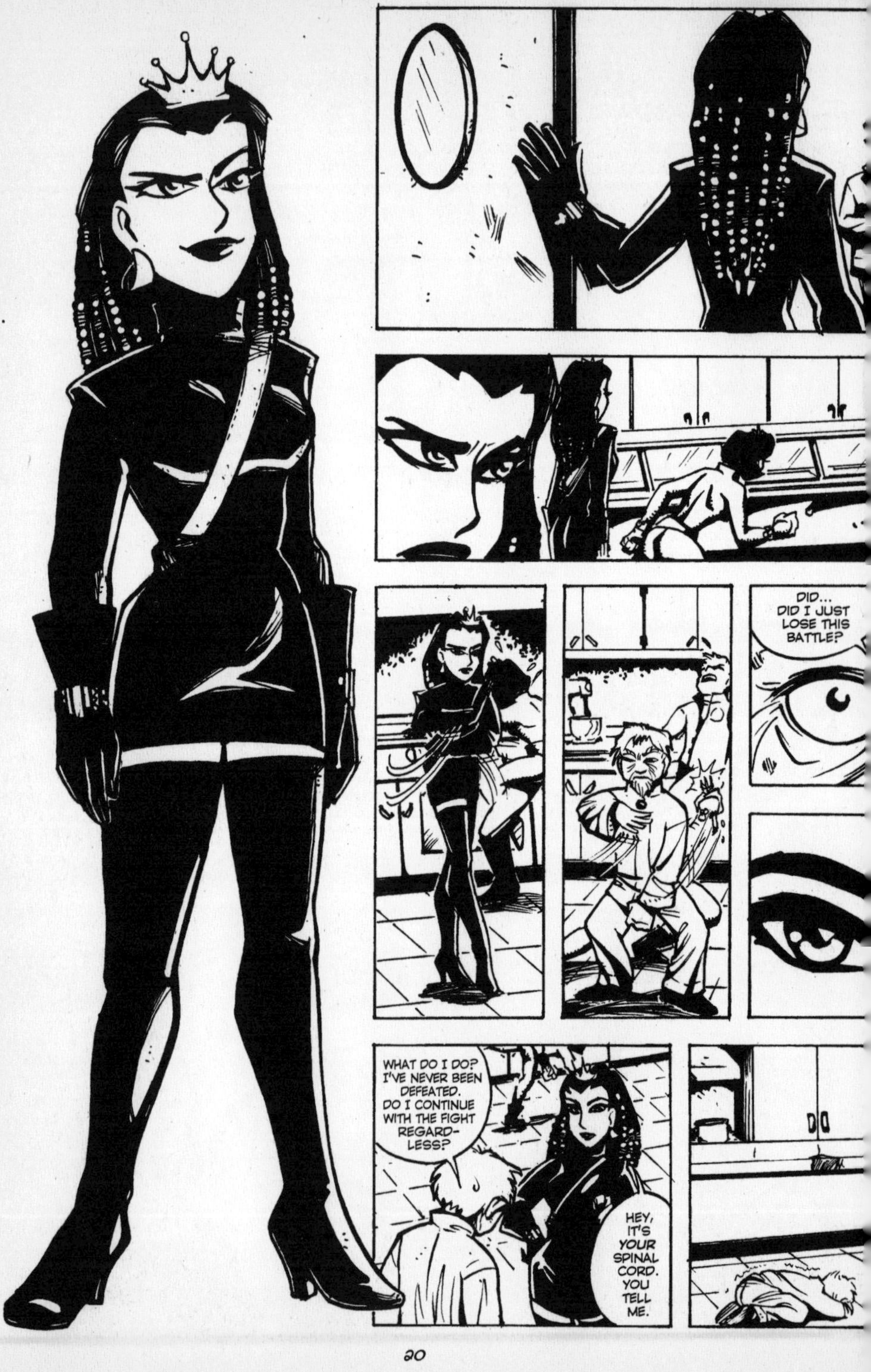
DID... DID I JUST LOSE THIS BATTLE?
WHAT DO I DO? I'VE NEVER BEEN DEFEATED. DO I CONTINUE WITH THE FIGHT REGARDLESS?
HEY, IT'S YOUR SPINAL CORD. YOU TELL ME.

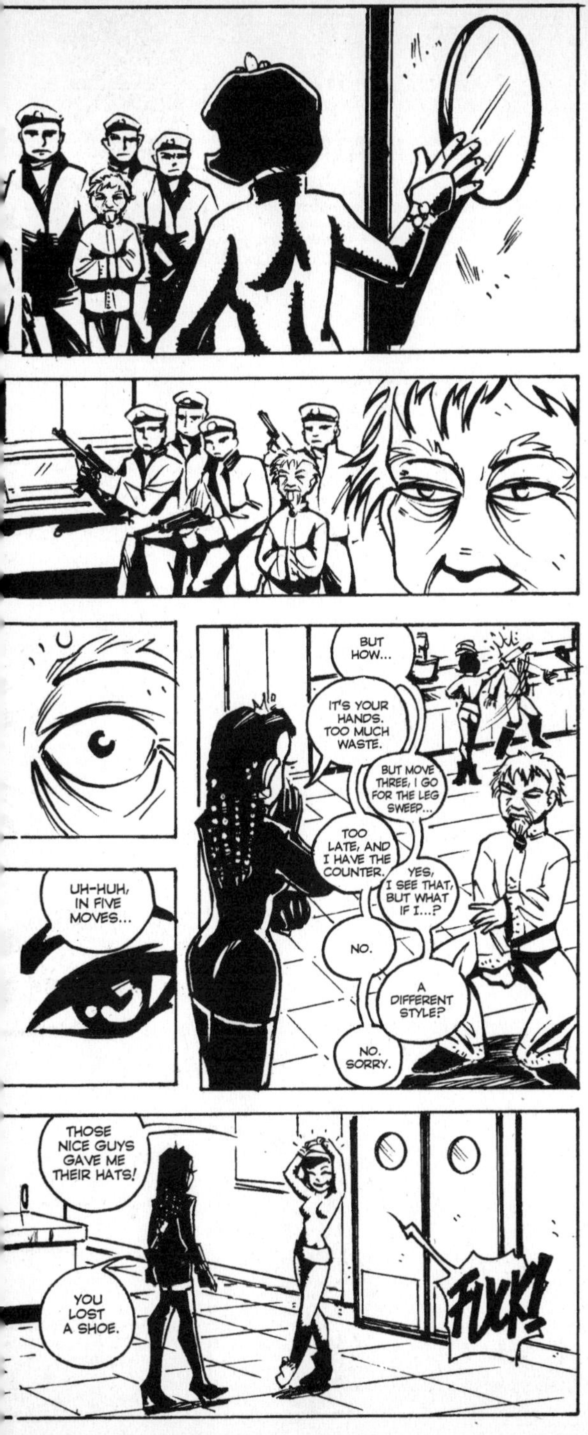
BUT HOW...
IT'S YOUR HANDS. TOO MUCH WASTE.
BUT MOVE THREE, I GO FOR THE LEG SWEEP...
TOO LATE, AND I HAVE THE COUNTER.
YES, I SEE THAT, BUT WHAT IF I...?
NO.
A DIFFERENT STYLE?
NO. SORRY.
UH-HUH, IN FIVE MOVES...
THOSE NICE GUYS GAVE ME THEIR HATS!
YOU LOST A SHOE.
FUCK!

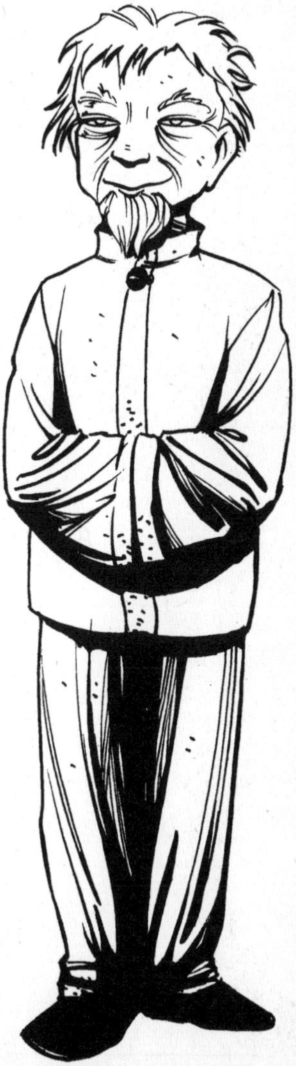

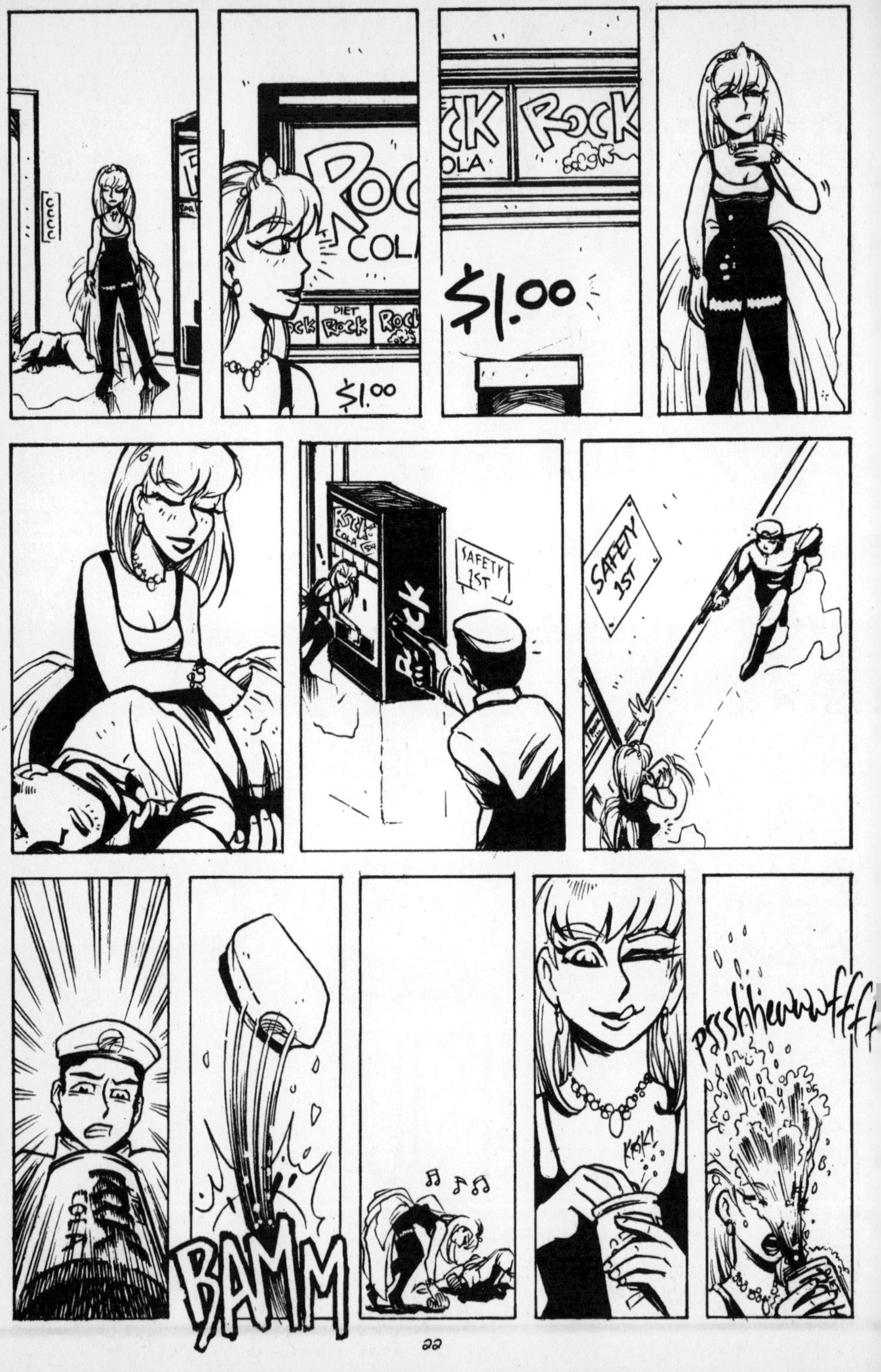
ROCK
COLA
DIET
ROCK
$1.00
ROCK
COLA
$1.00
SAFETY 1ST
SAFETY 1ST
BAMM
KAK!

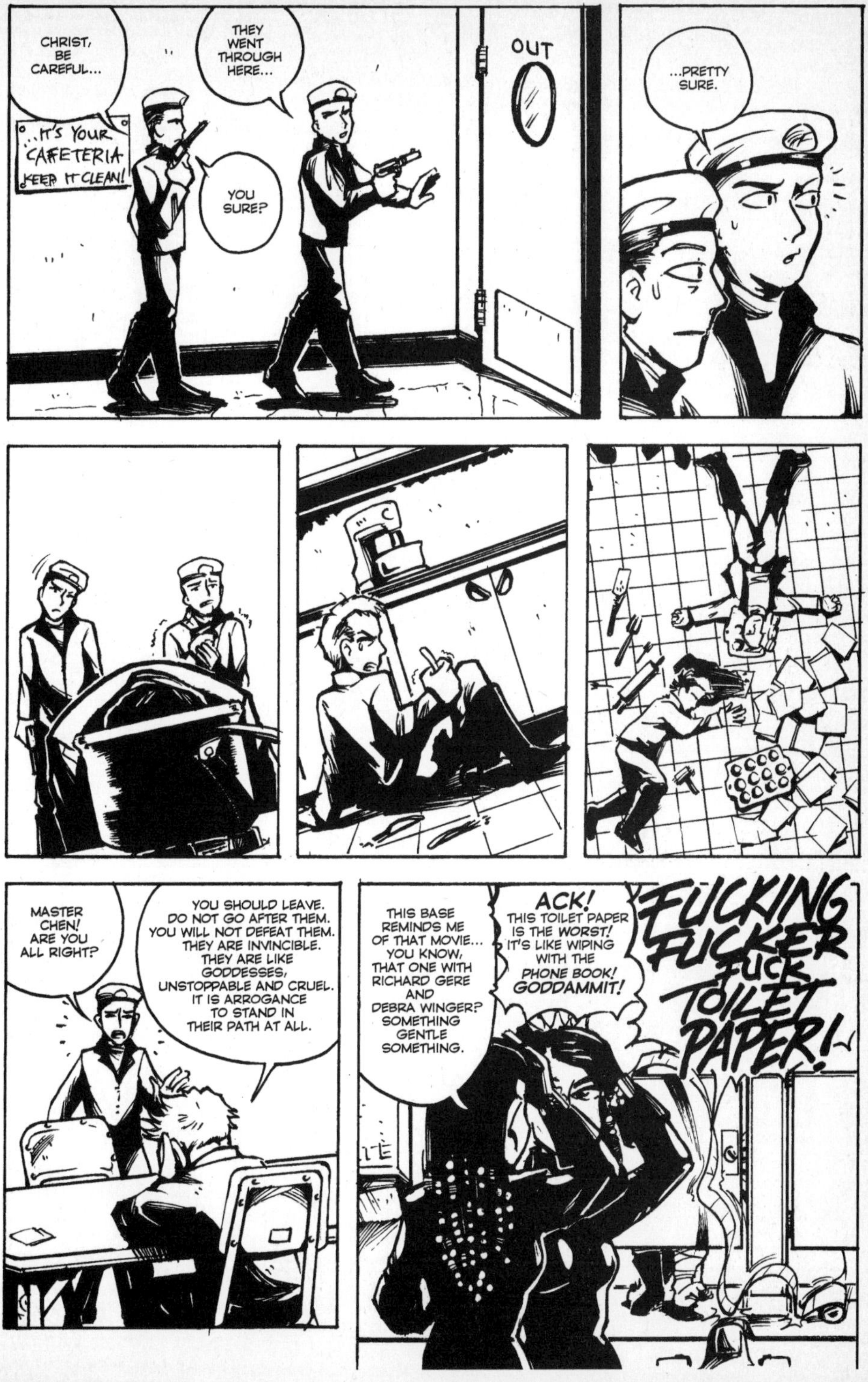
CHRIST, BE CAREFUL...
THEY WENT THROUGH HERE...
...IT'S YOUR CAFETERIA KEEP IT CLEAN!
YOU SURE?
OUT
...PRETTY SURE.
MASTER CHEN! ARE YOU ALL RIGHT?
YOU SHOULD LEAVE. DO NOT GO AFTER THEM. YOU WILL NOT DEFEAT THEM. THEY ARE INVINCIBLE. THEY ARE LIKE GODDESSES, UNSTOPPABLE AND CRUEL. IT IS ARROGANCE TO STAND IN THEIR PATH AT ALL.
THIS BASE REMINDS ME OF THAT MOVIE... YOU KNOW, THAT ONE WITH RICHARD GERE AND DEBRA WINGER? SOMETHING GENTLE SOMETHING.
ACK! THIS TOILET PAPER IS THE WORST! IT'S LIKE WIPING WITH THE PHONE BOOK! GODDAMMIT!
FUCKING FUCKER FUCK TOILET PAPER!

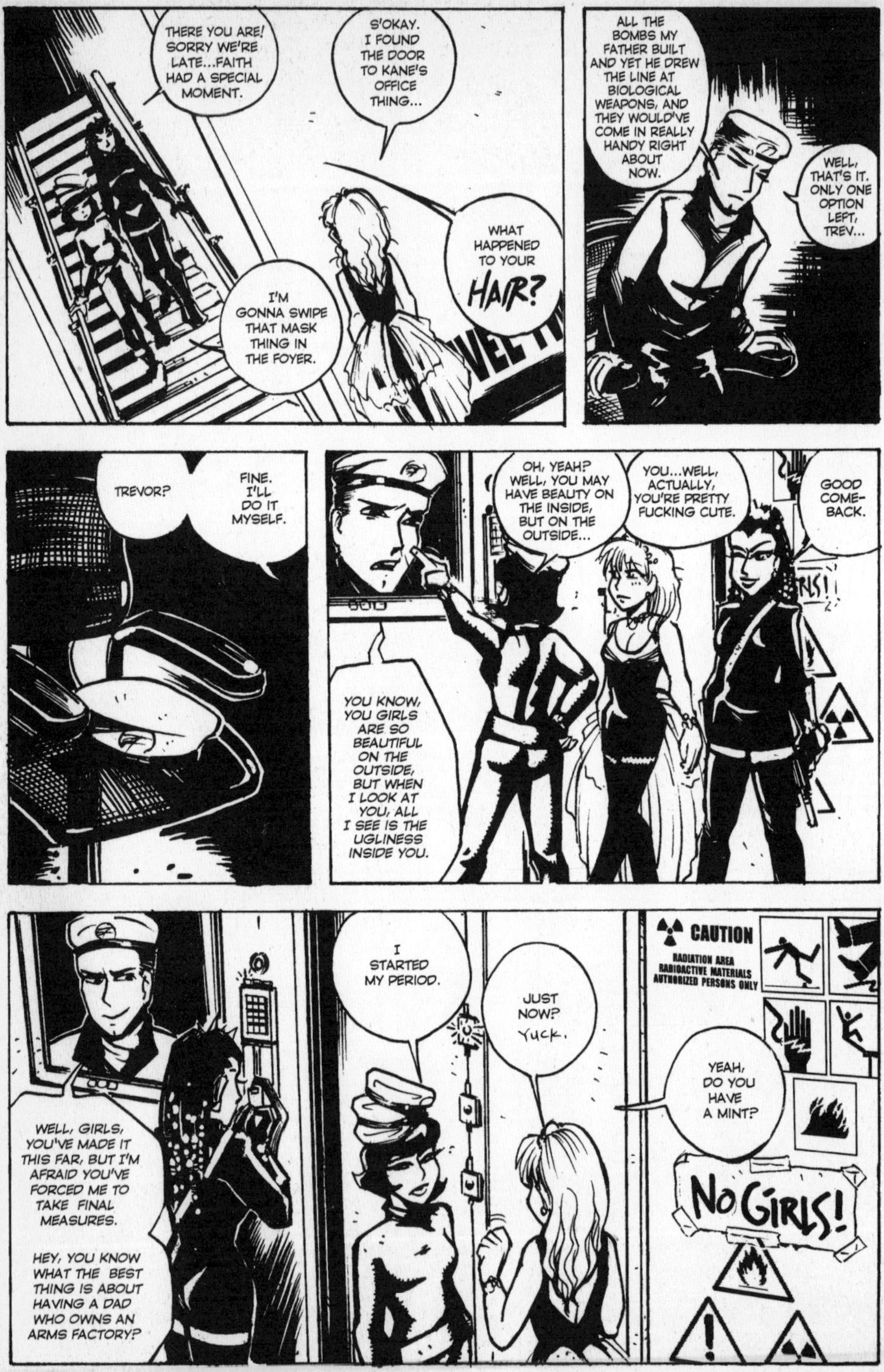
THERE YOU ARE! SORRY WE'RE LATE...FAITH HAD A SPECIAL MOMENT.
S'OKAY. I FOUND THE DOOR TO KANE'S OFFICE THING...
I'M GONNA SWIPE THAT MASK THING IN THE FOYER.
WHAT HAPPENED TO YOUR HAIR?
ALL THE BOMBS MY FATHER BUILT AND YET HE DREW THE LINE AT BIOLOGICAL WEAPONS, AND THEY WOULD'VE COME IN REALLY HANDY RIGHT ABOUT NOW.
WELL, THAT'S IT. ONLY ONE OPTION LEFT, TREV...
TREVOR?
FINE. I'LL DO IT MYSELF.
YOU KNOW, YOU GIRLS ARE SO BEAUTIFUL ON THE OUTSIDE, BUT WHEN I LOOK AT YOU, ALL I SEE IS THE UGLINESS INSIDE YOU.
OH, YEAH? WELL, YOU MAY HAVE BEAUTY ON THE INSIDE, BUT ON THE OUTSIDE...
YOU...WELL, ACTUALLY, YOU'RE PRETTY FUCKING CUTE.
GOOD COME-BACK.
WELL, GIRLS, YOU'VE MADE IT THIS FAR, BUT I'M AFRAID YOU'VE FORCED ME TO TAKE FINAL MEASURES.
HEY, YOU KNOW WHAT THE BEST THING IS ABOUT HAVING A DAD WHO OWNS AN ARMS FACTORY?
I STARTED MY PERIOD.
JUST NOW? Yuck.
CAUTION
RADIATION AREA
RADIOACTIVE MATERIALS
AUTHORIZED PERSONS ONLY
YEAH, DO YOU HAVE A MINT?
NO GIRLS!

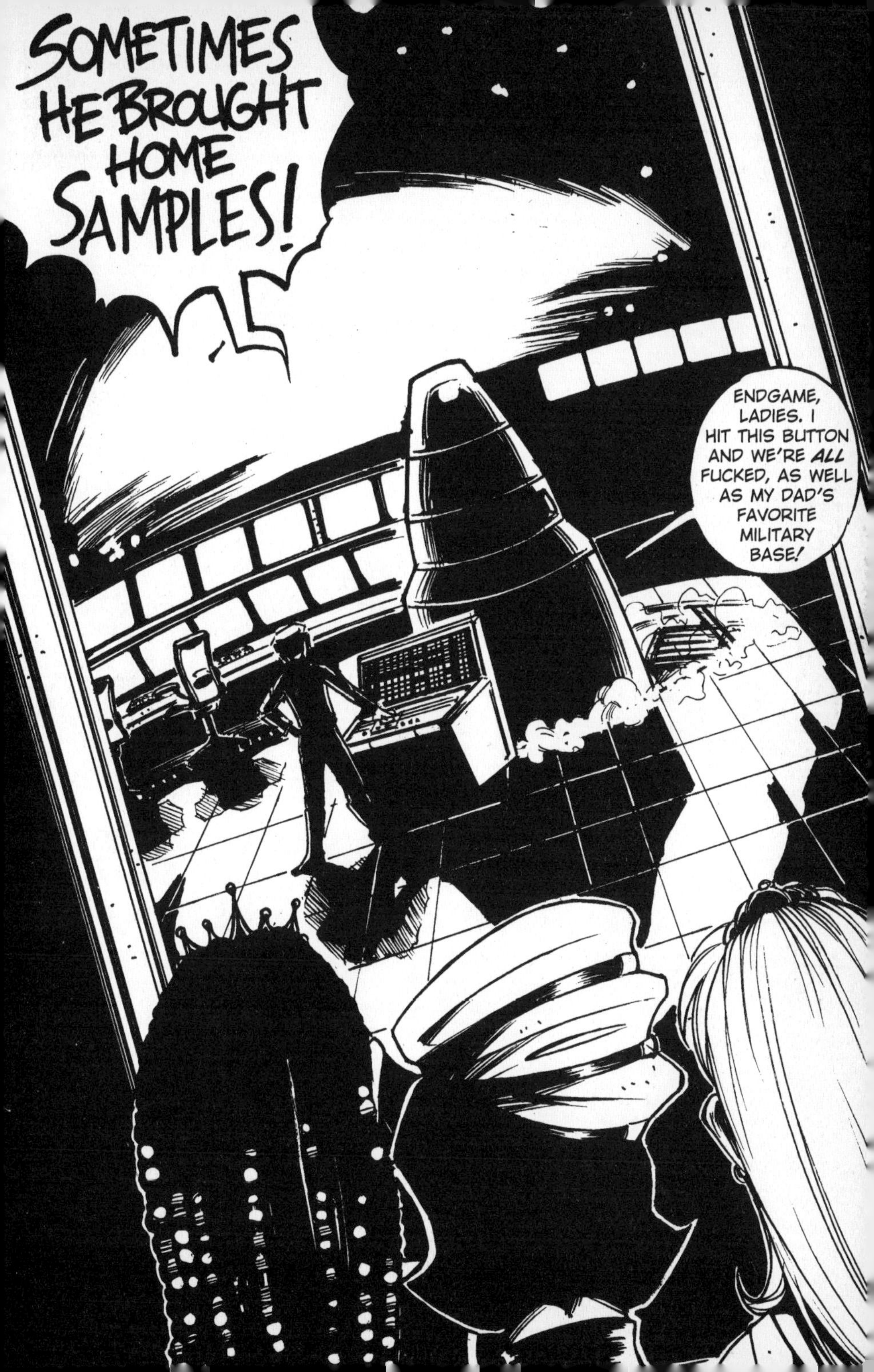
SOMETIMES HE BROUGHT HOME SAMPLES!
ENDGAME, LADIES. I HIT THIS BUTTON AND WE'RE ALL FUCKED, AS WELL AS MY DAD'S FAVORITE MILITARY BASE!

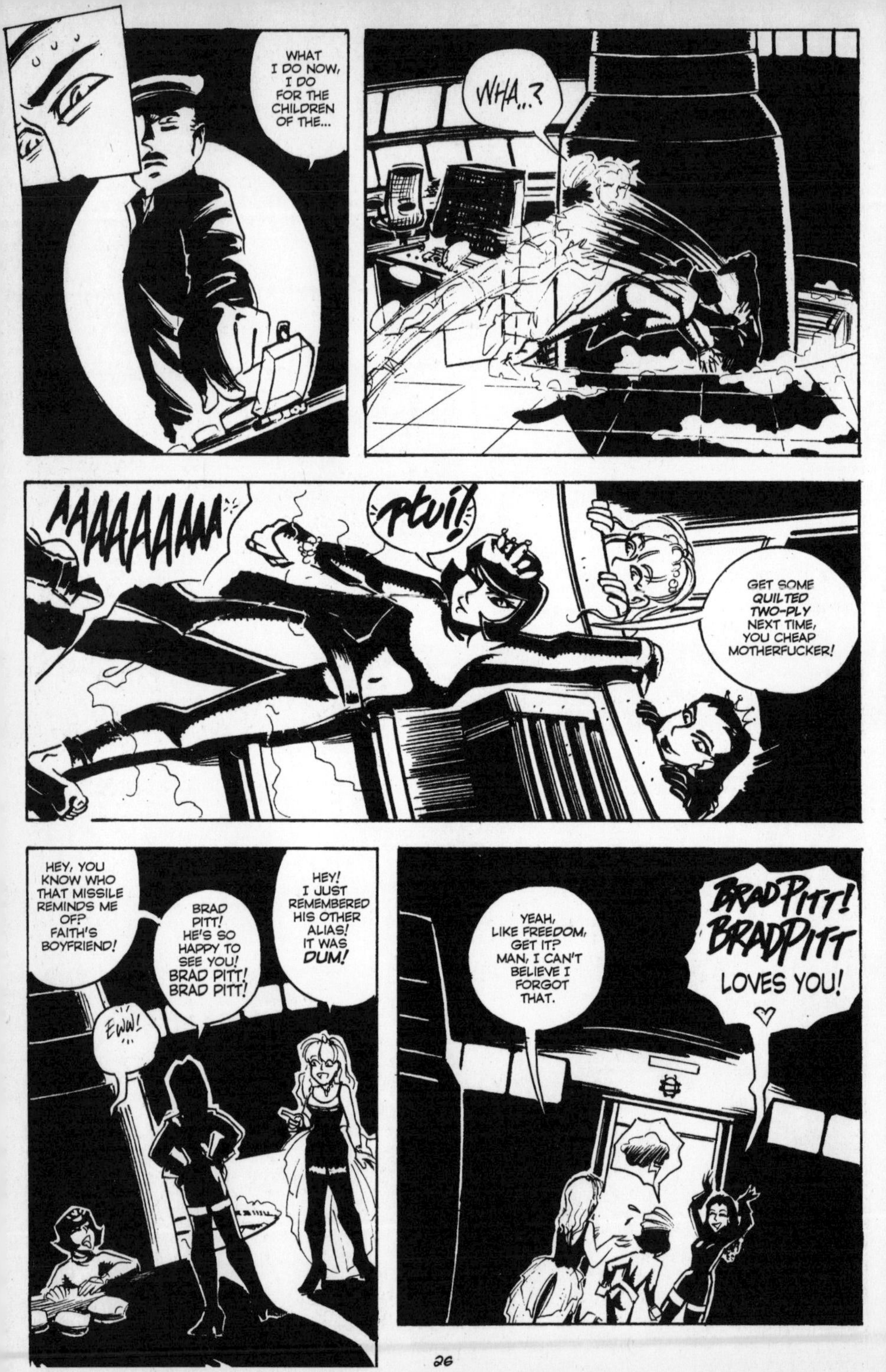
WHAT I DO NOW, I DO FOR THE CHILDREN OF THE...
WHA..?
AAAAAAAAAA
PTUI!
GET SOME QUILTED TWO-PLY NEXT TIME, YOU CHEAP MOTHERFUCKER!
HEY, YOU KNOW WHO THAT MISSILE REMINDS ME OF? FAITH'S BOYFRIEND!
BRAD PITT! HE'S SO HAPPY TO SEE YOU! BRAD PITT! BRAD PITT!
HEY! I JUST REMEMBERED HIS OTHER ALIAS! IT WAS DUM!
EWW!
YEAH, LIKE FREEDOM, GET IT? MAN, I CAN'T BELIEVE I FORGOT THAT.
BRAD PITT! BRAD PITT LOVES YOU!

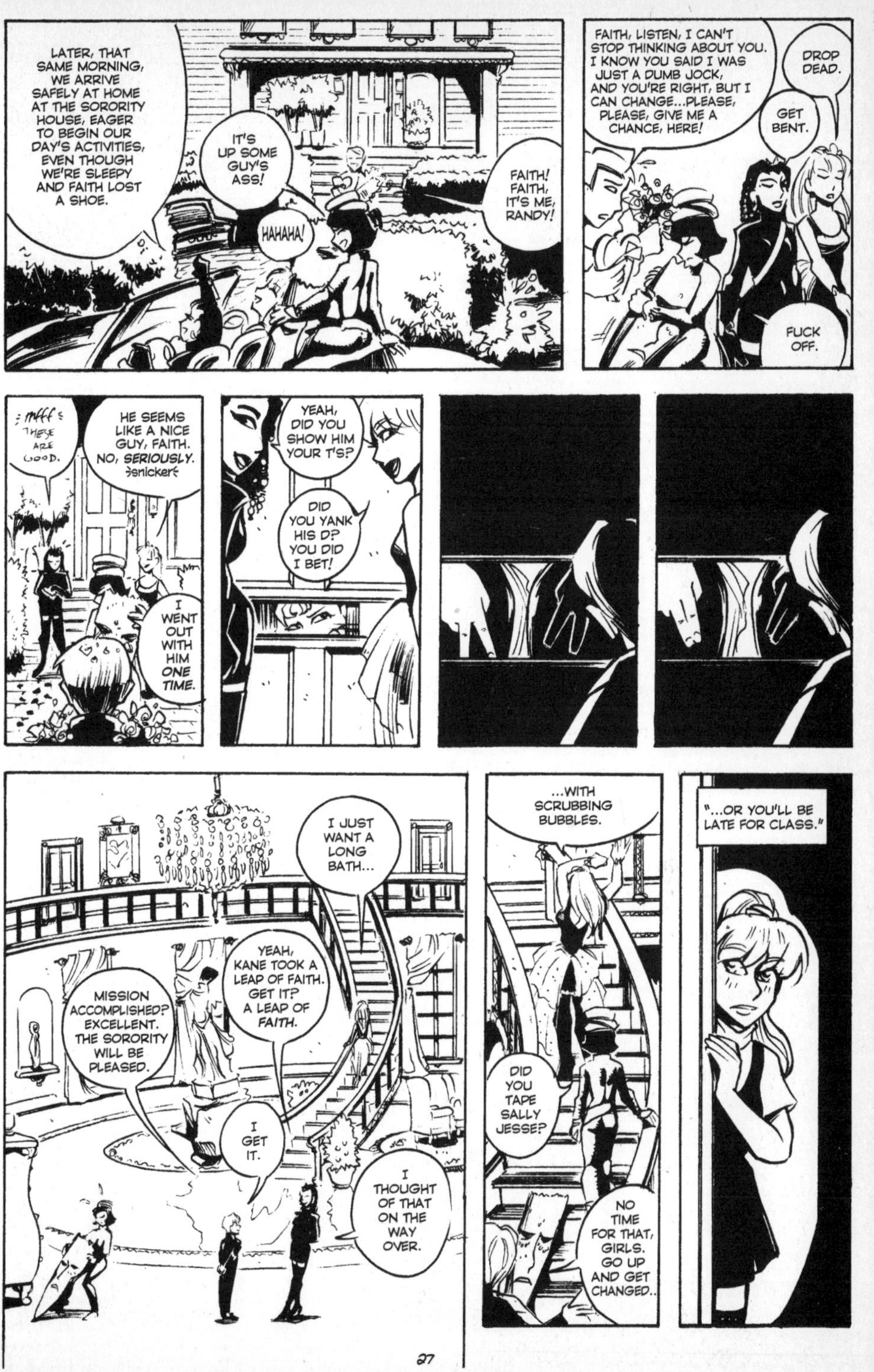
LATER, THAT SAME MORNING, WE ARRIVE SAFELY AT HOME AT THE SORORITY HOUSE, EAGER TO BEGIN OUR DAY'S ACTIVITIES, EVEN THOUGH WE'RE SLEEPY AND FAITH LOST A SHOE.
IT'S UP SOME GUY'S ASS!
HAHAHA!
FAITH! FAITH, IT'S ME, RANDY!
FAITH, LISTEN, I CAN'T STOP THINKING ABOUT YOU. I KNOW YOU SAID I WAS JUST A DUMB JOCK, AND YOU'RE RIGHT, BUT I CAN CHANGE...PLEASE, PLEASE, GIVE ME A CHANCE, HERE!
DROP DEAD.
GET BENT.
FUCK OFF.
mfff these are good.
HE SEEMS LIKE A NICE GUY, FAITH. NO, SERIOUSLY. snicker
I WENT OUT WITH HIM ONE TIME.
YEAH, DID YOU SHOW HIM YOUR T'S?
DID YOU YANK HIS D? YOU DID I BET!
I JUST WANT A LONG BATH...
YEAH, KANE TOOK A LEAP OF FAITH. GET IT? A LEAP OF FAITH.
MISSION ACCOMPLISHED? EXCELLENT. THE SORORITY WILL BE PLEASED.
I GET IT.
I THOUGHT OF THAT ON THE WAY OVER.
...WITH SCRUBBING BUBBLES.
DID YOU TAPE SALLY JESSE?
NO TIME FOR THAT, GIRLS. GO UP AND GET CHANGED..
"...OR YOU'LL BE LATE FOR CLASS."

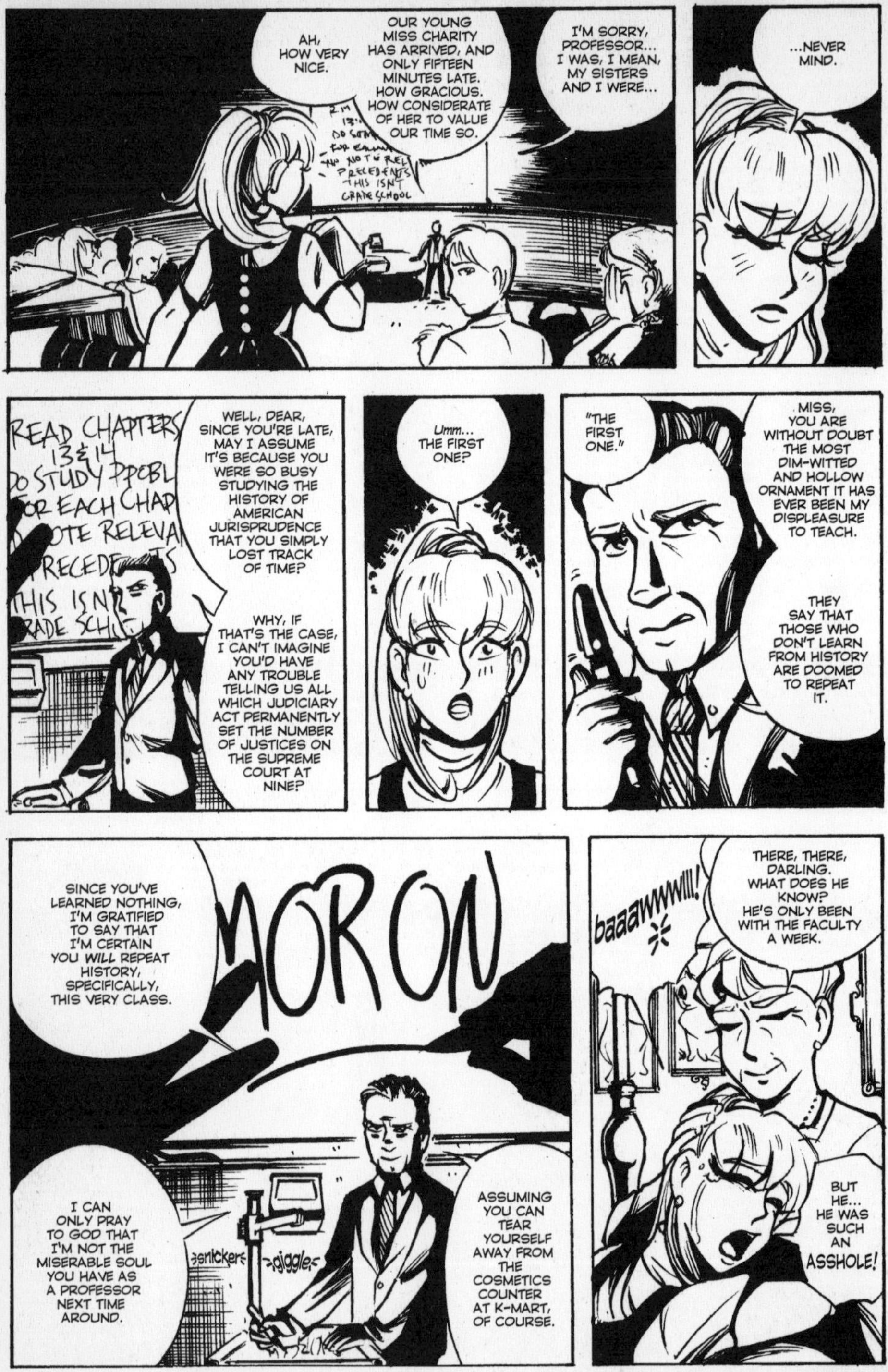

AH, HOW VERY NICE.
OUR YOUNG MISS CHARITY HAS ARRIVED, AND ONLY FIFTEEN MINUTES LATE. HOW GRACIOUS. HOW CONSIDERATE OF HER TO VALUE OUR TIME SO.
THIS ISN'T GRADE SCHOOL
I'M SORRY, PROFESSOR... I WAS, I MEAN, MY SISTERS AND I WERE...
...NEVER MIND.
READ CHAPTERS 13 & 14
WELL, DEAR, SINCE YOU'RE LATE, MAY I ASSUME IT'S BECAUSE YOU WERE SO BUSY STUDYING THE HISTORY OF AMERICAN JURISPRUDENCE THAT YOU SIMPLY LOST TRACK OF TIME?
WHY, IF THAT'S THE CASE, I CAN'T IMAGINE YOU'D HAVE ANY TROUBLE TELLING US ALL WHICH JUDICIARY ACT PERMANENTLY SET THE NUMBER OF JUSTICES ON THE SUPREME COURT AT NINE?
Umm... THE FIRST ONE?
"THE FIRST ONE."
MISS, YOU ARE WITHOUT DOUBT THE MOST DIM-WITTED AND HOLLOW ORNAMENT IT HAS EVER BEEN MY DISPLEASURE TO TEACH.
THEY SAY THAT THOSE WHO DON'T LEARN FROM HISTORY ARE DOOMED TO REPEAT IT.
SINCE YOU'VE LEARNED NOTHING, I'M GRATIFIED TO SAY THAT I'M CERTAIN YOU *WILL* REPEAT HISTORY, SPECIFICALLY, THIS VERY CLASS.
MORON
I CAN ONLY PRAY TO GOD THAT I'M NOT THE MISERABLE SOUL YOU HAVE AS A PROFESSOR NEXT TIME AROUND.
snicker
giggle
ASSUMING YOU CAN TEAR YOURSELF AWAY FROM THE COSMETICS COUNTER AT K-MART, OF COURSE.
baaawwwlll!
THERE, THERE, DARLING. WHAT DOES HE KNOW? HE'S ONLY BEEN WITH THE FACULTY A WEEK.
BUT HE... HE WAS SUCH AN ASSHOLE!

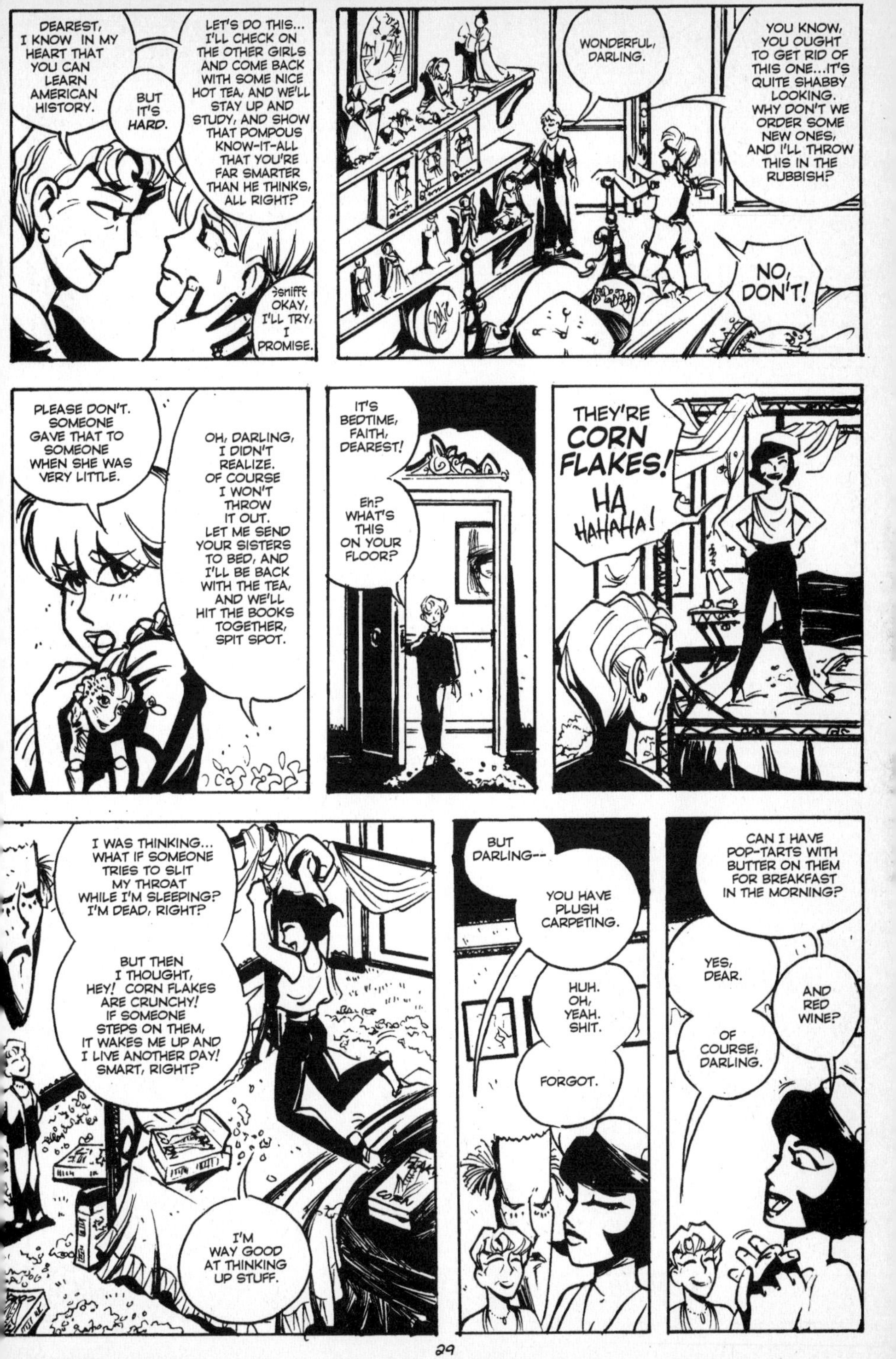

DEAREST, I KNOW IN MY HEART THAT YOU CAN LEARN AMERICAN HISTORY.
BUT IT'S HARD.
LET'S DO THIS... I'LL CHECK ON THE OTHER GIRLS AND COME BACK WITH SOME NICE HOT TEA, AND WE'LL STAY UP AND STUDY, AND SHOW THAT POMPOUS KNOW-IT-ALL THAT YOU'RE FAR SMARTER THAN HE THINKS, ALL RIGHT?
≶SNIFF≷ OKAY, I'LL TRY, I PROMISE.
WONDERFUL, DARLING.
YOU KNOW, YOU OUGHT TO GET RID OF THIS ONE...IT'S QUITE SHABBY LOOKING. WHY DON'T WE ORDER SOME NEW ONES, AND I'LL THROW THIS IN THE RUBBISH?
NO, DON'T!
PLEASE DON'T. SOMEONE GAVE THAT TO SOMEONE WHEN SHE WAS VERY LITTLE.
OH, DARLING, I DIDN'T REALIZE. OF COURSE I WON'T THROW IT OUT. LET ME SEND YOUR SISTERS TO BED, AND I'LL BE BACK WITH THE TEA, AND WE'LL HIT THE BOOKS TOGETHER, SPIT SPOT.
IT'S BEDTIME, FAITH, DEAREST!
Eh? WHAT'S THIS ON YOUR FLOOR?
THEY'RE CORN FLAKES! HA HAHAHA!
I WAS THINKING... WHAT IF SOMEONE TRIES TO SLIT MY THROAT WHILE I'M SLEEPING? I'M DEAD, RIGHT?
BUT THEN I THOUGHT, HEY! CORN FLAKES ARE CRUNCHY! IF SOMEONE STEPS ON THEM, IT WAKES ME UP AND I LIVE ANOTHER DAY! SMART, RIGHT?
I'M WAY GOOD AT THINKING UP STUFF.
BUT DARLING--
YOU HAVE PLUSH CARPETING.
HUH. OH, YEAH. SHIT.
FORGOT.
CAN I HAVE POP-TARTS WITH BUTTER ON THEM FOR BREAKFAST IN THE MORNING?
YES, DEAR.
AND RED WINE?
OF COURSE, DARLING.

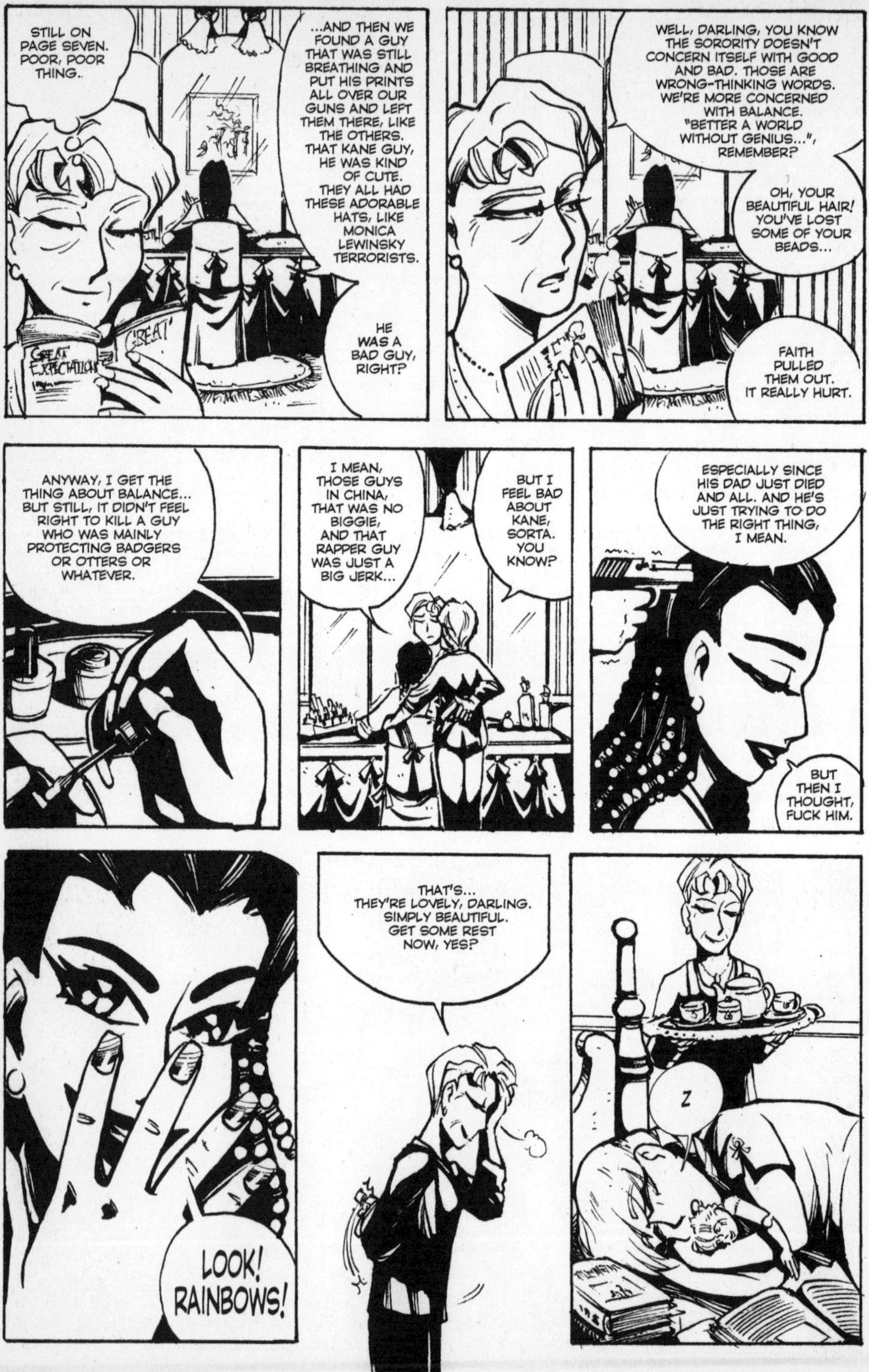
STILL ON PAGE SEVEN. POOR, POOR THING..
...AND THEN WE FOUND A GUY THAT WAS STILL BREATHING AND PUT HIS PRINTS ALL OVER OUR GUNS AND LEFT THEM THERE, LIKE THE OTHERS. THAT KANE GUY, HE WAS KIND OF CUTE. THEY ALL HAD THESE ADORABLE HATS, LIKE MONICA LEWINSKY TERRORISTS.
HE WAS A BAD GUY, RIGHT?
GREAT EXPECTATIONS
GREAT
WELL, DARLING, YOU KNOW THE SORORITY DOESN'T CONCERN ITSELF WITH GOOD AND BAD. THOSE ARE WRONG-THINKING WORDS. WE'RE MORE CONCERNED WITH BALANCE. "BETTER A WORLD WITHOUT GENIUS...", REMEMBER?
OH, YOUR BEAUTIFUL HAIR! YOU'VE LOST SOME OF YOUR BEADS...
FAITH PULLED THEM OUT. IT REALLY HURT.
ANYWAY, I GET THE THING ABOUT BALANCE... BUT STILL, IT DIDN'T FEEL RIGHT TO KILL A GUY WHO WAS MAINLY PROTECTING BADGERS OR OTTERS OR WHATEVER.
I MEAN, THOSE GUYS IN CHINA, THAT WAS NO BIGGIE, AND THAT RAPPER GUY WAS JUST A BIG JERK...
BUT I FEEL BAD ABOUT KANE, SORTA. YOU KNOW?
ESPECIALLY SINCE HIS DAD JUST DIED AND ALL. AND HE'S JUST TRYING TO DO THE RIGHT THING, I MEAN.
BUT THEN I THOUGHT, FUCK HIM.
LOOK! RAINBOWS!
THAT'S... THEY'RE LOVELY, DARLING. SIMPLY BEAUTIFUL. GET SOME REST NOW, YES?
Z

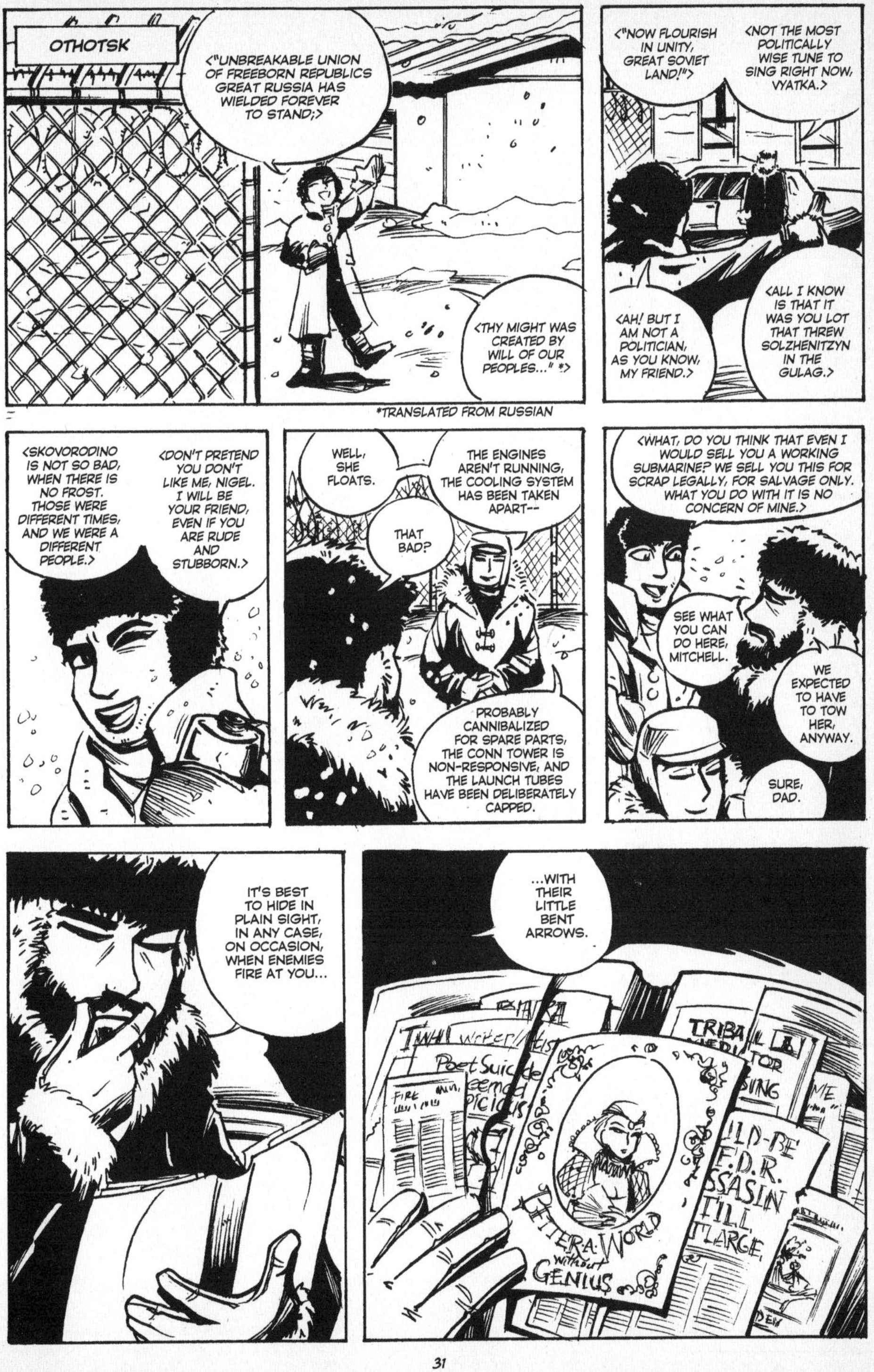
OTHOTSK
<"UNBREAKABLE UNION OF FREEBORN REPUBLICS GREAT RUSSIA HAS WIELDED FOREVER TO STAND;>
<THY MIGHT WAS CREATED BY WILL OF OUR PEOPLES..." *>
<"NOW FLOURISH IN UNITY, GREAT SOVIET LAND!">
<NOT THE MOST POLITICALLY WISE TUNE TO SING RIGHT NOW, VYATKA.>
<AH! BUT I AM NOT A POLITICIAN, AS YOU KNOW, MY FRIEND.>
<ALL I KNOW IS THAT IT WAS YOU LOT THAT THREW SOLZHENITZYN IN THE GULAG.>
*TRANSLATED FROM RUSSIAN
<SKOVORODINO IS NOT SO BAD, WHEN THERE IS NO FROST. THOSE WERE DIFFERENT TIMES, AND WE WERE A DIFFERENT PEOPLE.>
<DON'T PRETEND YOU DON'T LIKE ME, NIGEL. I WILL BE YOUR FRIEND, EVEN IF YOU ARE RUDE AND STUBBORN.>
WELL, SHE FLOATS.
THE ENGINES AREN'T RUNNING, THE COOLING SYSTEM HAS BEEN TAKEN APART--
THAT BAD?
PROBABLY CANNIBALIZED FOR SPARE PARTS, THE CONN TOWER IS NON-RESPONSIVE, AND THE LAUNCH TUBES HAVE BEEN DELIBERATELY CAPPED.
<WHAT, DO YOU THINK THAT EVEN I WOULD SELL YOU A WORKING SUBMARINE? WE SELL YOU THIS FOR SCRAP LEGALLY, FOR SALVAGE ONLY. WHAT YOU DO WITH IT IS NO CONCERN OF MINE.>
SEE WHAT YOU CAN DO HERE, MITCHELL.
WE EXPECTED TO HAVE TO TOW HER, ANYWAY.
SURE, DAD.
IT'S BEST TO HIDE IN PLAIN SIGHT, IN ANY CASE, ON OCCASION, WHEN ENEMIES FIRE AT YOU...
...WITH THEIR LITTLE BENT ARROWS.
BETTER A WORLD without GENIUS

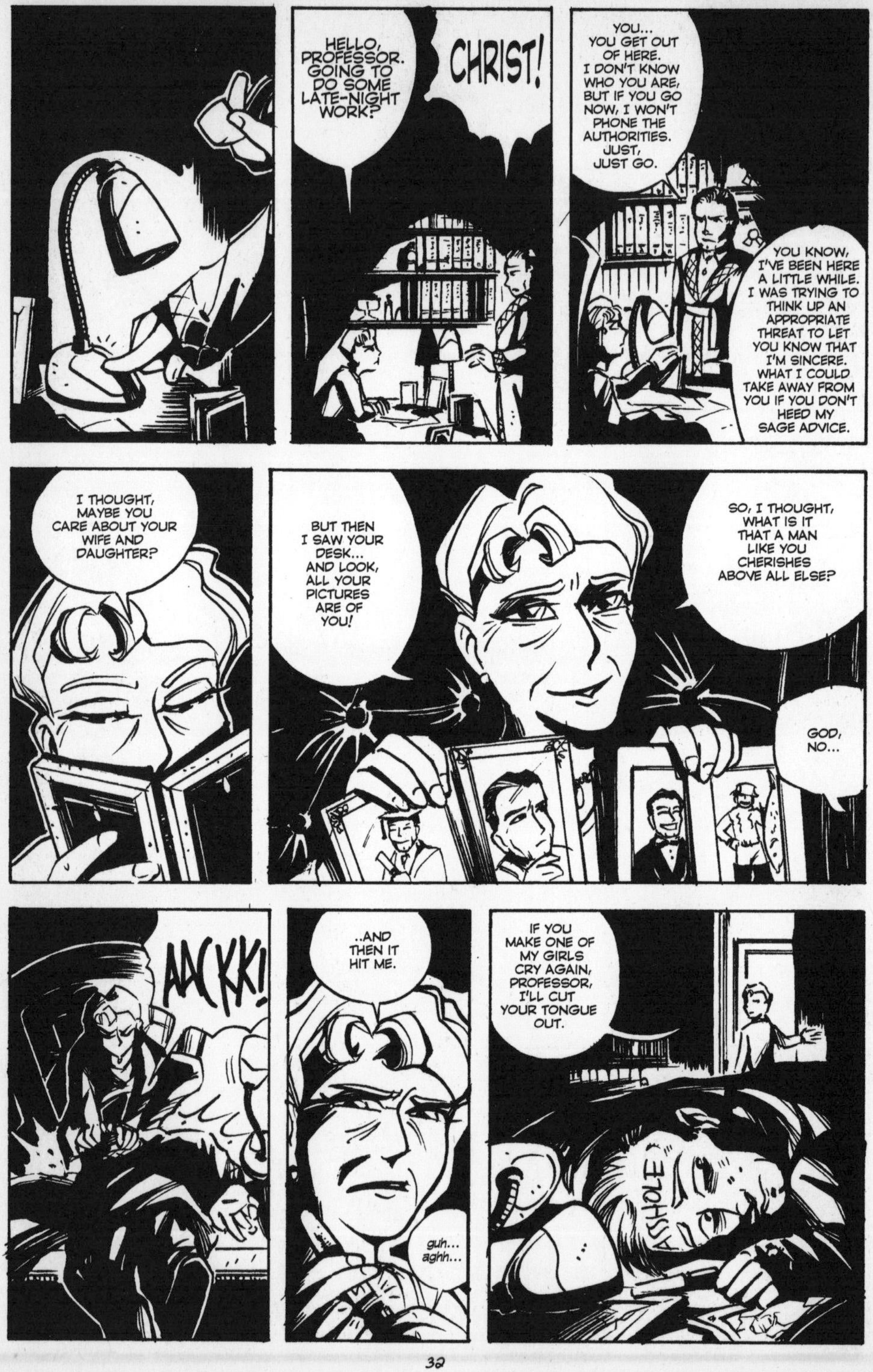

HELLO, PROFESSOR. GOING TO DO SOME LATE-NIGHT WORK?
CHRIST!
YOU... YOU GET OUT OF HERE. I DON'T KNOW WHO YOU ARE, BUT IF YOU GO NOW, I WON'T PHONE THE AUTHORITIES. JUST, JUST GO.
YOU KNOW, I'VE BEEN HERE A LITTLE WHILE. I WAS TRYING TO THINK UP AN APPROPRIATE THREAT TO LET YOU KNOW THAT I'M SINCERE. WHAT I COULD TAKE AWAY FROM YOU IF YOU DON'T HEED MY SAGE ADVICE.
I THOUGHT, MAYBE YOU CARE ABOUT YOUR WIFE AND DAUGHTER?
BUT THEN I SAW YOUR DESK... AND LOOK, ALL YOUR PICTURES ARE OF YOU!
SO, I THOUGHT, WHAT IS IT THAT A MAN LIKE YOU CHERISHES ABOVE ALL ELSE?
GOD, NO...
AACKK!
..AND THEN IT HIT ME.
guh... aghh...
IF YOU MAKE ONE OF MY GIRLS CRY AGAIN, PROFESSOR, I'LL CUT YOUR TONGUE OUT.
...
ASSHOLE

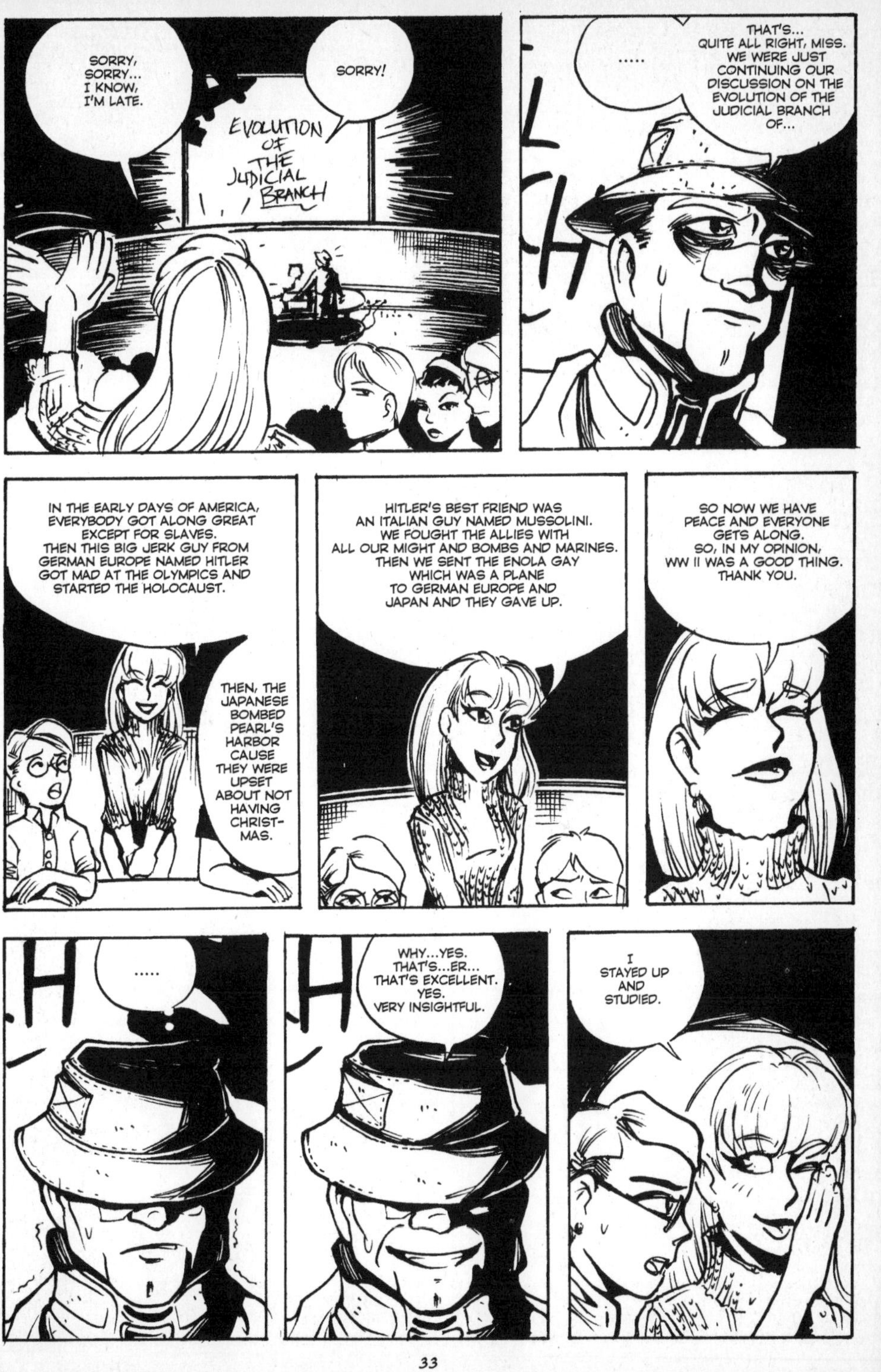
SORRY, SORRY... I KNOW, I'M LATE.
SORRY!
EVOLUTION OF THE JUDICIAL BRANCH
.....
THAT'S... QUITE ALL RIGHT, MISS. WE WERE JUST CONTINUING OUR DISCUSSION ON THE EVOLUTION OF THE JUDICIAL BRANCH OF...
IN THE EARLY DAYS OF AMERICA, EVERYBODY GOT ALONG GREAT EXCEPT FOR SLAVES. THEN THIS BIG JERK GUY FROM GERMAN EUROPE NAMED HITLER GOT MAD AT THE OLYMPICS AND STARTED THE HOLOCAUST.
THEN, THE JAPANESE BOMBED PEARL'S HARBOR CAUSE THEY WERE UPSET ABOUT NOT HAVING CHRIST-MAS.
HITLER'S BEST FRIEND WAS AN ITALIAN GUY NAMED MUSSOLINI. WE FOUGHT THE ALLIES WITH ALL OUR MIGHT AND BOMBS AND MARINES. THEN WE SENT THE ENOLA GAY WHICH WAS A PLANE TO GERMAN EUROPE AND JAPAN AND THEY GAVE UP.
SO NOW WE HAVE PEACE AND EVERYONE GETS ALONG. SO, IN MY OPINION, WW II WAS A GOOD THING. THANK YOU.
.....
WHY...YES. THAT'S...ER... THAT'S EXCELLENT. YES. VERY INSIGHTFUL.
I STAYED UP AND STUDIED.

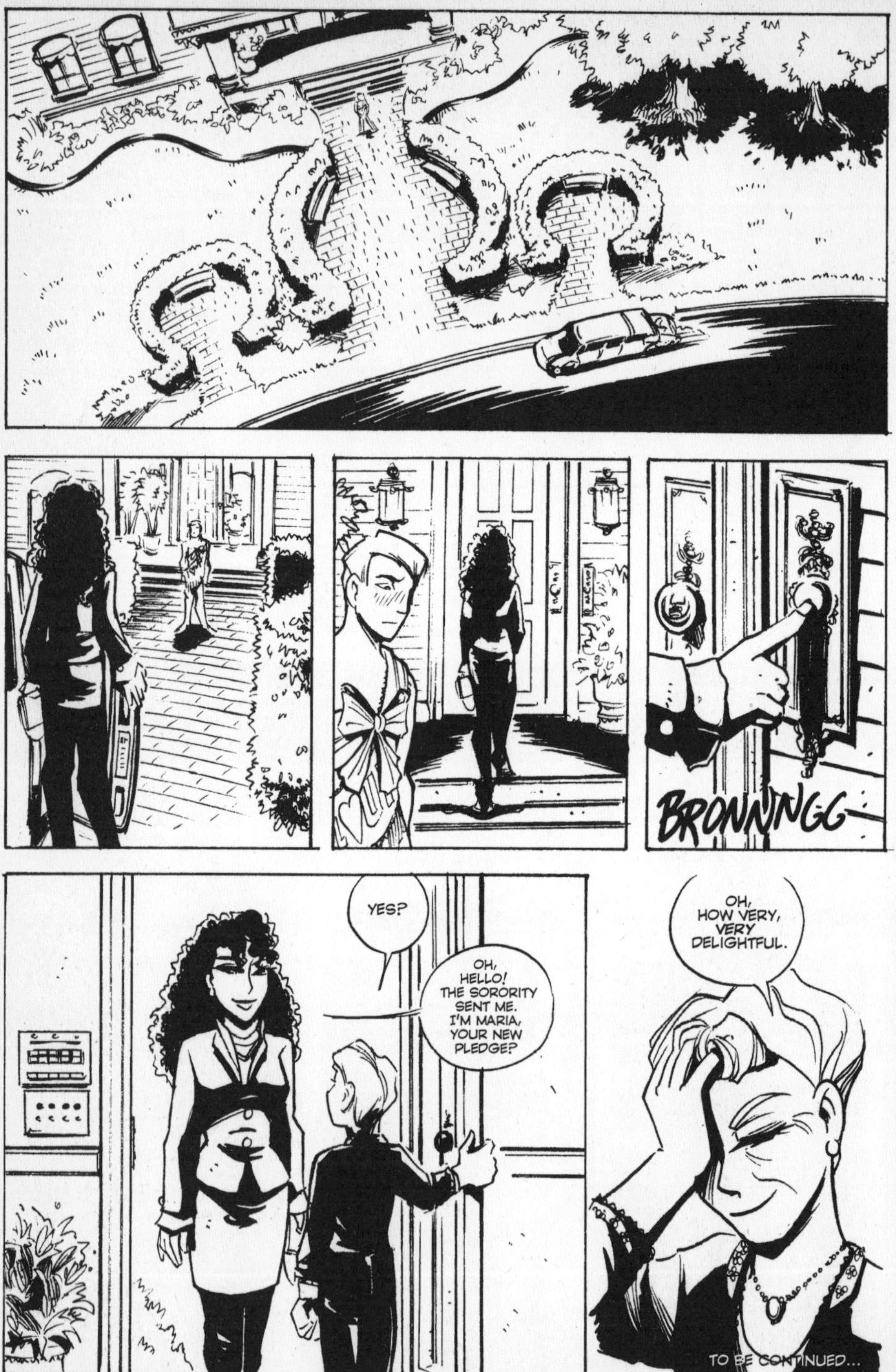
BRONNNGG
YES?
OH, HELLO! THE SORORITY SENT ME. I'M MARIA, YOUR NEW PLEDGE?
OH, HOW VERY, VERY DELIGHTFUL.
TO BE CONTINUED...

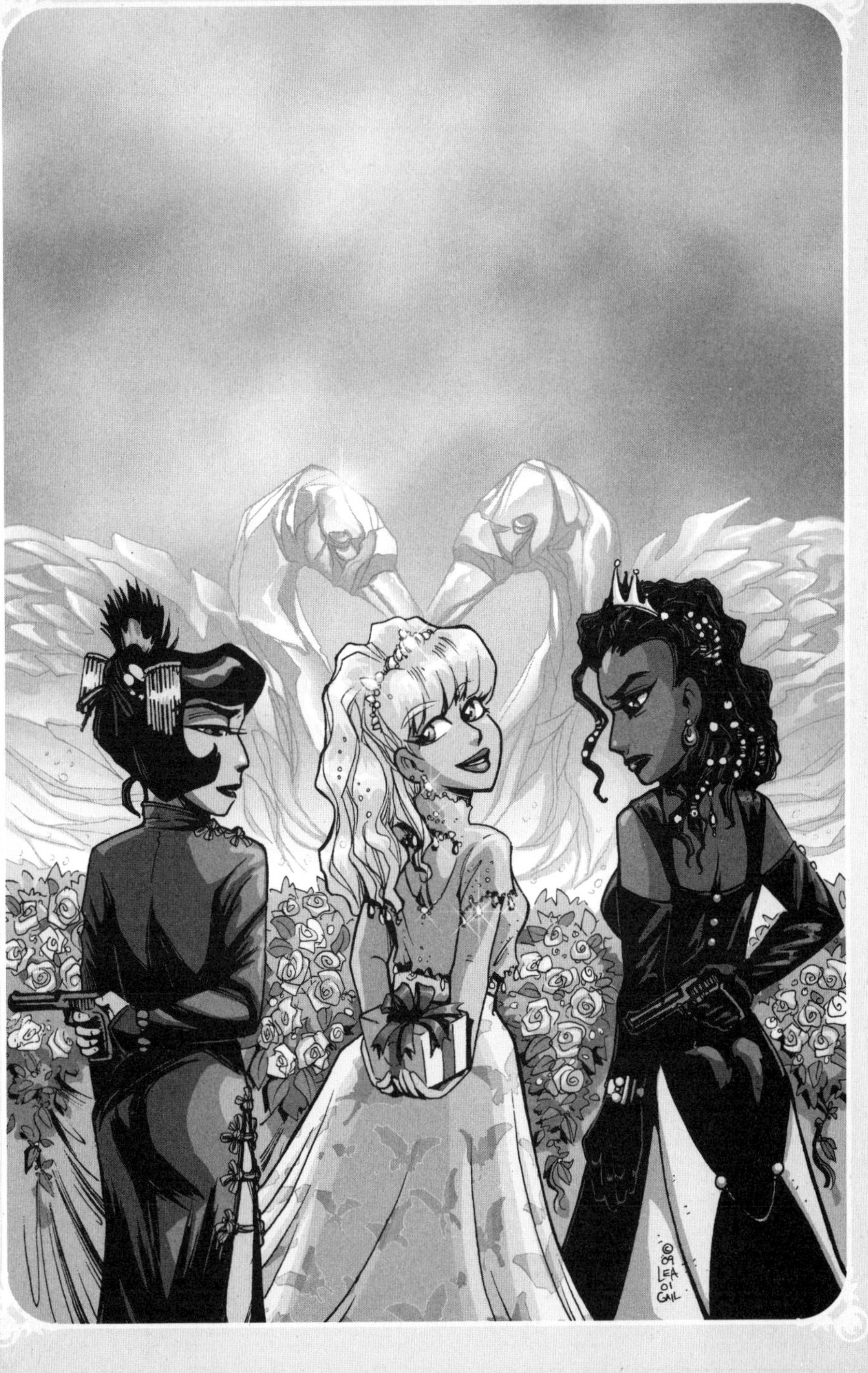
©
'09
LEA
01
GAIL

Chapter 2

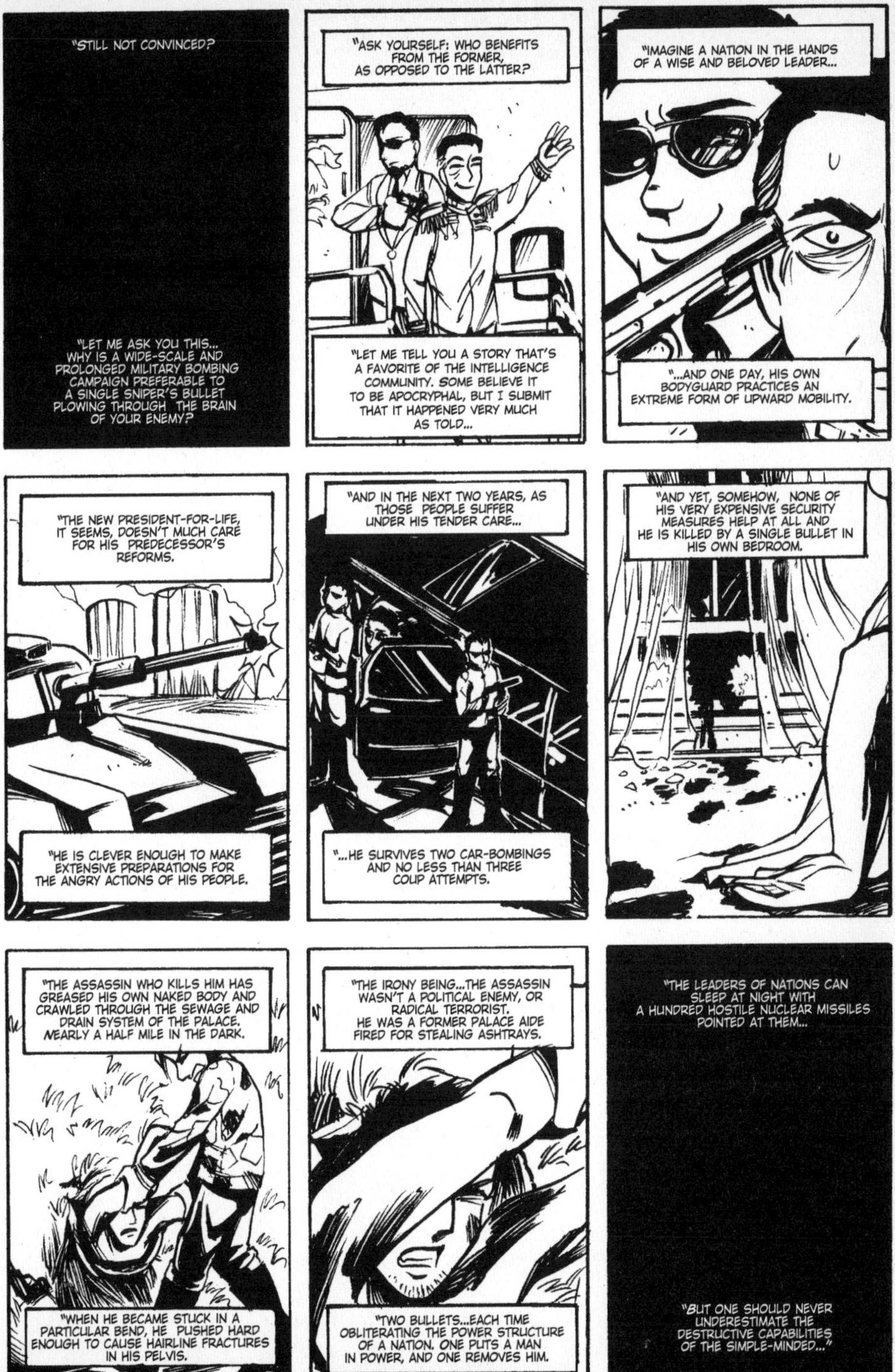
"STILL NOT CONVINCED?
"LET ME ASK YOU THIS... WHY IS A WIDE-SCALE AND PROLONGED MILITARY BOMBING CAMPAIGN PREFERABLE TO A SINGLE SNIPER'S BULLET PLOWING THROUGH THE BRAIN OF YOUR ENEMY?
"ASK YOURSELF: WHO BENEFITS FROM THE FORMER, AS OPPOSED TO THE LATTER?
"LET ME TELL YOU A STORY THAT'S A FAVORITE OF THE INTELLIGENCE COMMUNITY. SOME BELIEVE IT TO BE APOCRYPHAL, BUT I SUBMIT THAT IT HAPPENED VERY MUCH AS TOLD...
"IMAGINE A NATION IN THE HANDS OF A WISE AND BELOVED LEADER...
"...AND ONE DAY, HIS OWN BODYGUARD PRACTICES AN EXTREME FORM OF UPWARD MOBILITY.
"THE NEW PRESIDENT-FOR-LIFE, IT SEEMS, DOESN'T MUCH CARE FOR HIS PREDECESSOR'S REFORMS.
"HE IS CLEVER ENOUGH TO MAKE EXTENSIVE PREPARATIONS FOR THE ANGRY ACTIONS OF HIS PEOPLE.
"AND IN THE NEXT TWO YEARS, AS THOSE PEOPLE SUFFER UNDER HIS TENDER CARE...
"...HE SURVIVES TWO CAR-BOMBINGS AND NO LESS THAN THREE COUP ATTEMPTS.
"AND YET, SOMEHOW, NONE OF HIS VERY EXPENSIVE SECURITY MEASURES HELP AT ALL AND HE IS KILLED BY A SINGLE BULLET IN HIS OWN BEDROOM.
"THE ASSASSIN WHO KILLS HIM HAS GREASED HIS OWN NAKED BODY AND CRAWLED THROUGH THE SEWAGE AND DRAIN SYSTEM OF THE PALACE. NEARLY A HALF MILE IN THE DARK.
"WHEN HE BECAME STUCK IN A PARTICULAR BEND, HE PUSHED HARD ENOUGH TO CAUSE HAIRLINE FRACTURES IN HIS PELVIS.
"THE IRONY BEING...THE ASSASSIN WASN'T A POLITICAL ENEMY, OR RADICAL TERRORIST. HE WAS A FORMER PALACE AIDE FIRED FOR STEALING ASHTRAYS.
"TWO BULLETS...EACH TIME OBLITERATING THE POWER STRUCTURE OF A NATION. ONE PUTS A MAN IN POWER, AND ONE REMOVES HIM.
"THE LEADERS OF NATIONS CAN SLEEP AT NIGHT WITH A HUNDRED HOSTILE NUCLEAR MISSILES POINTED AT THEM...
"BUT ONE SHOULD NEVER UNDERESTIMATE THE DESTRUCTIVE CAPABILITIES OF THE SIMPLE-MINDED..."

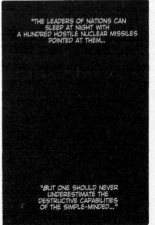

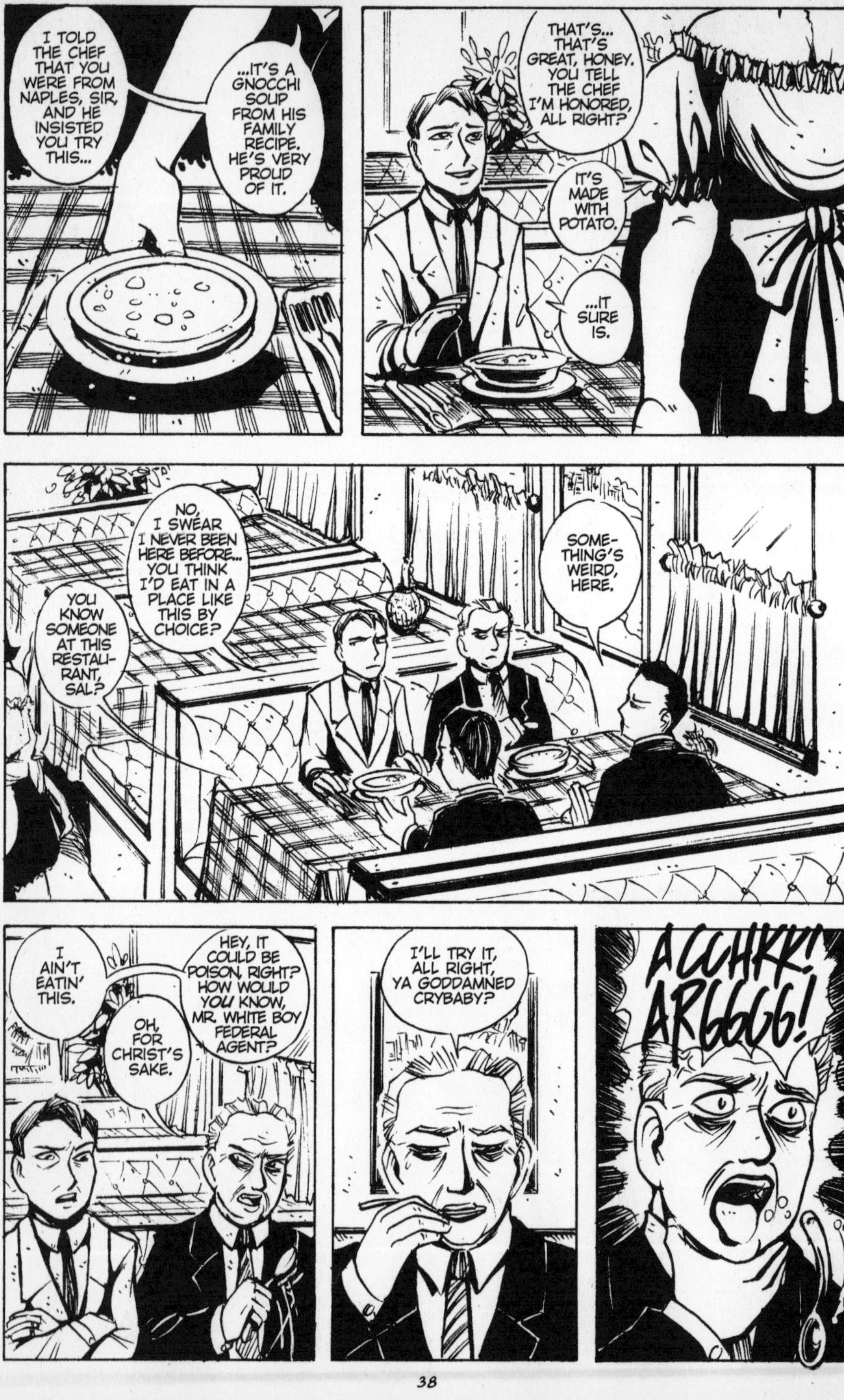
I TOLD THE CHEF THAT YOU WERE FROM NAPLES, SIR, AND HE INSISTED YOU TRY THIS...
...IT'S A GNOCCHI SOUP FROM HIS FAMILY RECIPE. HE'S VERY PROUD OF IT.
THAT'S... THAT'S GREAT, HONEY. YOU TELL THE CHEF I'M HONORED, ALL RIGHT?
IT'S MADE WITH POTATO.
...IT SURE IS.
YOU KNOW SOMEONE AT THIS RESTAURANT, SAL?
NO, I SWEAR I NEVER BEEN HERE BEFORE... YOU THINK I'D EAT IN A PLACE LIKE THIS BY CHOICE?
SOME-THING'S WEIRD, HERE.
I AIN'T EATIN' THIS.
HEY, IT COULD BE POISON, RIGHT? HOW WOULD *YOU* KNOW, MR. WHITE BOY FEDERAL AGENT?
OH, FOR CHRIST'S SAKE.
I'LL TRY IT, ALL RIGHT, YA GODDAMNED CRYBABY?
ACCHRR! ARGGGG!

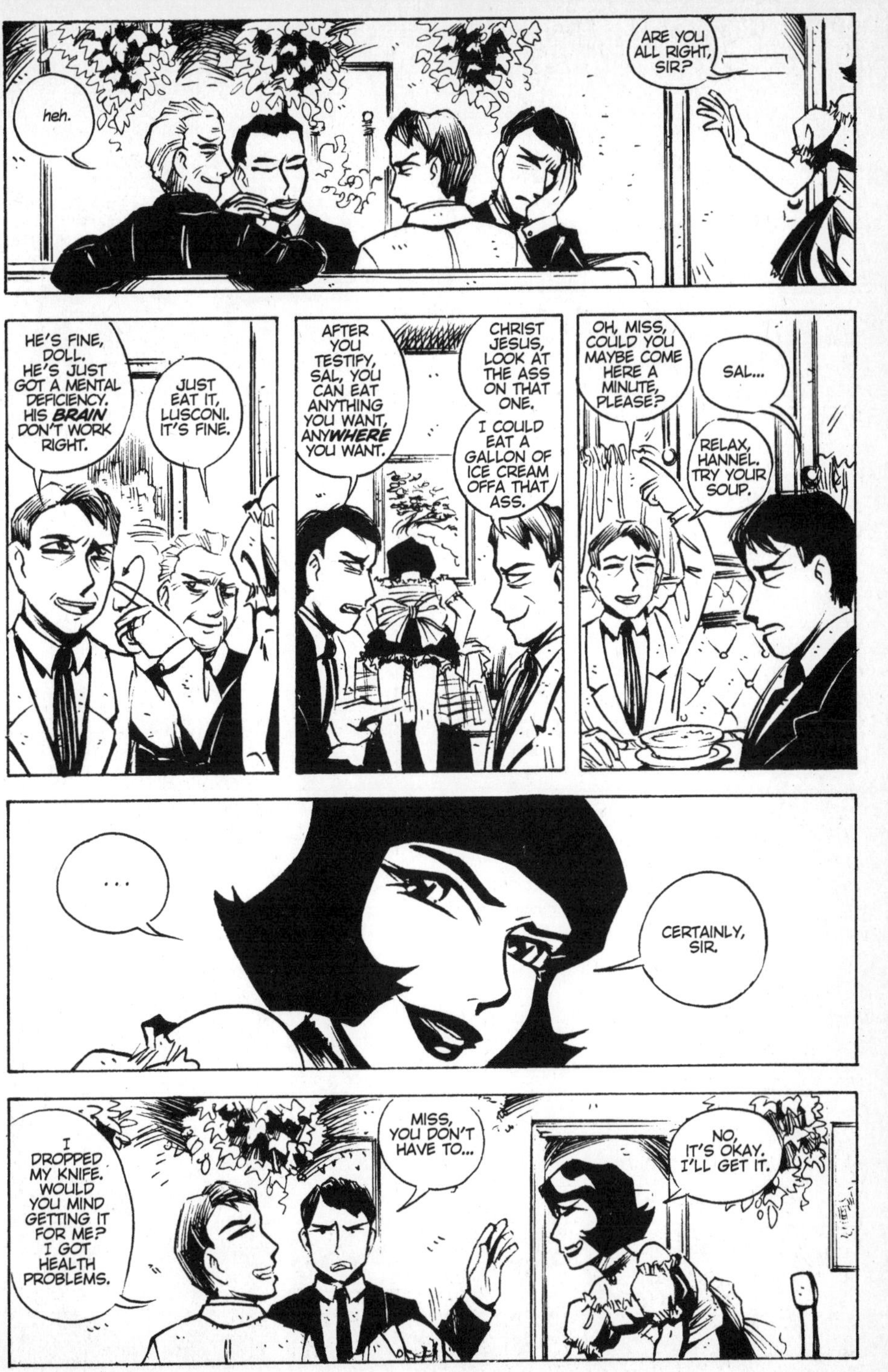
ARE YOU ALL RIGHT, SIR?
heh.
HE'S FINE, DOLL. HE'S JUST GOT A MENTAL DEFICIENCY. HIS **BRAIN** DON'T WORK RIGHT.
JUST EAT IT, LUSCONI. IT'S FINE.
AFTER YOU TESTIFY, SAL, YOU CAN EAT ANYTHING YOU WANT, ANY***WHERE*** YOU WANT.
CHRIST JESUS, LOOK AT THE ASS ON THAT ONE.
I COULD EAT A GALLON OF ICE CREAM OFFA THAT ASS.
OH, MISS, COULD YOU MAYBE COME HERE A MINUTE, PLEASE?
SAL...
RELAX, HANNEL. TRY YOUR SOUP.
...
CERTAINLY, SIR.
I DROPPED MY KNIFE. WOULD YOU MIND GETTING IT FOR ME? I GOT HEALTH PROBLEMS.
MISS, YOU DON'T HAVE TO...
NO, IT'S OKAY. I'LL GET IT.

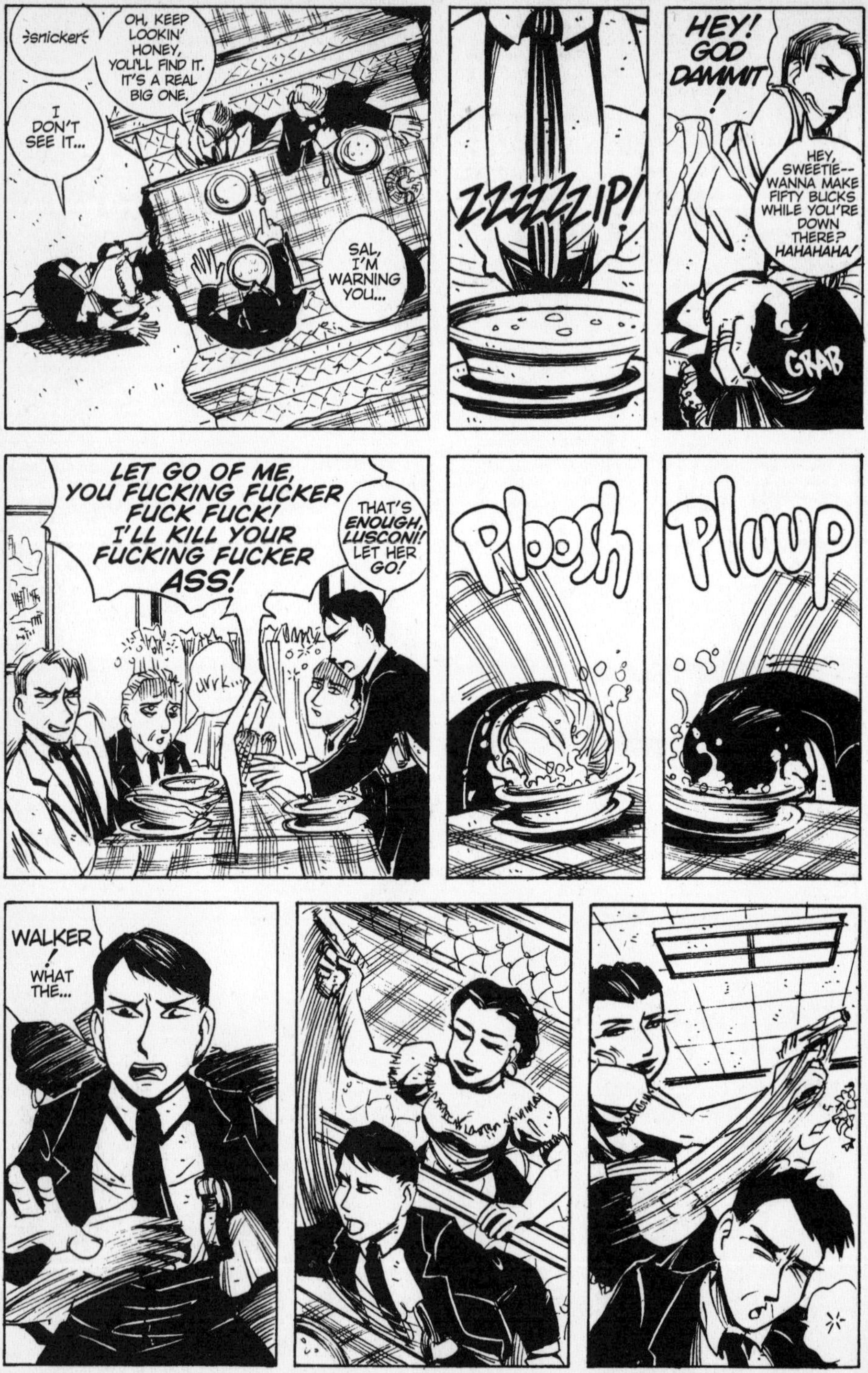

snicker
OH, KEEP LOOKIN' HONEY, YOU'LL FIND IT. IT'S A REAL BIG ONE.
I DON'T SEE IT...
SAL, I'M WARNING YOU...
ZZZZZZIP!
HEY! GOD DAMMIT!
HEY, SWEETIE-- WANNA MAKE FIFTY BUCKS WHILE YOU'RE DOWN THERE? HAHAHAHA!
GRAB
LET GO OF ME, YOU FUCKING FUCKER FUCK FUCK! I'LL KILL YOUR FUCKING FUCKER ASS!
THAT'S ENOUGH, LUSCONI! LET HER GO!
urrk...
Ploosh
Pluup
WALKER! WHAT THE...

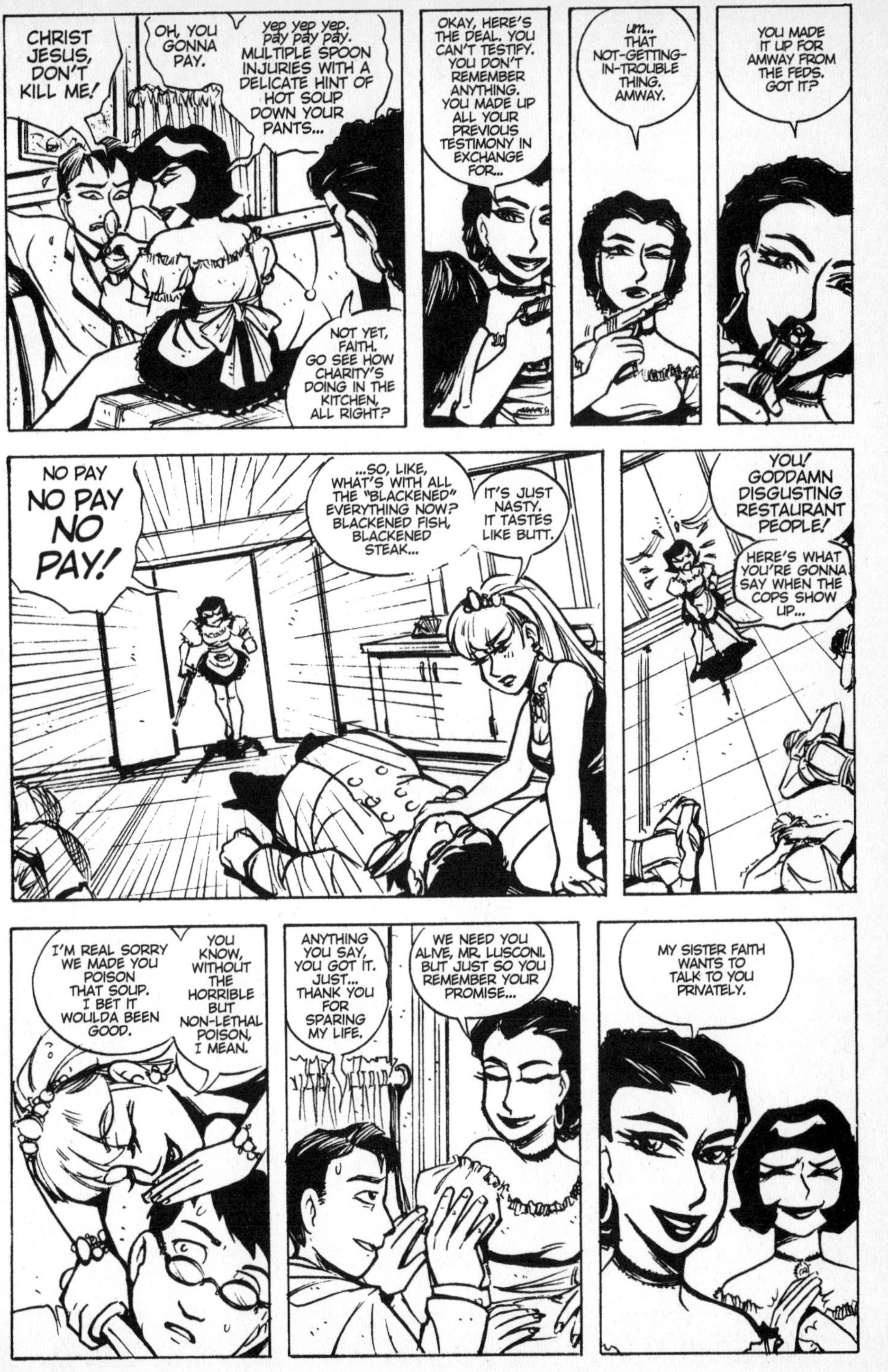
CHRIST JESUS, DON'T KILL ME!
OH, YOU GONNA PAY.
yep yep yep. pay pay pay. MULTIPLE SPOON INJURIES WITH A DELICATE HINT OF HOT SOUP DOWN YOUR PANTS...
NOT YET, FAITH. GO SEE HOW CHARITY'S DOING IN THE KITCHEN, ALL RIGHT?
OKAY, HERE'S THE DEAL. YOU CAN'T TESTIFY. YOU DON'T REMEMBER ANYTHING. YOU MADE UP ALL YOUR PREVIOUS TESTIMONY IN EXCHANGE FOR...
um... THAT NOT-GETTING-IN-TROUBLE THING. AMWAY.
YOU MADE IT UP FOR AMWAY FROM THE FEDS. GOT IT?
NO PAY NO PAY NO PAY!
...SO, LIKE, WHAT'S WITH ALL THE "BLACKENED" EVERYTHING NOW? BLACKENED FISH, BLACKENED STEAK...
IT'S JUST NASTY. IT TASTES LIKE BUTT.
YOU! GODDAMN DISGUSTING RESTAURANT PEOPLE!
HERE'S WHAT YOU'RE GONNA SAY WHEN THE COPS SHOW UP...
I'M REAL SORRY WE MADE YOU POISON THAT SOUP. I BET IT WOULDA BEEN GOOD.
YOU KNOW, WITHOUT THE HORRIBLE BUT NON-LETHAL POISON, I MEAN.
ANYTHING YOU SAY, YOU GOT IT. JUST... THANK YOU FOR SPARING MY LIFE.
WE NEED YOU ALIVE, MR. LUSCONI. BUT JUST SO YOU REMEMBER YOUR PROMISE...
MY SISTER FAITH WANTS TO TALK TO YOU PRIVATELY.

JESUS CHRI-

SILVIO LUSCONI A-0959-0311 04.13
Silver Oaks Hospital   L. ARM

GODDAMMIT STOP!

SILVIO LUSCONI A-0959-0311 04.13
Silver Oaks Hospital   R. FOOT

NOT THE FA...

OWW!

SILVIO LUSCONI A-0959-0311 04.13   L. MANDI
Silver Oaks Hospital

Mfffannd!
Mmffikkin
AAAnwx!

SILVIO LUSCON
Silver Oaks H   R. HAND

I LOVE MY JOB!

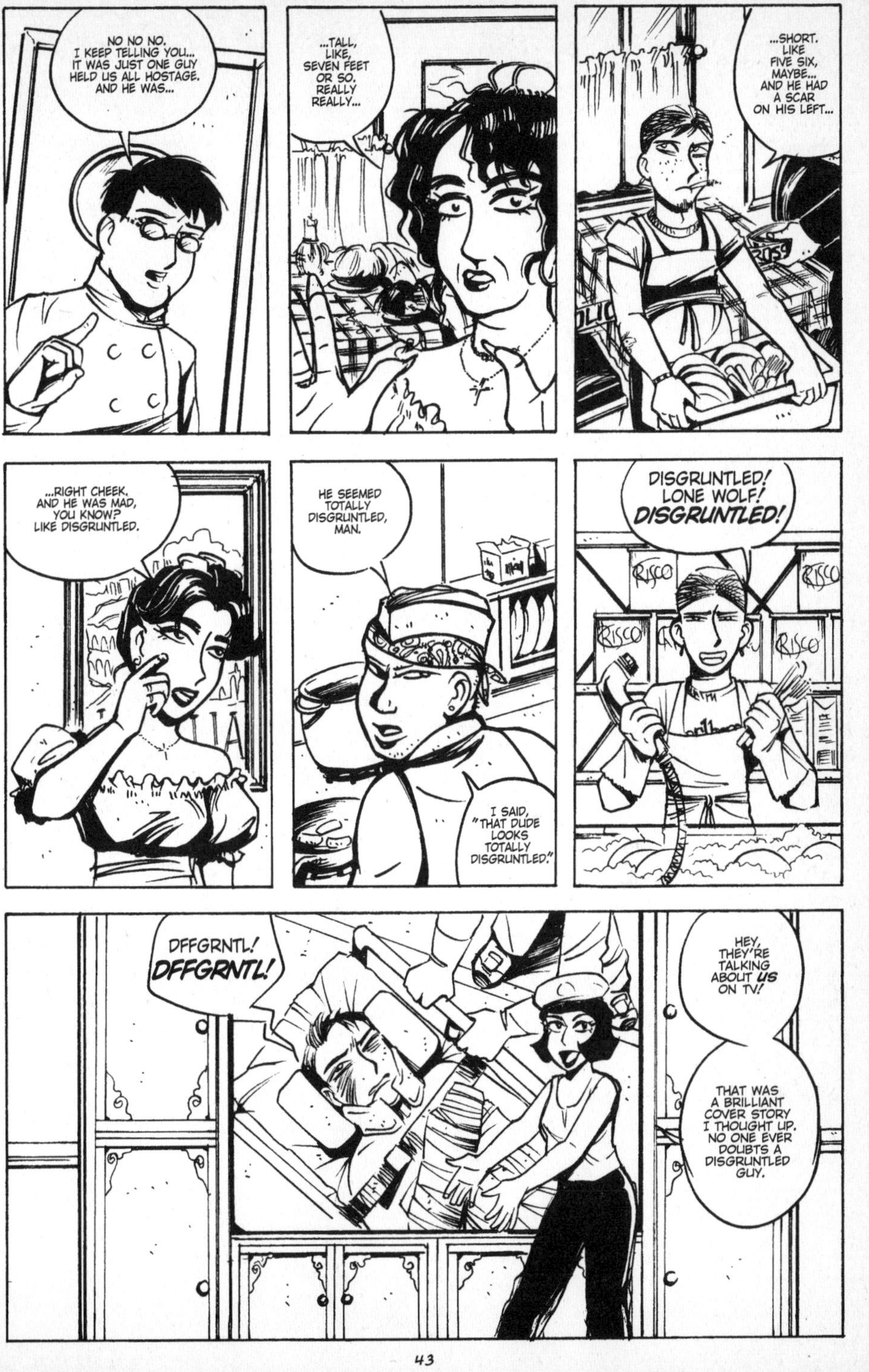
NO NO NO. I KEEP TELLING YOU... IT WAS JUST ONE GUY HELD US ALL HOSTAGE. AND HE WAS...
...TALL, LIKE, SEVEN FEET OR SO. REALLY REALLY...
...SHORT. LIKE FIVE SIX, MAYBE... AND HE HAD A SCAR ON HIS LEFT...
...RIGHT CHEEK. AND HE WAS MAD, YOU KNOW? LIKE DISGRUNTLED.
HE SEEMED TOTALLY DISGRUNTLED, MAN.
I SAID, "THAT DUDE LOOKS TOTALLY DISGRUNTLED."
DISGRUNTLED! LONE WOLF! DISGRUNTLED!
RISCO
DFFGRNTL! DFFGRNTL!
HEY, THEY'RE TALKING ABOUT US ON TV!
THAT WAS A BRILLIANT COVER STORY I THOUGHT UP. NO ONE EVER DOUBTS A DISGRUNTLED GUY.

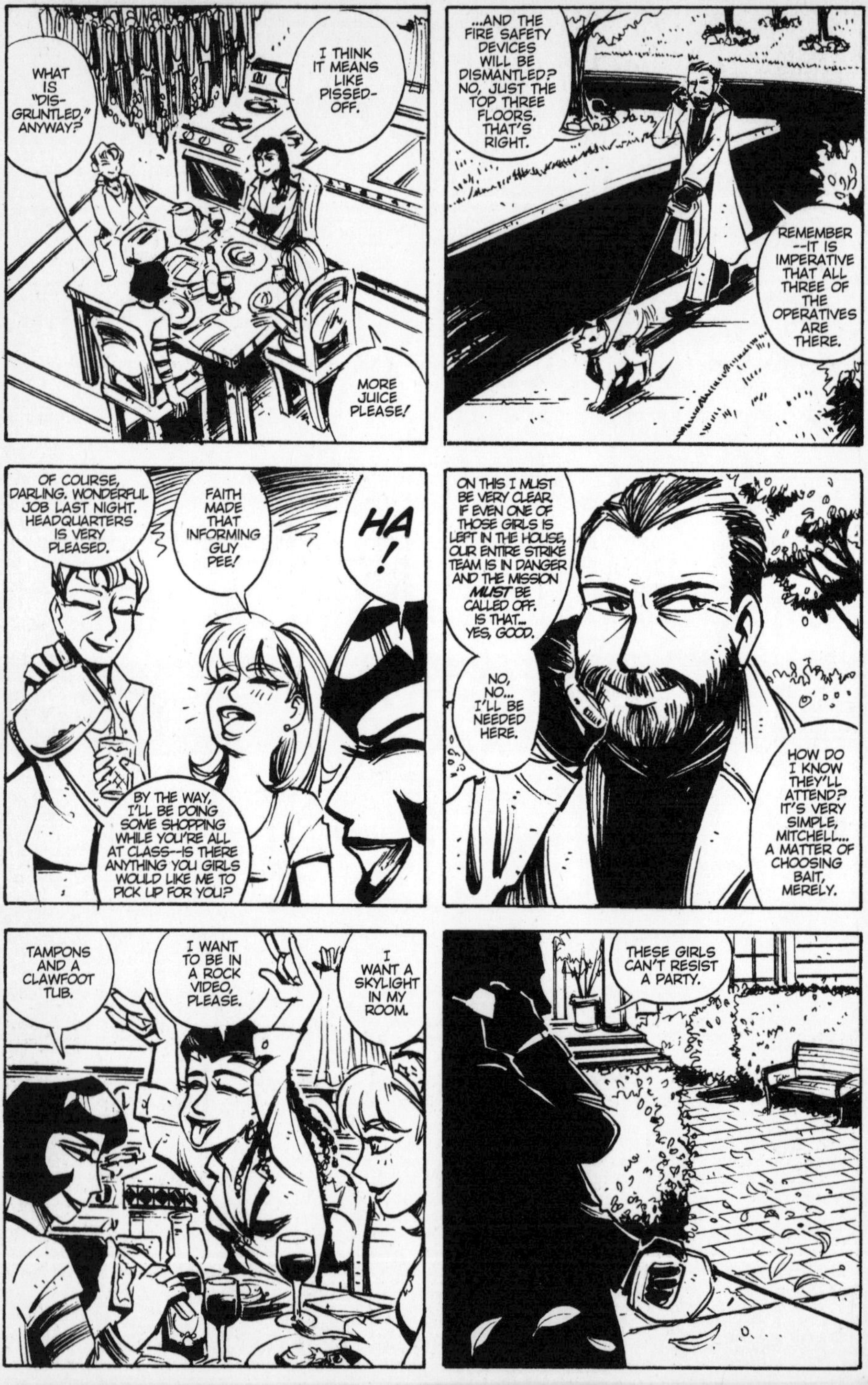
WHAT IS "DIS-GRUNTLED," ANYWAY?
I THINK IT MEANS LIKE PISSED-OFF.
MORE JUICE PLEASE!
...AND THE FIRE SAFETY DEVICES WILL BE DISMANTLED? NO, JUST THE TOP THREE FLOORS. THAT'S RIGHT.
REMEMBER --IT IS IMPERATIVE THAT ALL THREE OF THE OPERATIVES ARE THERE.
OF COURSE, DARLING. WONDERFUL JOB LAST NIGHT. HEADQUARTERS IS VERY PLEASED.
FAITH MADE THAT INFORMING GUY PEE!
HA!
BY THE WAY, I'LL BE DOING SOME SHOPPING WHILE YOU'RE ALL AT CLASS--IS THERE ANYTHING YOU GIRLS WOULD LIKE ME TO PICK UP FOR YOU?
ON THIS I MUST BE VERY CLEAR. IF EVEN ONE OF THOSE GIRLS IS LEFT IN THE HOUSE, OUR ENTIRE STRIKE TEAM IS IN DANGER AND THE MISSION MUST BE CALLED OFF. IS THAT... YES, GOOD.
NO, NO... I'LL BE NEEDED HERE.
HOW DO I KNOW THEY'LL ATTEND? IT'S VERY SIMPLE, MITCHELL... A MATTER OF CHOOSING BAIT, MERELY.
TAMPONS AND A CLAWFOOT TUB.
I WANT TO BE IN A ROCK VIDEO, PLEASE.
I WANT A SKYLIGHT IN MY ROOM.
THESE GIRLS CAN'T RESIST A PARTY.

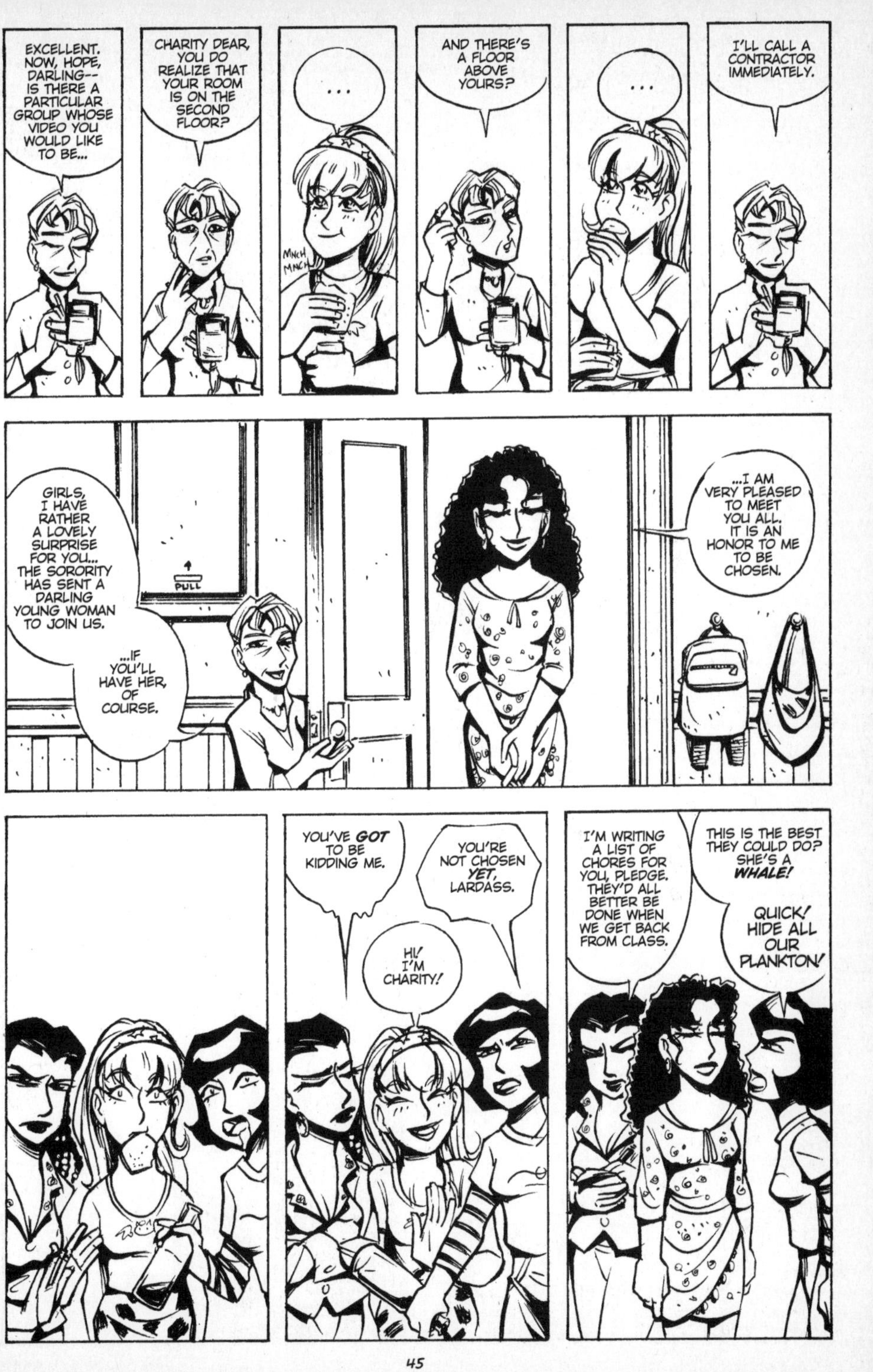

EXCELLENT. NOW, HOPE, DARLING-- IS THERE A PARTICULAR GROUP WHOSE VIDEO YOU WOULD LIKE TO BE...
CHARITY DEAR, YOU DO REALIZE THAT YOUR ROOM IS ON THE SECOND FLOOR?
...
MNCH MNCH
AND THERE'S A FLOOR ABOVE YOURS?
...
I'LL CALL A CONTRACTOR IMMEDIATELY.
GIRLS, I HAVE RATHER A LOVELY SURPRISE FOR YOU... THE SORORITY HAS SENT A DARLING YOUNG WOMAN TO JOIN US.
...IF YOU'LL HAVE HER, OF COURSE.
PULL
...I AM VERY PLEASED TO MEET YOU ALL. IT IS AN HONOR TO ME TO BE CHOSEN.
YOU'VE **GOT** TO BE KIDDING ME.
YOU'RE NOT CHOSEN **YET**, LARDASS.
HI! I'M CHARITY!
I'M WRITING A LIST OF CHORES FOR YOU, PLEDGE. THEY'D ALL BETTER BE DONE WHEN WE GET BACK FROM CLASS.
THIS IS THE BEST THEY COULD DO? SHE'S A **WHALE!**
QUICK! HIDE ALL OUR PLANKTON!

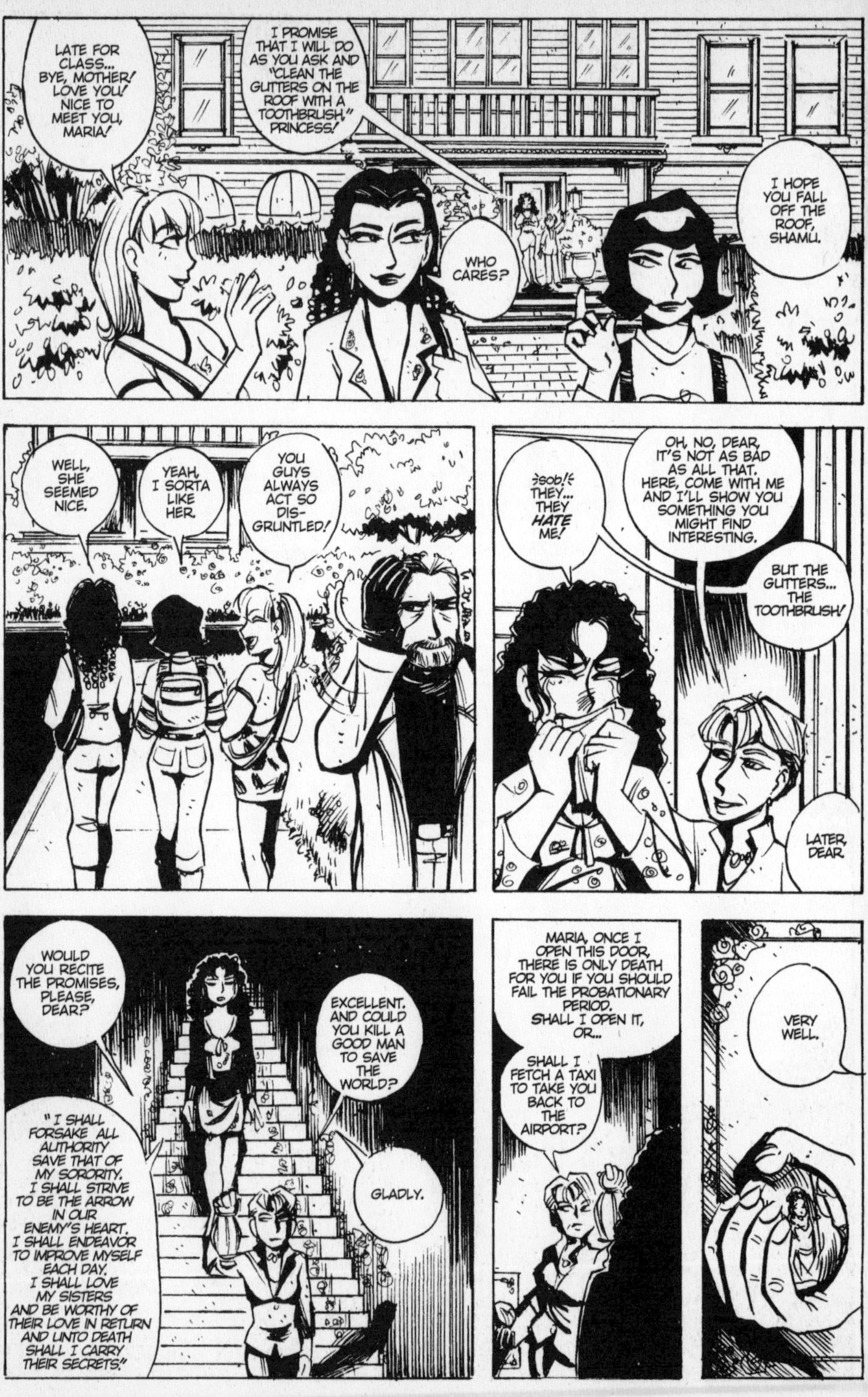
LATE FOR CLASS... BYE, MOTHER! LOVE YOU! NICE TO MEET YOU, MARIA!
I PROMISE THAT I WILL DO AS YOU ASK AND "CLEAN THE GUTTERS ON THE ROOF WITH A TOOTHBRUSH," PRINCESS!
WHO CARES?
I HOPE YOU FALL OFF THE ROOF, SHAMU.
WELL, SHE SEEMED NICE.
YEAH, I SORTA LIKE HER.
YOU GUYS ALWAYS ACT SO DIS-GRUNTLED!
sob! THEY... THEY *HATE* ME!
OH, NO, DEAR, IT'S NOT AS BAD AS ALL THAT. HERE, COME WITH ME AND I'LL SHOW YOU SOMETHING YOU MIGHT FIND INTERESTING.
BUT THE GUTTERS... THE TOOTHBRUSH!
LATER, DEAR
WOULD YOU RECITE THE PROMISES, PLEASE, DEAR?
"I SHALL FORSAKE ALL AUTHORITY SAVE THAT OF MY SORORITY. I SHALL STRIVE TO BE THE ARROW IN OUR ENEMY'S HEART. I SHALL ENDEAVOR TO IMPROVE MYSELF EACH DAY. I SHALL LOVE MY SISTERS AND BE WORTHY OF THEIR LOVE IN RETURN AND UNTO DEATH SHALL I CARRY THEIR SECRETS."
EXCELLENT. AND COULD YOU KILL A GOOD MAN TO SAVE THE WORLD?
GLADLY.
MARIA, ONCE I OPEN THIS DOOR, THERE IS ONLY DEATH FOR YOU IF YOU SHOULD FAIL THE PROBATIONARY PERIOD. SHALL I OPEN IT, OR...
SHALL I FETCH A TAXI TO TAKE YOU BACK TO THE AIRPORT?
VERY WELL.

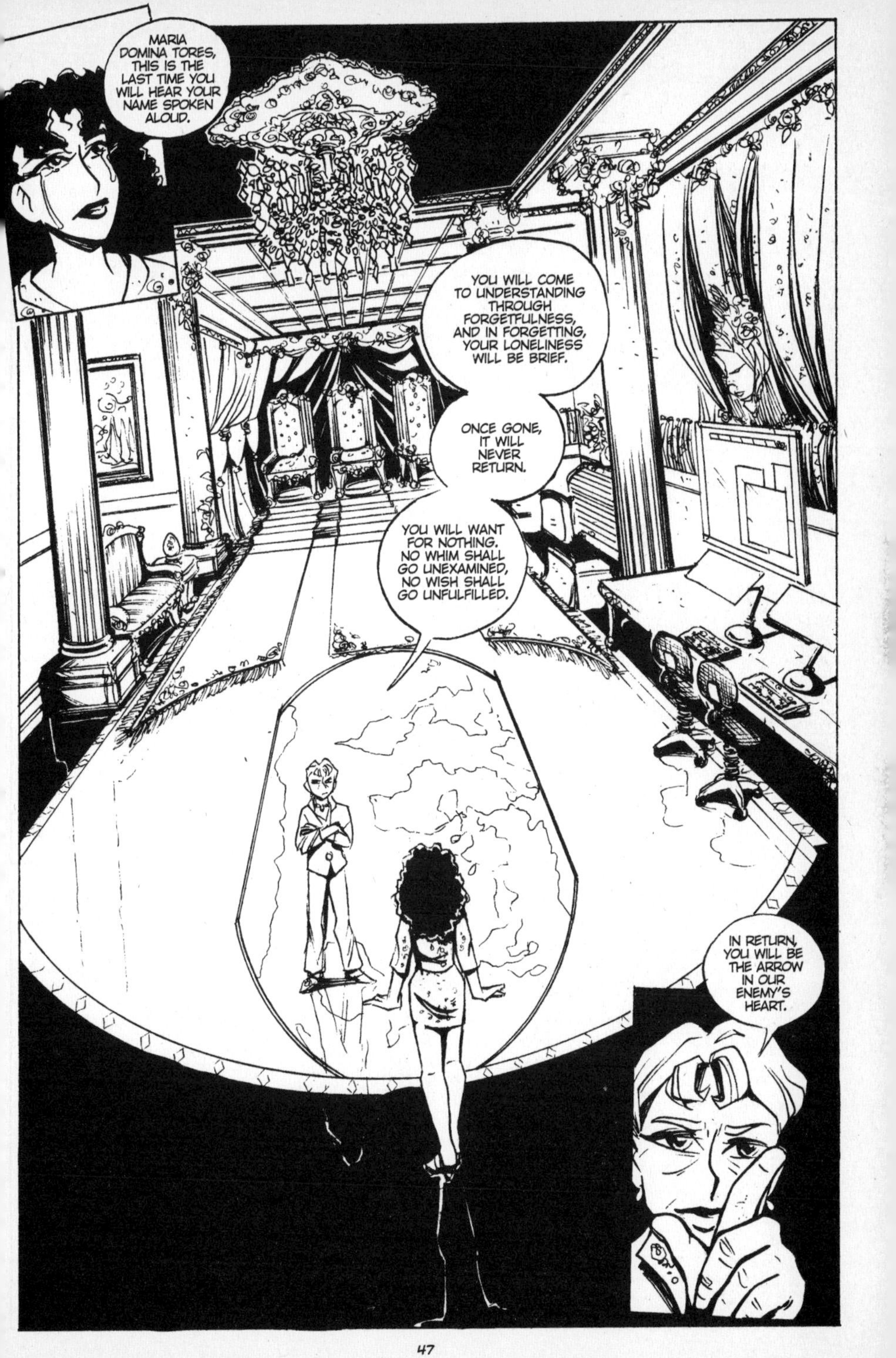
MARIA DOMINA TORES, THIS IS THE LAST TIME YOU WILL HEAR YOUR NAME SPOKEN ALOUD.
YOU WILL COME TO UNDERSTANDING THROUGH FORGETFULNESS, AND IN FORGETTING, YOUR LONELINESS WILL BE BRIEF.
ONCE GONE, IT WILL NEVER RETURN.
YOU WILL WANT FOR NOTHING. NO WHIM SHALL GO UNEXAMINED, NO WISH SHALL GO UNFULFILLED.
IN RETURN, YOU WILL BE THE ARROW IN OUR ENEMY'S HEART.

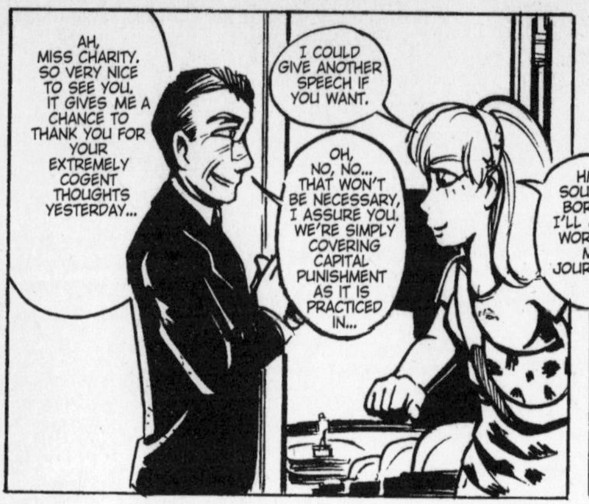
AH, MISS CHARITY. SO VERY NICE TO SEE YOU. IT GIVES ME A CHANCE TO THANK YOU FOR YOUR EXTREMELY COGENT THOUGHTS YESTERDAY...
I COULD GIVE ANOTHER SPEECH IF YOU WANT.
OH, NO, NO... THAT WON'T BE NECESSARY, I ASSURE YOU. WE'RE SIMPLY COVERING CAPITAL PUNISHMENT AS IT IS PRACTICED IN...
HM. SOUNDS BORING. I'LL JUST WORK IN MY JOURNAL!

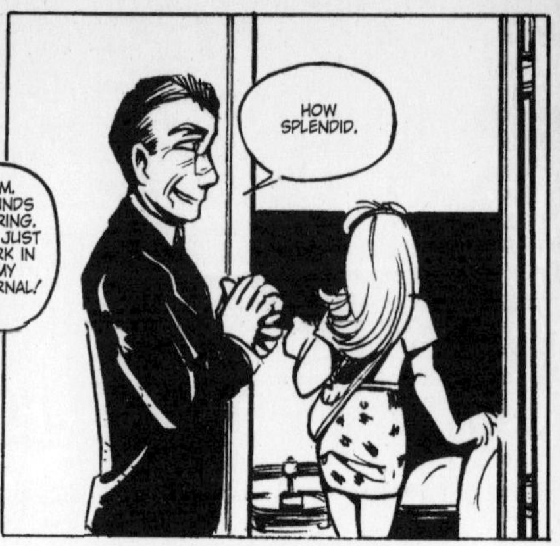
HOW SPLENDID.

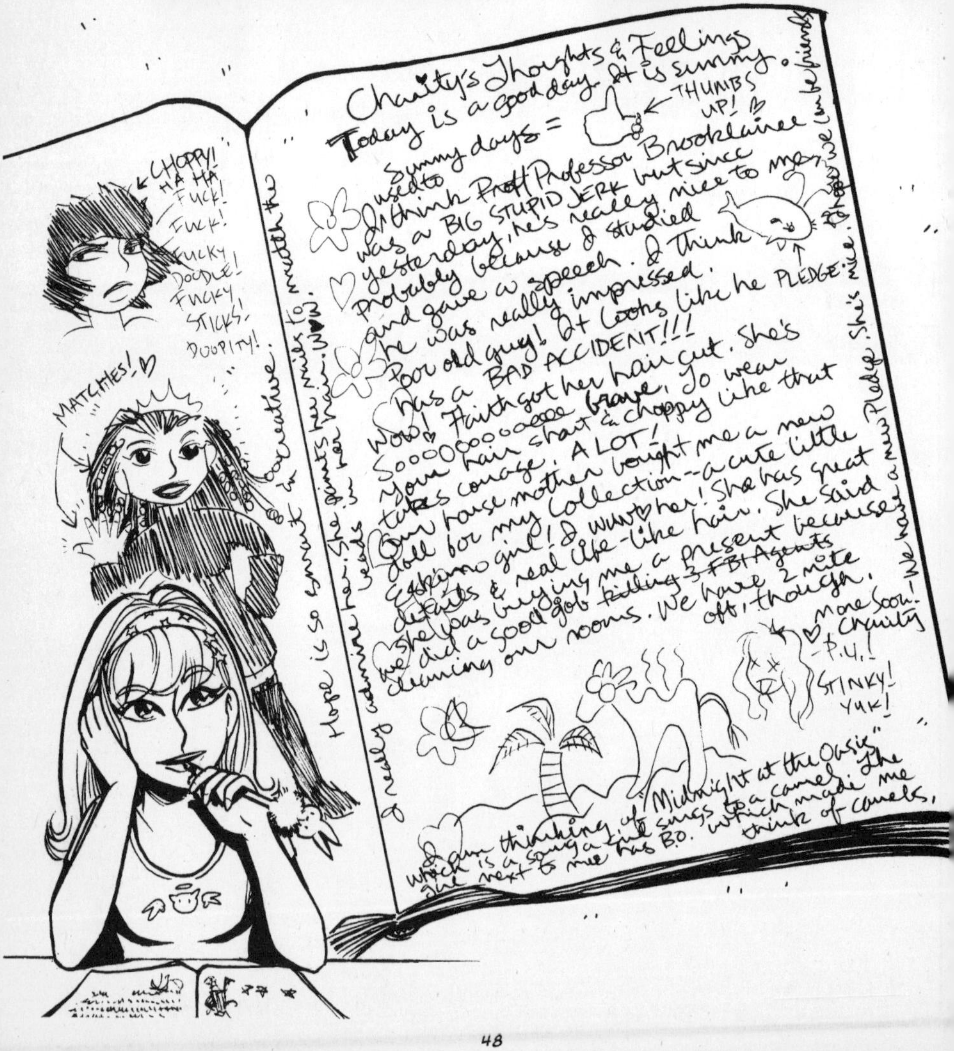
Charity's Thoughts & Feelings
Today is a good day. It is sunny.
Sunny days = [thumbs up] ← THUMBS UP! ♡
I used to think Prof Professor Brooklaine was a BIG STUPID JERK but since yesterday, he's really nice to me. Probably because I studied and gave a speech. I think he was really impressed.
Poor old guy! It looks like he has a BAD ACCIDENT!!!
WOW! Faith got her hair cut. She's Soooooooooooo brave. To wear your hair short & choppy like that takes courage. A LOT!
Our house mother bought me a new doll for my collection -- a cute little Eskimo girl! I luv♡ her! She has great details & real life-like hair. She said she was buying me a present because we did a good job killing 3 FBI Agents cleaning our rooms. We have 2 more off, though.
♡ more soon! Charity
PLEDGE:
-P.U.! STINKY! YUK!
I am thinking of "Midnight at the Oasis" which is a song a girl sings to a camel. The girl next to me has B.O. which made me think of camels.
We have a new Pledge. She's nice. I hope we can be friends.
← CHOPPY! HA HA FUCK! FUCK! FUCKY DOODLE! FUCKY STICKS! DOOPITY!
MATCHES! ♡
Hope is so smart & creative.
I really admire her. She paints her nails to match the words in her hair. WOW.

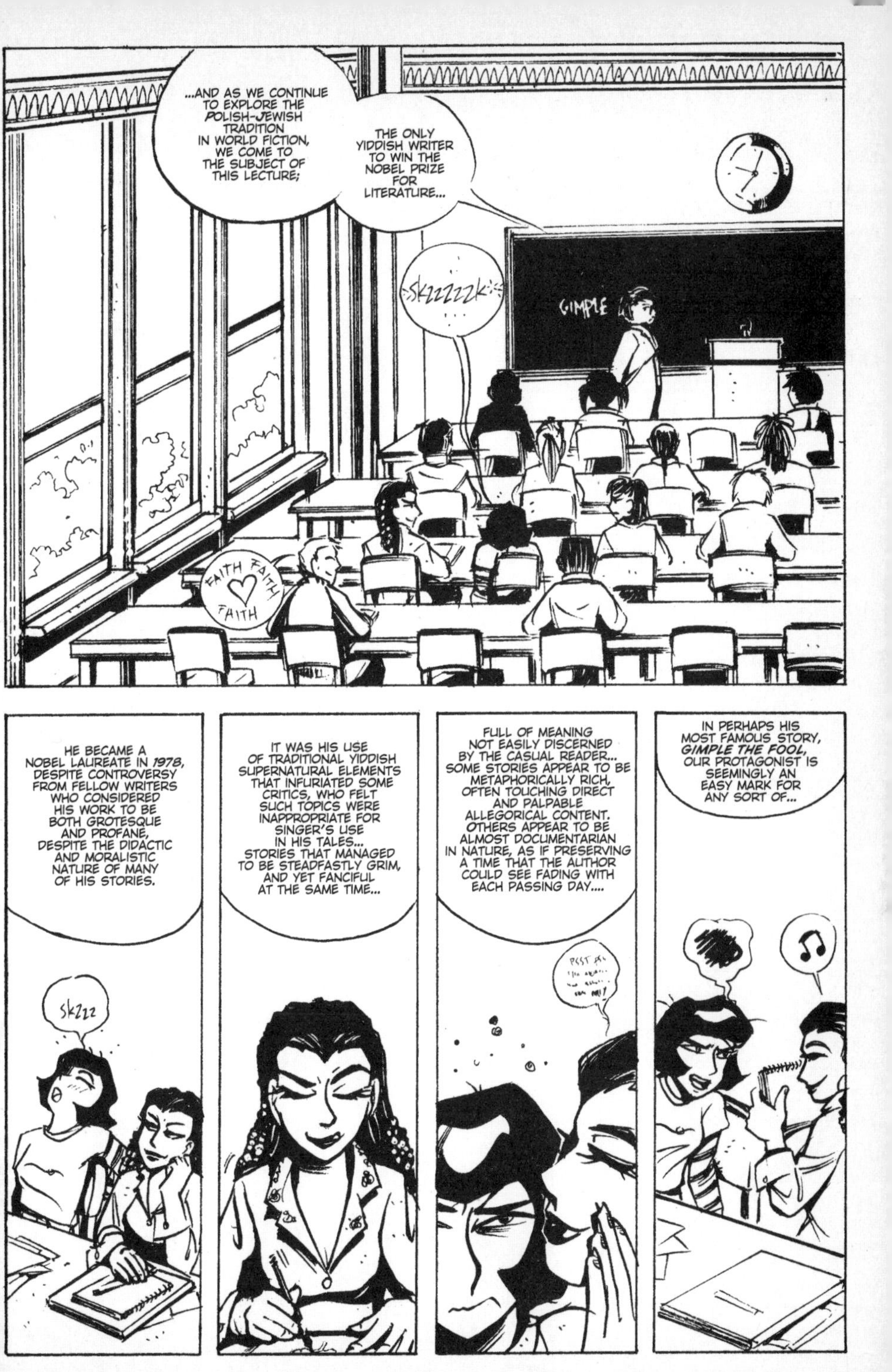

...AND AS WE CONTINUE TO EXPLORE THE *POLISH-JEWISH* TRADITION IN WORLD FICTION, WE COME TO THE SUBJECT OF THIS LECTURE;
THE ONLY YIDDISH WRITER TO WIN THE NOBEL PRIZE FOR LITERATURE...
SKZZZZZK
GIMPLE
FAITH FAITH FAITH
HE BECAME A NOBEL LAUREATE IN *1978*, DESPITE CONTROVERSY FROM FELLOW WRITERS WHO CONSIDERED HIS WORK TO BE BOTH GROTESQUE AND PROFANE, DESPITE THE DIDACTIC AND MORALISTIC NATURE OF MANY OF HIS STORIES.
SKZZZ
IT WAS HIS USE OF TRADITIONAL YIDDISH SUPERNATURAL ELEMENTS THAT INFURIATED SOME CRITICS, WHO FELT SUCH TOPICS WERE INAPPROPRIATE FOR SINGER'S USE IN HIS TALES... STORIES THAT MANAGED TO BE STEADFASTLY GRIM, AND YET FANCIFUL AT THE SAME TIME...
FULL OF MEANING NOT EASILY DISCERNED BY THE CASUAL READER... SOME STORIES APPEAR TO BE METAPHORICALLY RICH, OFTEN TOUCHING DIRECT AND PALPABLE ALLEGORICAL CONTENT. OTHERS APPEAR TO BE ALMOST DOCUMENTARIAN IN NATURE, AS IF PRESERVING A TIME THAT THE AUTHOR COULD SEE FADING WITH EACH PASSING DAY....
PSST
IN PERHAPS HIS MOST FAMOUS STORY, ***GIMPLE THE FOOL***, OUR PROTAGONIST IS SEEMINGLY AN EASY MARK FOR ANY SORT OF...

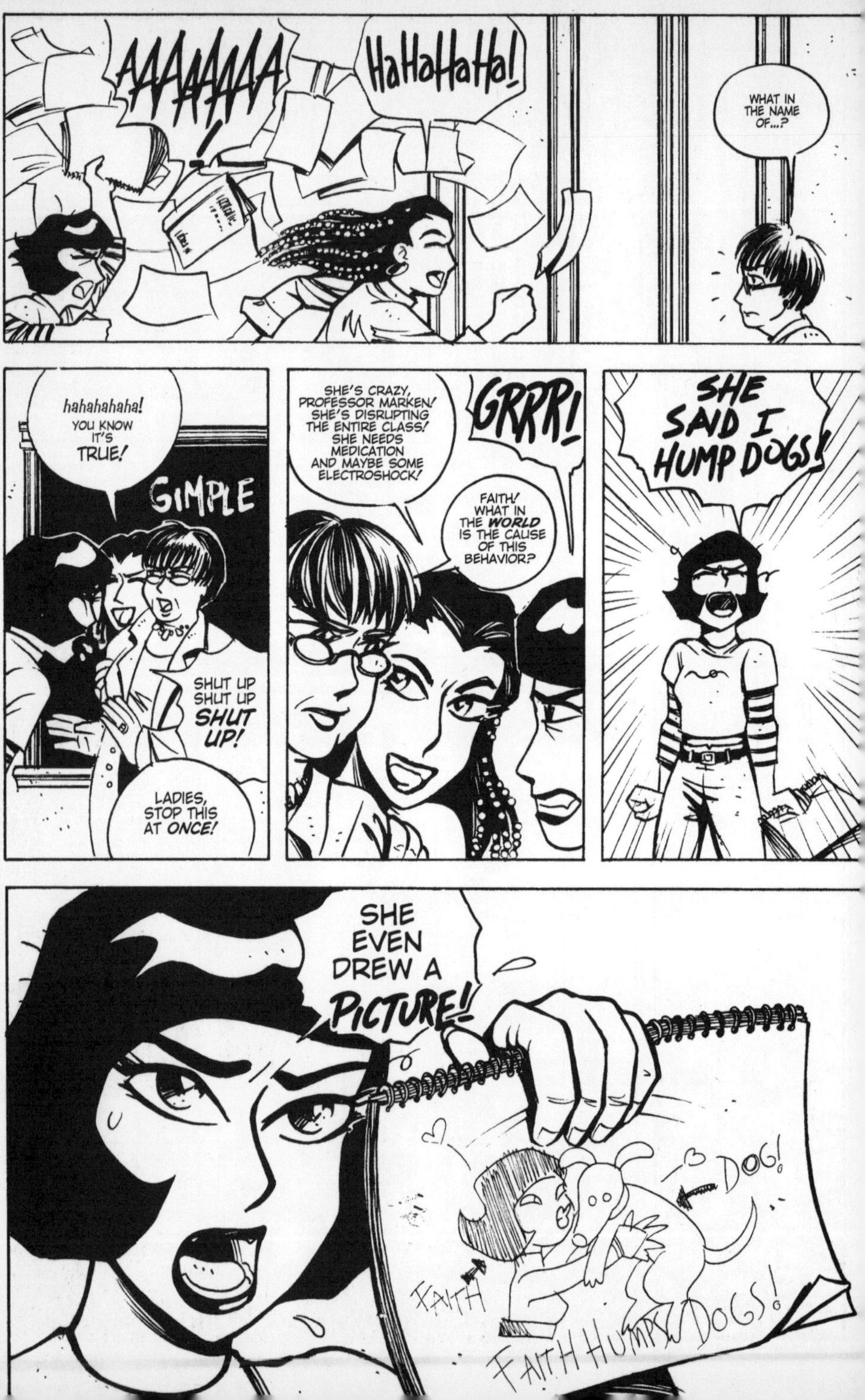
AAAAAAAA
HaHaHaHa!
WHAT IN THE NAME OF...?
hahahahaha! YOU KNOW IT'S TRUE!
GIMPLE
SHUT UP SHUT UP SHUT UP!
LADIES, STOP THIS AT ONCE!
SHE'S CRAZY, PROFESSOR MARKEN! SHE'S DISRUPTING THE ENTIRE CLASS! SHE NEEDS MEDICATION AND MAYBE SOME ELECTROSHOCK!
GRRR!
FAITH! WHAT IN THE WORLD IS THE CAUSE OF THIS BEHAVIOR?
SHE SAID I HUMP DOGS!
SHE EVEN DREW A PICTURE!
DOG!
FAITH
FAITH HUMPS DOGS!

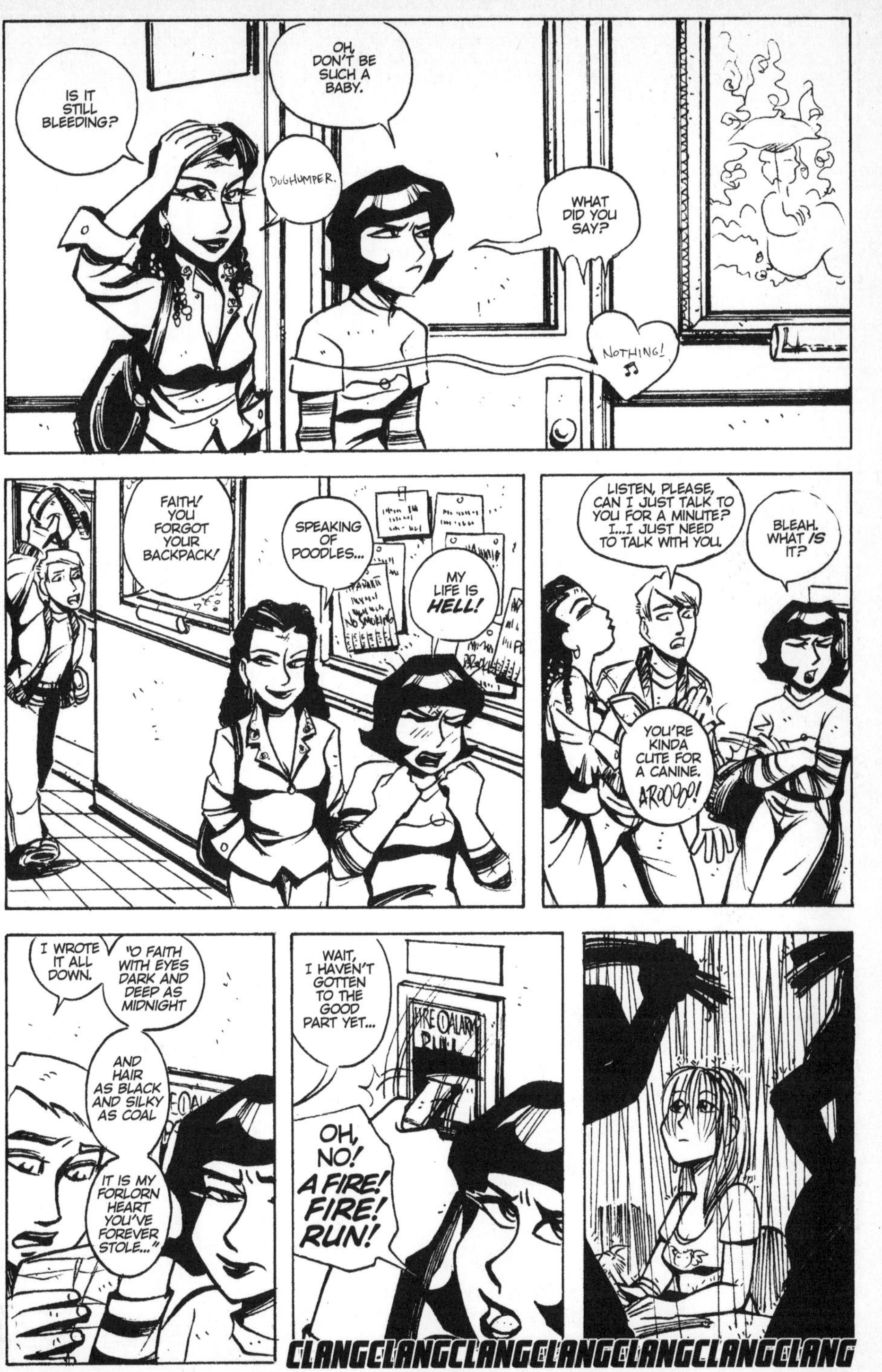

IS IT STILL BLEEDING?
OH, DON'T BE SUCH A BABY.
DOGHUMPER.
WHAT DID YOU SAY?
NOTHING! ♫
FAITH! YOU FORGOT YOUR BACKPACK!
SPEAKING OF POODLES...
MY LIFE IS HELL!
NO SMOKING
LISTEN, PLEASE, CAN I JUST TALK TO YOU FOR A MINUTE? I...I JUST NEED TO TALK WITH YOU.
BLEAH. WHAT IS IT?
YOU'RE KINDA CUTE FOR A CANINE. AROOOO!
I WROTE IT ALL DOWN.
"O FAITH WITH EYES DARK AND DEEP AS MIDNIGHT
AND HAIR AS BLACK AND SILKY AS COAL
IT IS MY FORLORN HEART YOU'VE FOREVER STOLE..."
WAIT, I HAVEN'T GOTTEN TO THE GOOD PART YET...
FIRE ALARM PULL
OH, NO! A FIRE! FIRE! RUN!
CLANGCLANGCLANGCLANGCLANGCLANGCLANG

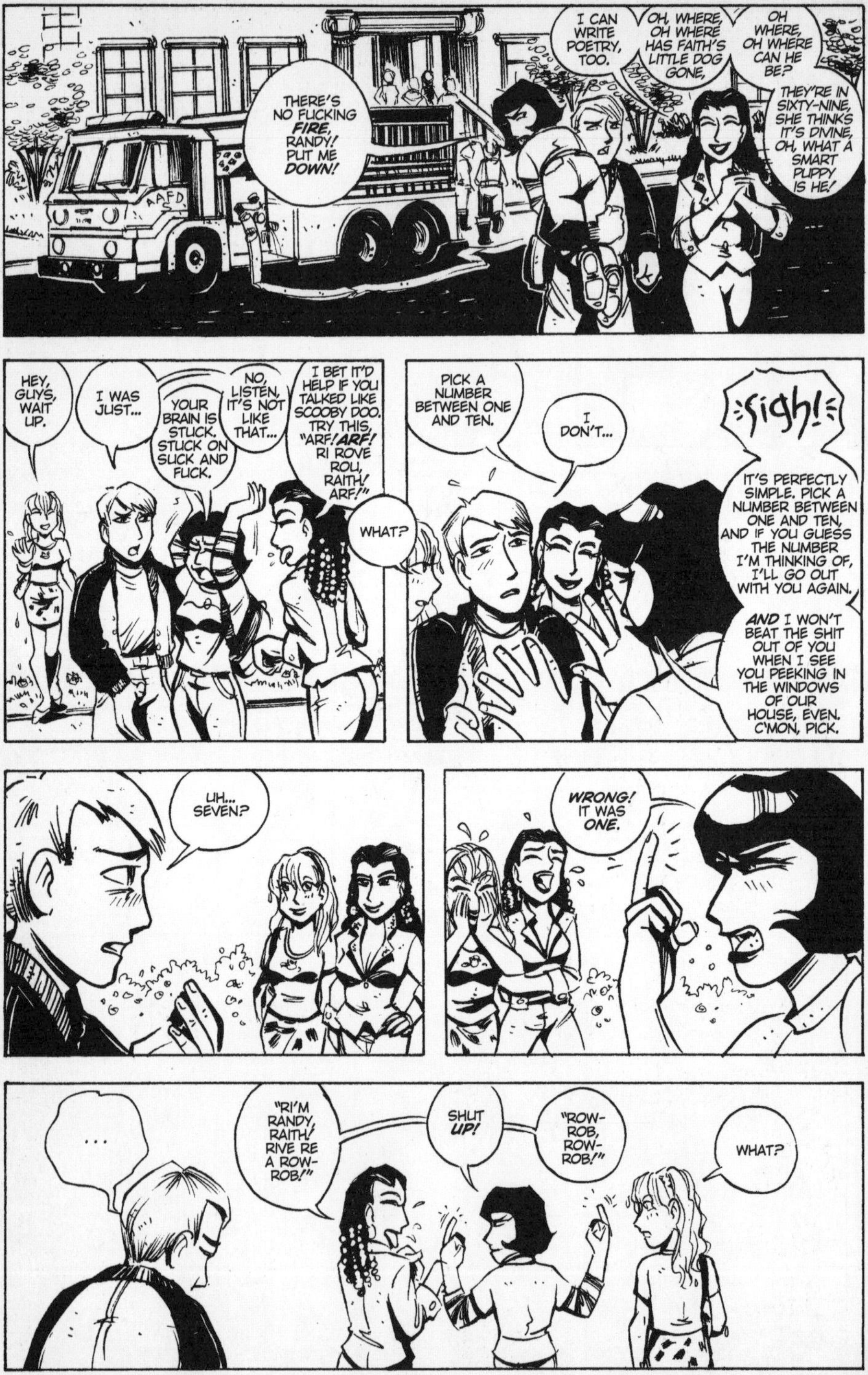
THERE'S NO FUCKING FIRE, RANDY! PUT ME DOWN!
I CAN WRITE POETRY, TOO.
OH, WHERE, OH WHERE HAS FAITH'S LITTLE DOG GONE,
OH WHERE, OH WHERE CAN HE BE?
THEY'RE IN SIXTY-NINE, SHE THINKS IT'S DIVINE, OH, WHAT A SMART PUPPY IS HE!
AAFD
HEY, GUYS, WAIT UP.
I WAS JUST...
YOUR BRAIN IS STUCK. STUCK ON SUCK AND FUCK.
NO, LISTEN, IT'S NOT LIKE THAT...
I BET IT'D HELP IF YOU TALKED LIKE SCOOBY DOO. TRY THIS, "ARF! ARF! RI ROVE ROU, RAITH! ARF!"
WHAT?
PICK A NUMBER BETWEEN ONE AND TEN.
I DON'T...
SIGH!
IT'S PERFECTLY SIMPLE. PICK A NUMBER BETWEEN ONE AND TEN, AND IF YOU GUESS THE NUMBER I'M THINKING OF, I'LL GO OUT WITH YOU AGAIN.
AND I WON'T BEAT THE SHIT OUT OF YOU WHEN I SEE YOU PEEKING IN THE WINDOWS OF OUR HOUSE, EVEN. C'MON, PICK.
UH... SEVEN?
WRONG! IT WAS ONE.
...
"RI'M RANDY, RAITH! RIVE RE A ROW-ROB!"
SHUT UP!
"ROW-ROB, ROW-ROB!"
WHAT?

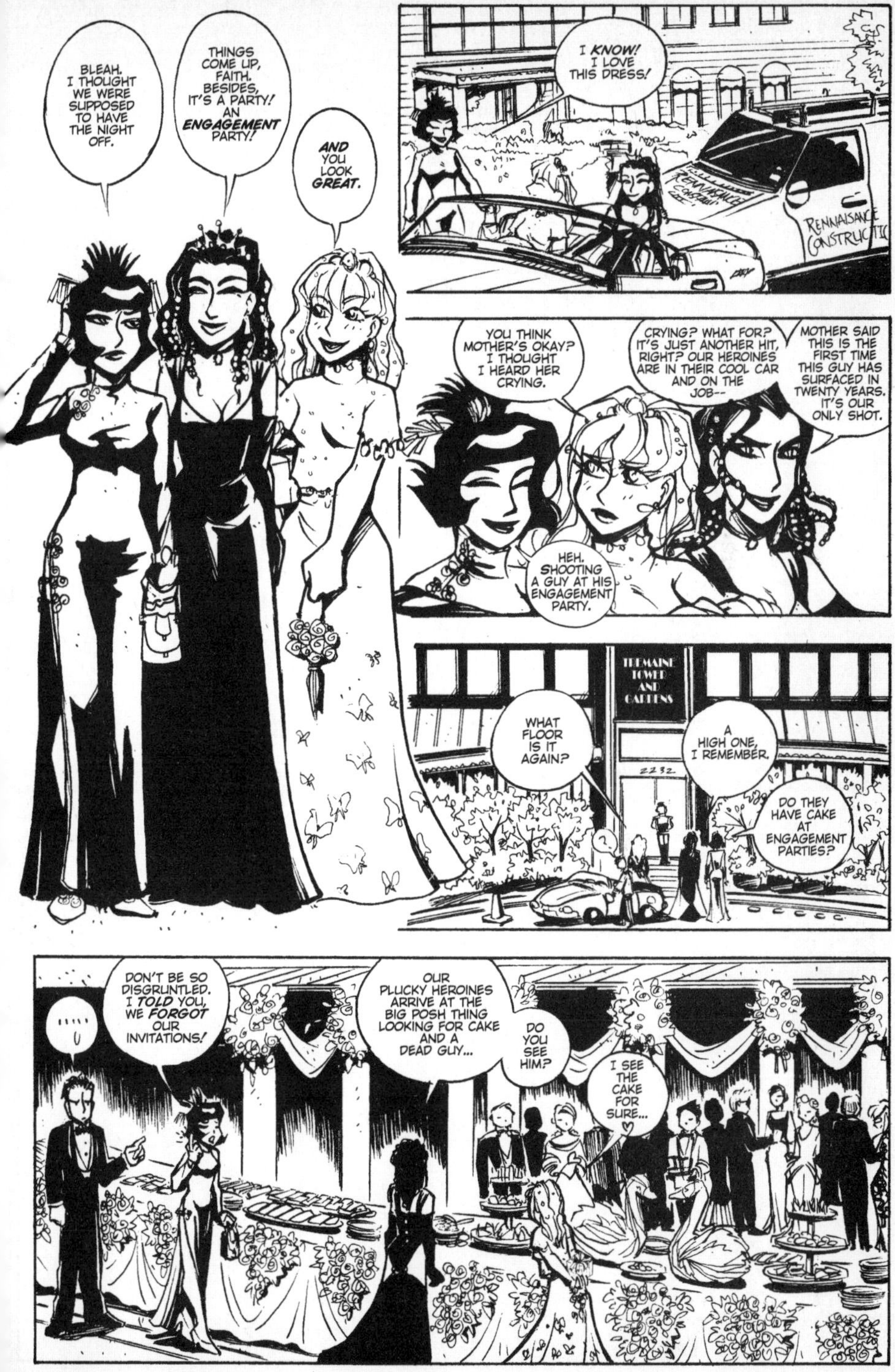
BLEAH. I THOUGHT WE WERE SUPPOSED TO HAVE THE NIGHT OFF.
THINGS COME UP, FAITH. BESIDES, IT'S A PARTY! AN ENGAGEMENT PARTY!
AND YOU LOOK GREAT.
I KNOW! I LOVE THIS DRESS!
RENNAISANCE CONSTRUCTIO
YOU THINK MOTHER'S OKAY? I THOUGHT I HEARD HER CRYING.
CRYING? WHAT FOR? IT'S JUST ANOTHER HIT, RIGHT? OUR HEROINES ARE IN THEIR COOL CAR AND ON THE JOB--
MOTHER SAID THIS IS THE FIRST TIME THIS GUY HAS SURFACED IN TWENTY YEARS. IT'S OUR ONLY SHOT.
HEH. SHOOTING A GUY AT HIS ENGAGEMENT PARTY.
TREMAINE TOWER AND GARDENS
2232
WHAT FLOOR IS IT AGAIN?
A HIGH ONE, I REMEMBER.
DO THEY HAVE CAKE AT ENGAGEMENT PARTIES?
?
.....
DON'T BE SO DISGRUNTLED. I TOLD YOU, WE FORGOT OUR INVITATIONS!
OUR PLUCKY HEROINES ARRIVE AT THE BIG POSH THING LOOKING FOR CAKE AND A DEAD GUY...
DO YOU SEE HIM?
I SEE THE CAKE FOR SURE...

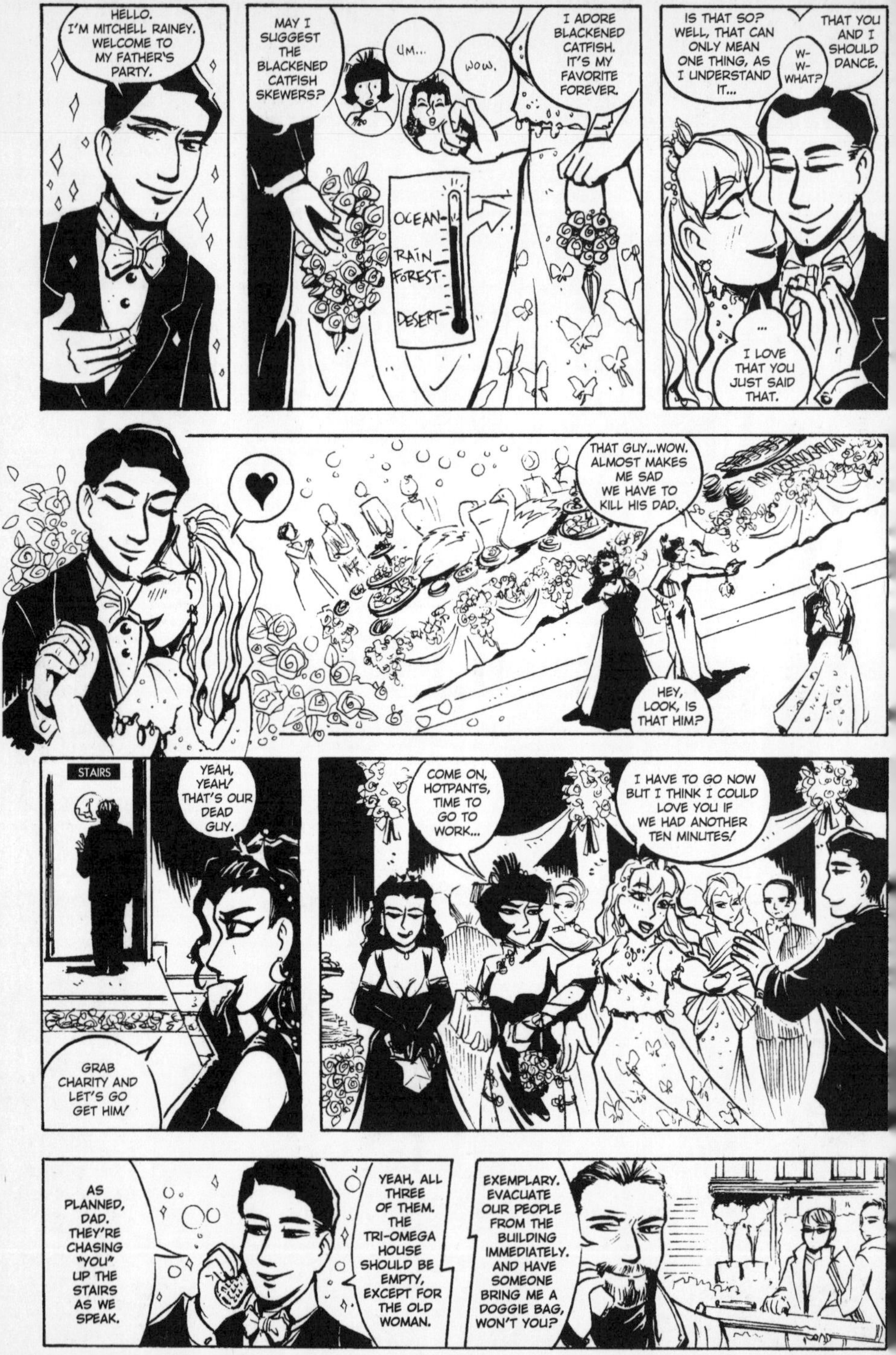
HELLO. I'M MITCHELL RAINEY. WELCOME TO MY FATHER'S PARTY.
MAY I SUGGEST THE BLACKENED CATFISH SKEWERS?
UM...
WOW.
I ADORE BLACKENED CATFISH. IT'S MY FAVORITE FOREVER.
OCEAN
RAIN FOREST
DESERT
IS THAT SO? WELL, THAT CAN ONLY MEAN ONE THING, AS I UNDERSTAND IT...
W-W-WHAT?
THAT YOU AND I SHOULD DANCE.
...
I LOVE THAT YOU JUST SAID THAT.
THAT GUY...WOW. ALMOST MAKES ME SAD WE HAVE TO KILL HIS DAD.
HEY, LOOK, IS THAT HIM?
STAIRS
YEAH, YEAH! THAT'S OUR DEAD GUY.
GRAB CHARITY AND LET'S GO GET HIM!
COME ON, HOTPANTS, TIME TO GO TO WORK...
I HAVE TO GO NOW BUT I THINK I COULD LOVE YOU IF WE HAD ANOTHER TEN MINUTES!
AS PLANNED, DAD. THEY'RE CHASING "YOU" UP THE STAIRS AS WE SPEAK.
YEAH, ALL THREE OF THEM. THE TRI-OMEGA HOUSE SHOULD BE EMPTY, EXCEPT FOR THE OLD WOMAN.
EXEMPLARY. EVACUATE OUR PEOPLE FROM THE BUILDING IMMEDIATELY. AND HAVE SOMEONE BRING ME A DOGGIE BAG, WON'T YOU?

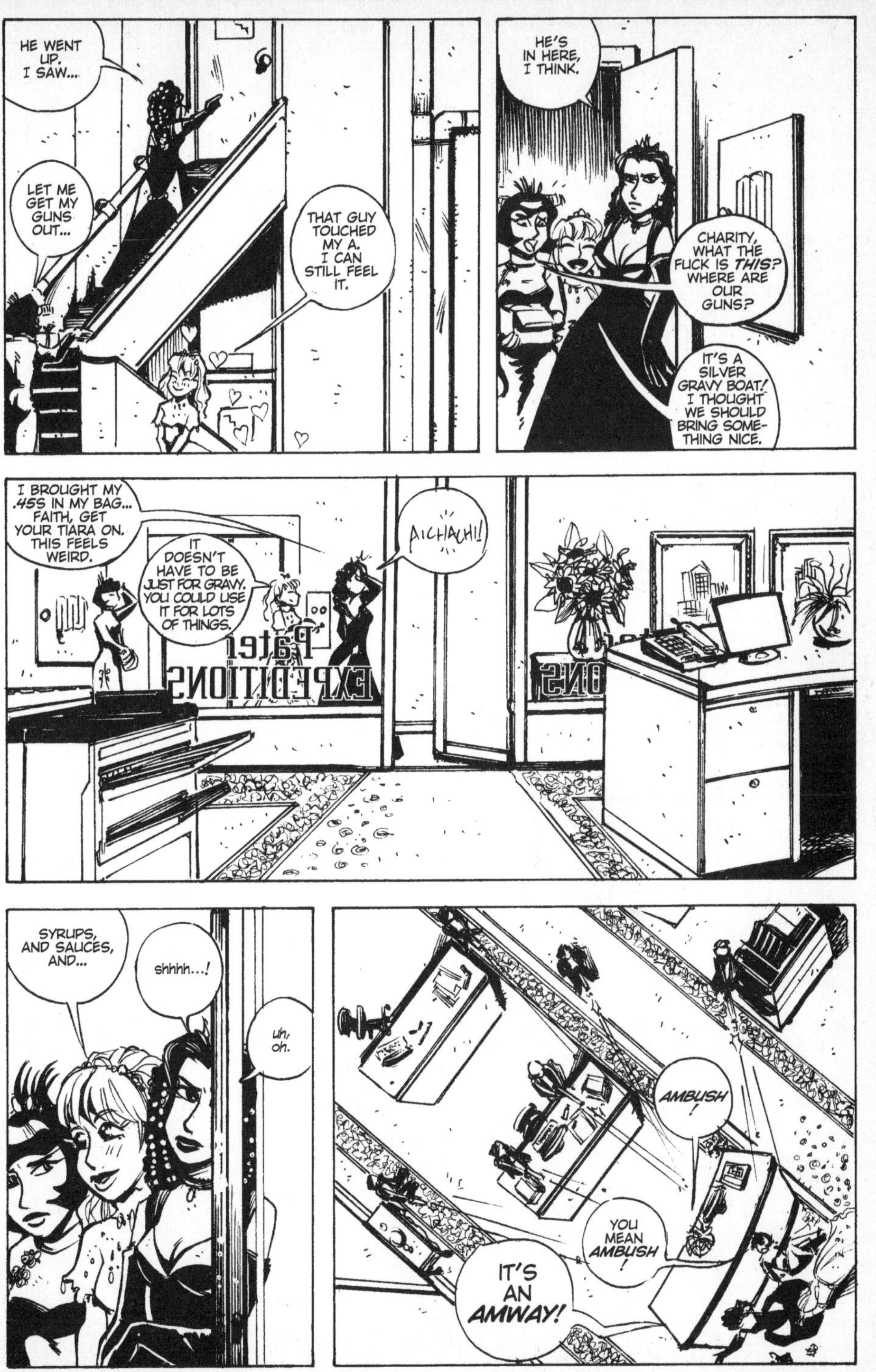
HE WENT UP. I SAW...
LET ME GET MY GUNS OUT...
THAT GUY TOUCHED MY A. I CAN STILL FEEL IT.
HE'S IN HERE, I THINK.
CHARITY, WHAT THE FUCK IS *THIS*? WHERE ARE OUR GUNS?
IT'S A SILVER GRAVY BOAT! I THOUGHT WE SHOULD BRING SOME-THING NICE.
I BROUGHT MY .45S IN MY BAG... FAITH, GET YOUR TIARA ON. THIS FEELS WEIRD.
IT DOESN'T HAVE TO BE JUST FOR GRAVY. YOU COULD USE IT FOR LOTS OF THINGS.
AICHACHI!!
Pater EXPEDITIONS
SYRUPS, AND SAUCES, AND...
shhhh...!
uh, oh.
AMBUSH!
YOU MEAN AMBUSH!
IT'S AN AMWAY!

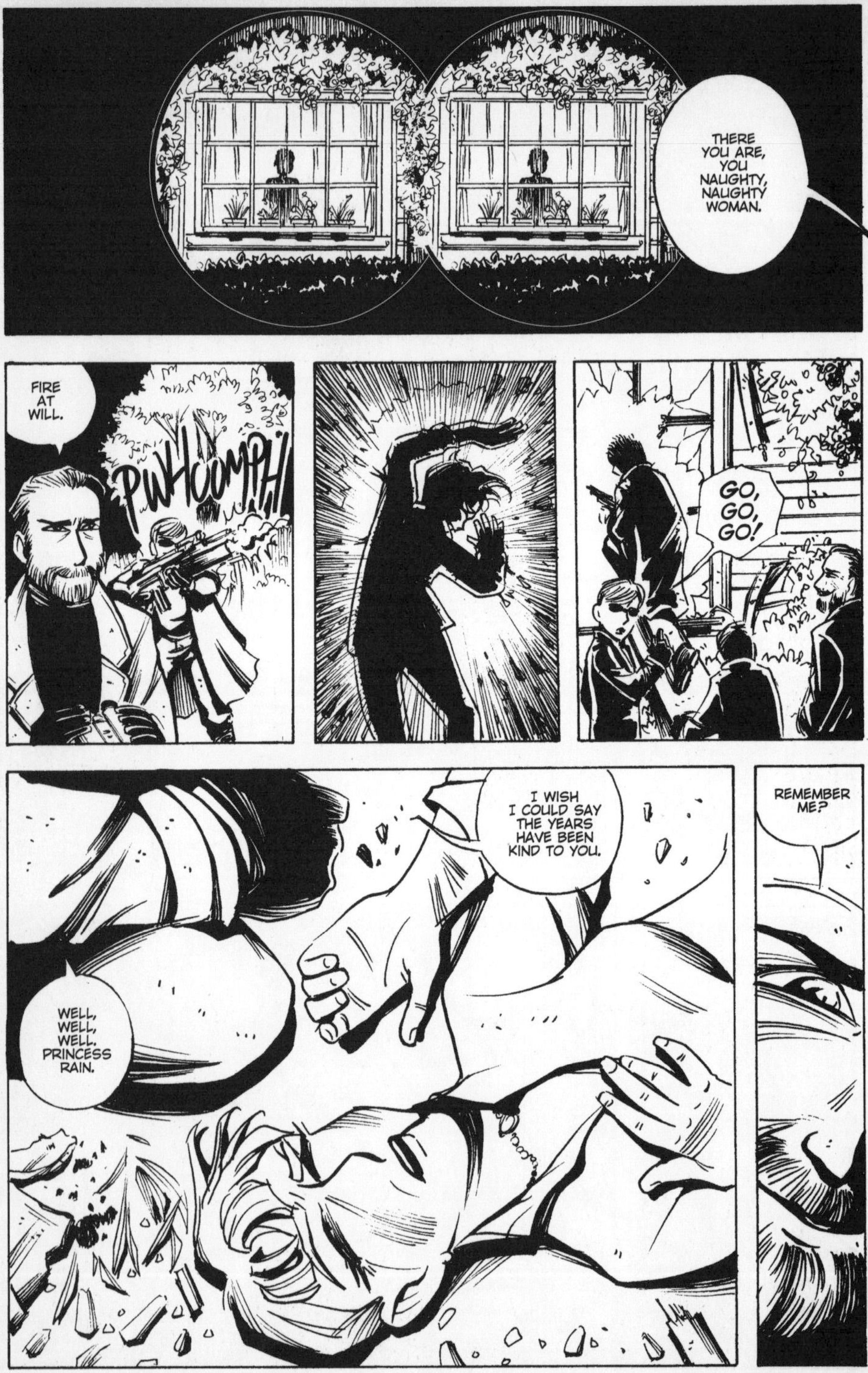
THERE YOU ARE, YOU NAUGHTY, NAUGHTY WOMAN.
FIRE AT WILL.
PWHOOMPH!
GO, GO, GO!
I WISH I COULD SAY THE YEARS HAVE BEEN KIND TO YOU.
WELL, WELL, WELL. PRINCESS RAIN.
REMEMBER ME?

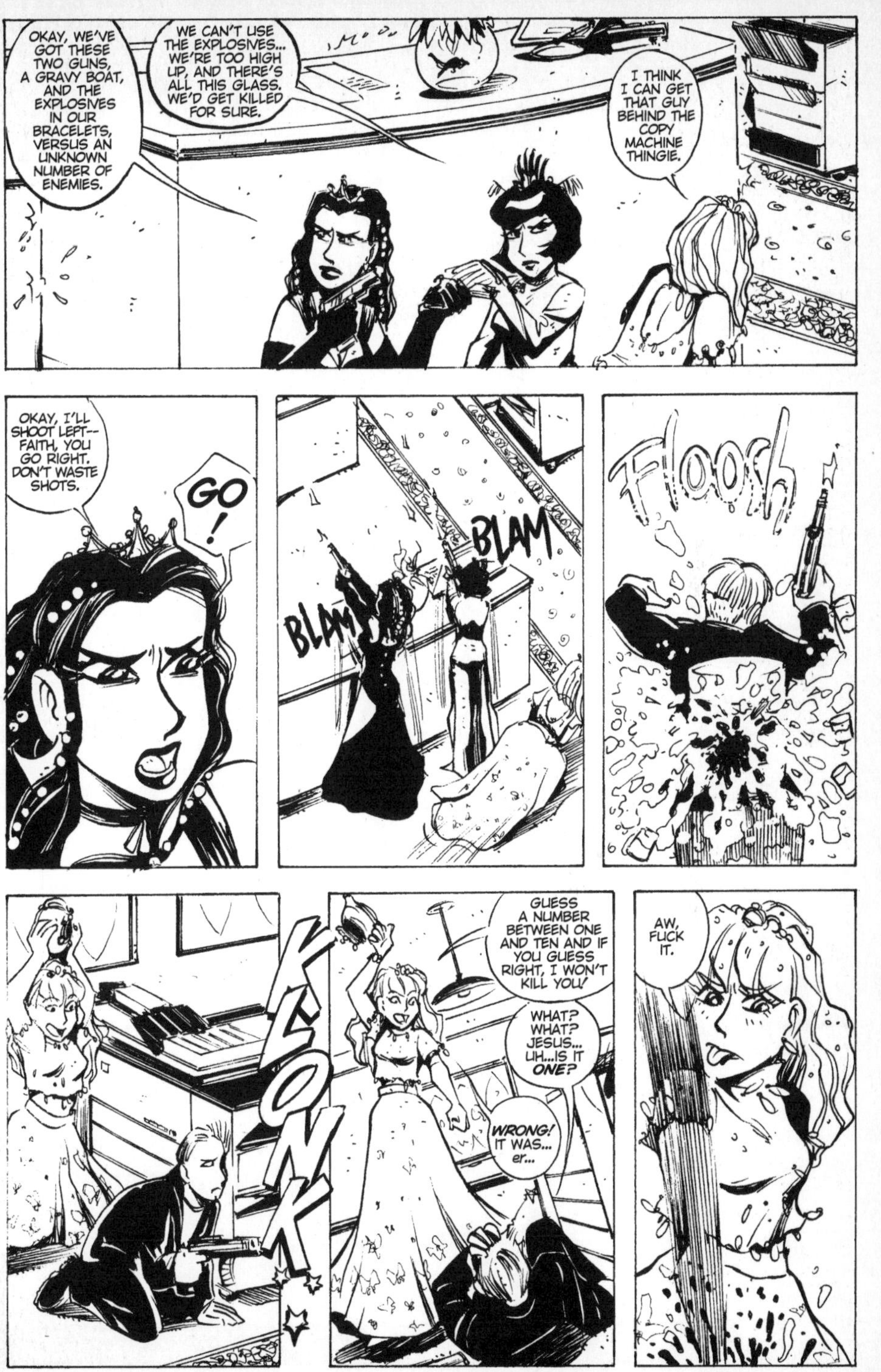

OKAY, WE'VE GOT THESE TWO GUNS, A GRAVY BOAT, AND THE EXPLOSIVES IN OUR BRACELETS, VERSUS AN UNKNOWN NUMBER OF ENEMIES.
WE CAN'T USE THE EXPLOSIVES... WE'RE TOO HIGH UP, AND THERE'S ALL THIS GLASS. WE'D GET KILLED FOR SURE.
I THINK I CAN GET THAT GUY BEHIND THE COPY MACHINE THINGIE.
OKAY, I'LL SHOOT LEFT-- FAITH, YOU GO RIGHT. DON'T WASTE SHOTS.
GO!
BLAM
BLAM
FLOOSH
KLONK
GUESS A NUMBER BETWEEN ONE AND TEN AND IF YOU GUESS RIGHT, I WON'T KILL YOU!
WHAT? WHAT? JESUS... UH...IS IT ONE?
WRONG! IT WAS... er...
AW, FUCK IT.

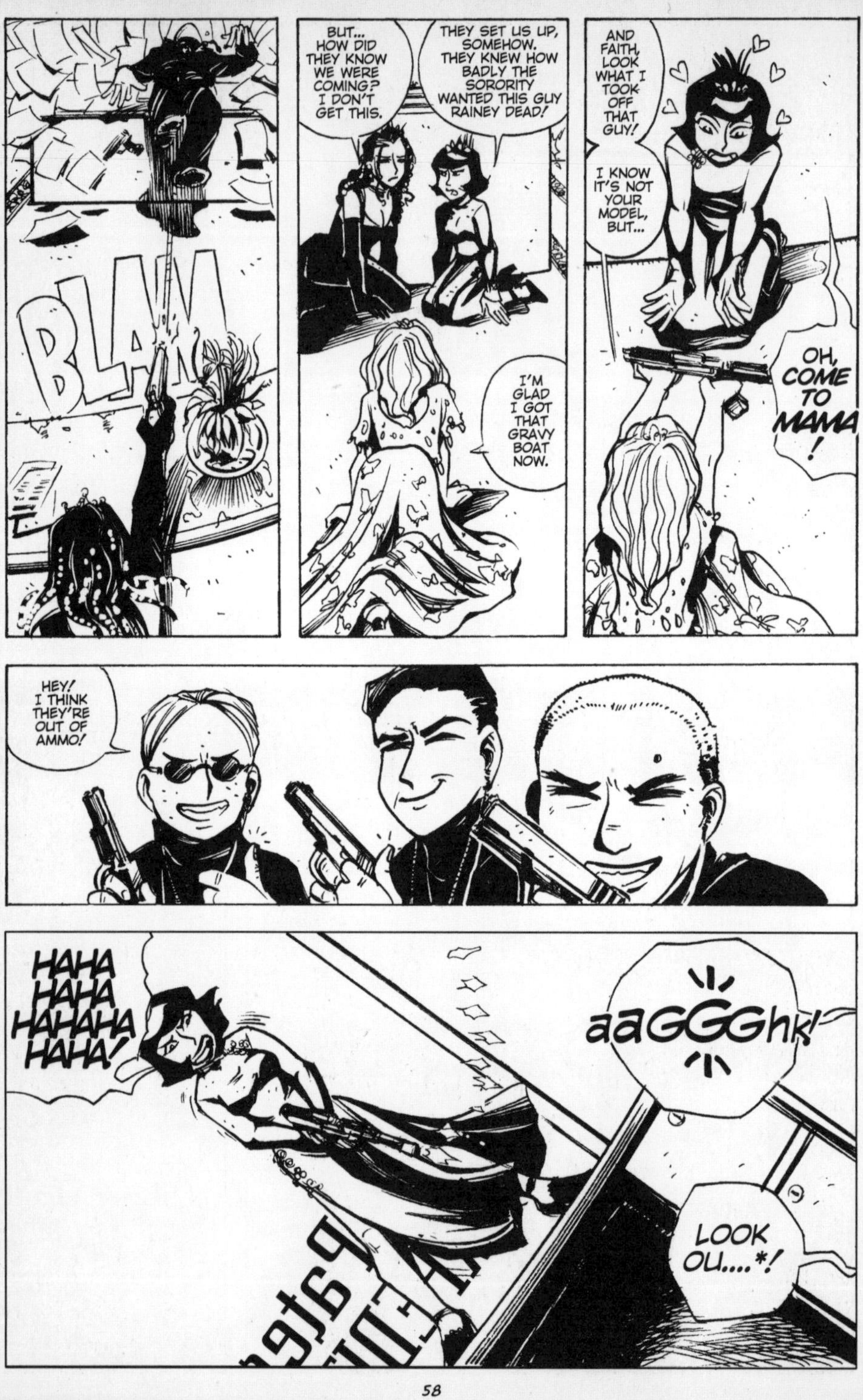
BLAM
BUT... HOW DID THEY KNOW WE WERE COMING? I DON'T GET THIS.
THEY SET US UP, SOMEHOW. THEY KNEW HOW BADLY THE SORORITY WANTED THIS GUY RAINEY DEAD!
I'M GLAD I GOT THAT GRAVY BOAT NOW.
AND FAITH, LOOK WHAT I TOOK OFF THAT GUY!
I KNOW IT'S NOT YOUR MODEL, BUT...
OH, COME TO MAMA!
HEY! I THINK THEY'RE OUT OF AMMO!
HAHA HAHA HAHAHA HAHA!
aaGGGhk!
LOOK OU....*!

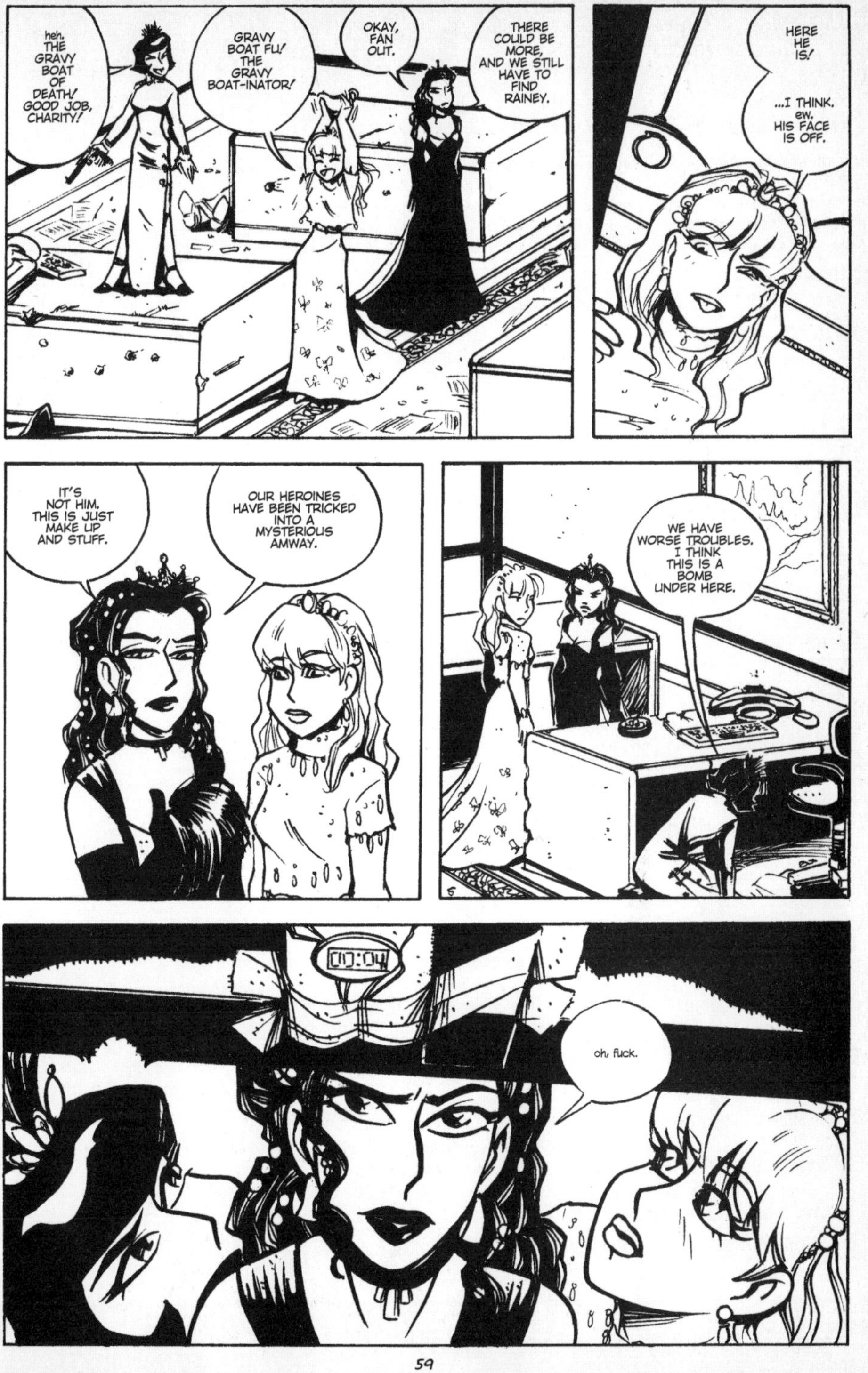
heh. THE GRAVY BOAT OF DEATH! GOOD JOB, CHARITY!
GRAVY BOAT FU! THE GRAVY BOAT-INATOR!
OKAY, FAN OUT.
THERE COULD BE MORE, AND WE STILL HAVE TO FIND RAINEY.
HERE HE IS!
...I THINK. ew. HIS FACE IS OFF.
IT'S NOT HIM. THIS IS JUST MAKE UP AND STUFF.
OUR HEROINES HAVE BEEN TRICKED INTO A MYSTERIOUS AMWAY.
WE HAVE WORSE TROUBLES. I THINK THIS IS A BOMB UNDER HERE.
00:04
oh, fuck.

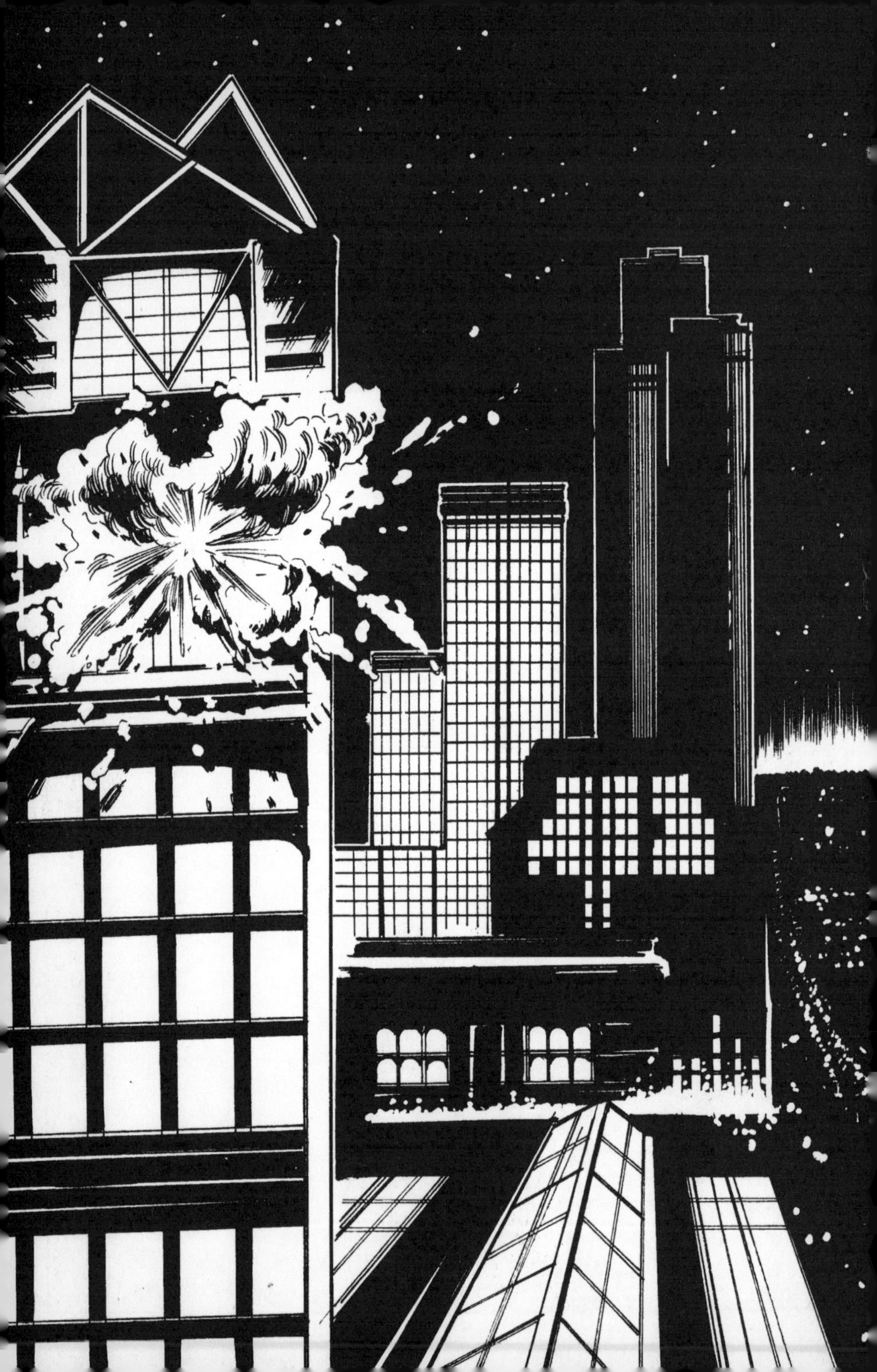

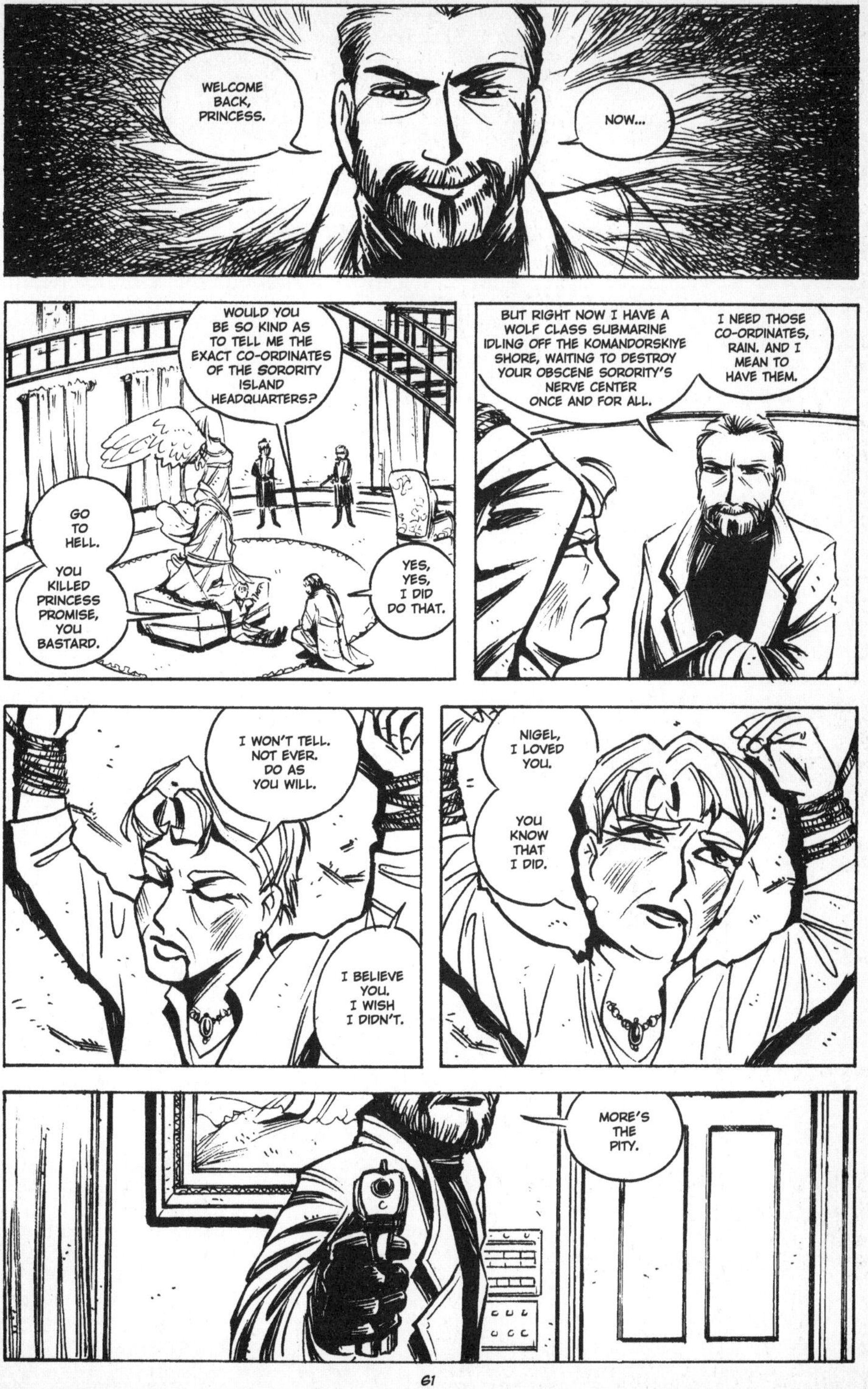

WELCOME BACK, PRINCESS.
NOW...
WOULD YOU BE SO KIND AS TO TELL ME THE EXACT CO-ORDINATES OF THE SORORITY ISLAND HEADQUARTERS?
GO TO HELL.
YOU KILLED PRINCESS PROMISE, YOU BASTARD.
YES, YES, I DID DO THAT.
BUT RIGHT NOW I HAVE A WOLF CLASS SUBMARINE IDLING OFF THE KOMANDORSKIYE SHORE, WAITING TO DESTROY YOUR OBSCENE SORORITY'S NERVE CENTER ONCE AND FOR ALL.
I NEED THOSE CO-ORDINATES, RAIN. AND I MEAN TO HAVE THEM.
I WON'T TELL. NOT EVER. DO AS YOU WILL.
I BELIEVE YOU. I WISH I DIDN'T.
NIGEL, I LOVED YOU.
YOU KNOW THAT I DID.
MORE'S THE PITY.

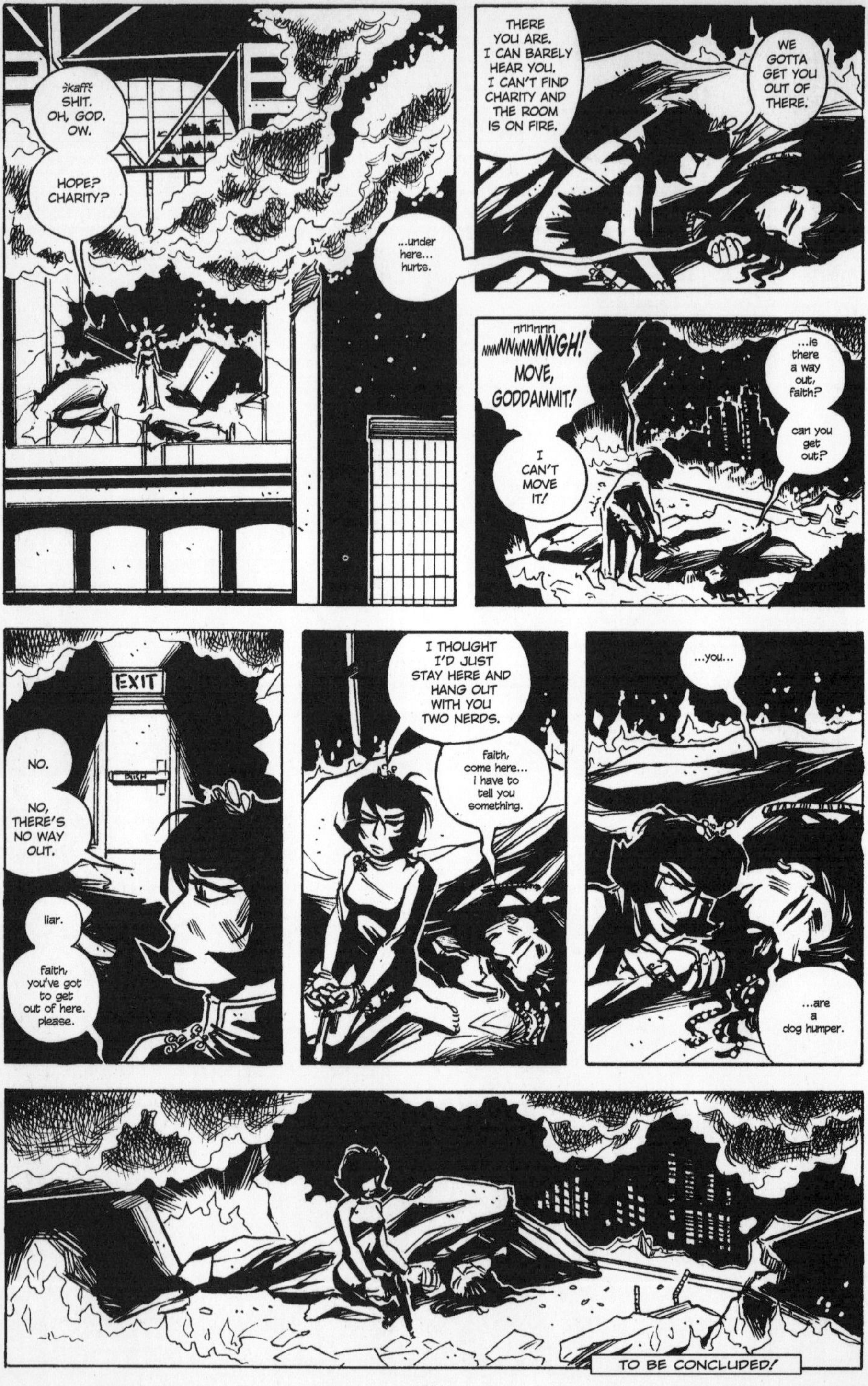

kaff SHIT. OH, GOD. OW.
HOPE? CHARITY?
...under here... hurts.
THERE YOU ARE. I CAN BARELY HEAR YOU. I CAN'T FIND CHARITY AND THE ROOM IS ON FIRE.
WE GOTTA GET YOU OUT OF THERE.
nnnnnn NNNNNNNNNGH! MOVE, GODDAMMIT!
I CAN'T MOVE IT!
...is there a way out, faith?
can you get out?
EXIT
NO.
NO, THERE'S NO WAY OUT.
liar.
faith, you've got to get out of here. please.
I THOUGHT I'D JUST STAY HERE AND HANG OUT WITH YOU TWO NERDS.
faith, come here... i have to tell you something.
...you...
...are a dog humper.
TO BE CONCLUDED!

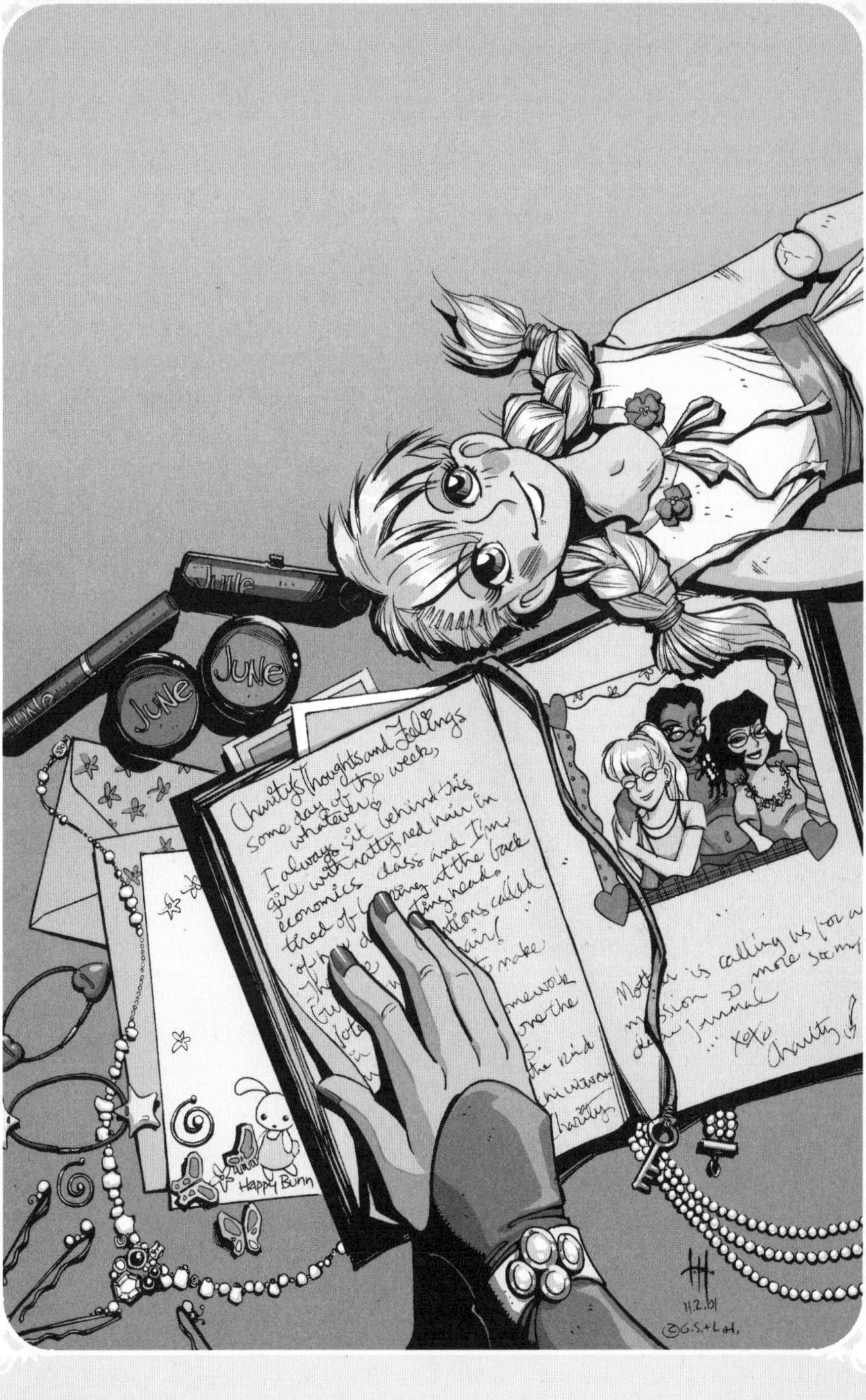

JUNE
JUNE
JUNE
Charity's Thoughts and Feelings
some day of the week, whatever
I always sit behind this
girl with ratty red hair in
economics class and I'm
Happy Bunn
XOXO
Charity
11.2.01
©G.S.+L.H.

Chapter 3

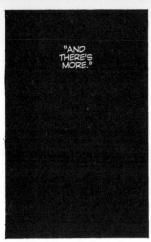

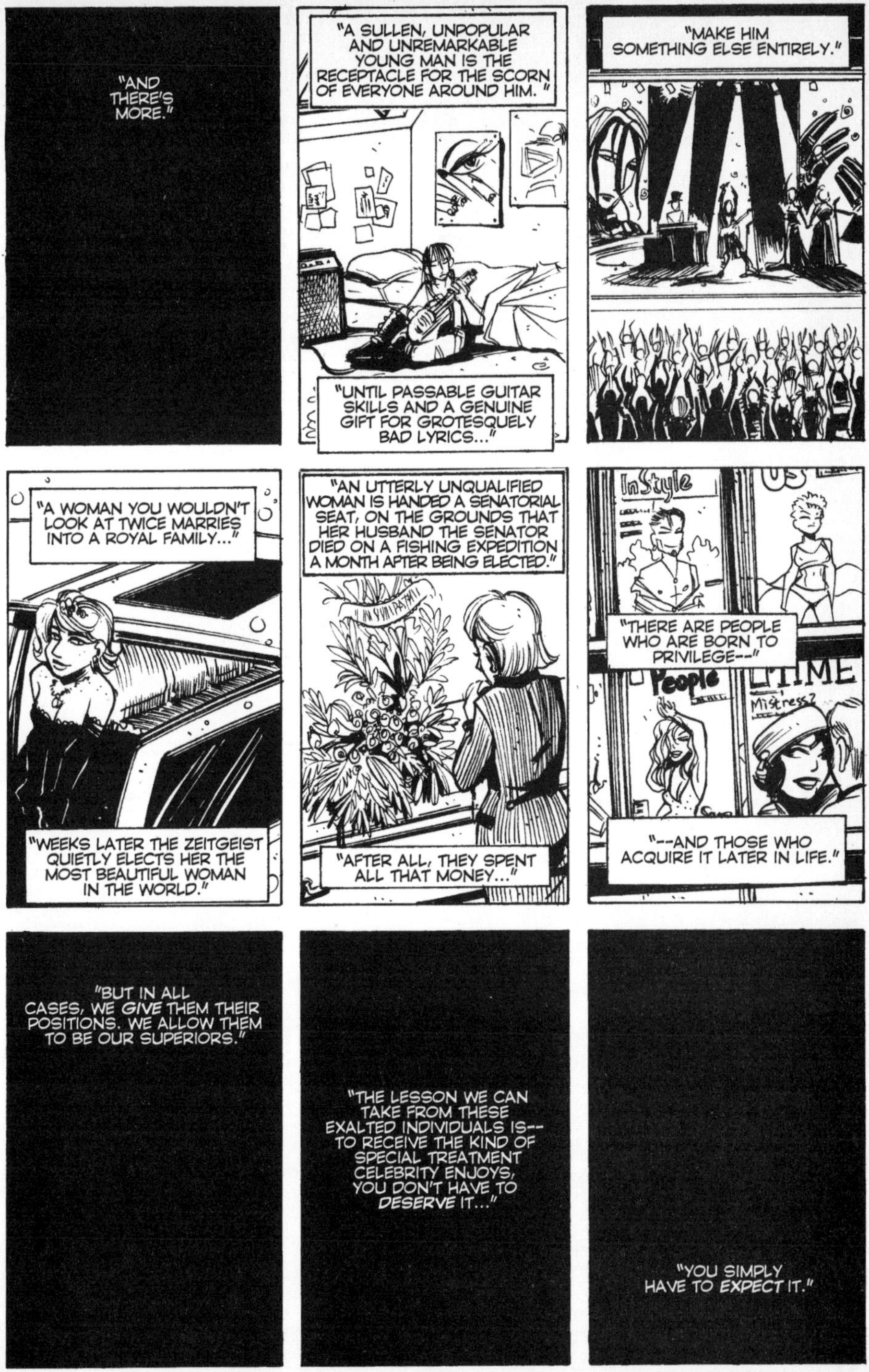
"AND THERE'S MORE."
"A SULLEN, UNPOPULAR AND UNREMARKABLE YOUNG MAN IS THE RECEPTACLE FOR THE SCORN OF EVERYONE AROUND HIM."
"UNTIL PASSABLE GUITAR SKILLS AND A GENUINE GIFT FOR GROTESQUELY BAD LYRICS..."
"MAKE HIM SOMETHING ELSE ENTIRELY."
"A WOMAN YOU WOULDN'T LOOK AT TWICE MARRIES INTO A ROYAL FAMILY..."
"WEEKS LATER THE ZEITGEIST QUIETLY ELECTS HER THE MOST BEAUTIFUL WOMAN IN THE WORLD."
"AN UTTERLY UNQUALIFIED WOMAN IS HANDED A SENATORIAL SEAT, ON THE GROUNDS THAT HER HUSBAND THE SENATOR DIED ON A FISHING EXPEDITION A MONTH AFTER BEING ELECTED."
"AFTER ALL, THEY SPENT ALL THAT MONEY..."
InStyle
"THERE ARE PEOPLE WHO ARE BORN TO PRIVILEGE--"
People
Mistress?
"--AND THOSE WHO ACQUIRE IT LATER IN LIFE."
"BUT IN ALL CASES, WE *GIVE* THEM THEIR POSITIONS. WE ALLOW THEM TO BE OUR SUPERIORS."
"THE LESSON WE CAN TAKE FROM THESE EXALTED INDIVIDUALS IS-- TO RECEIVE THE KIND OF SPECIAL TREATMENT CELEBRITY ENJOYS, YOU DON'T HAVE TO *DESERVE* IT..."
"YOU SIMPLY HAVE TO *EXPECT* IT."

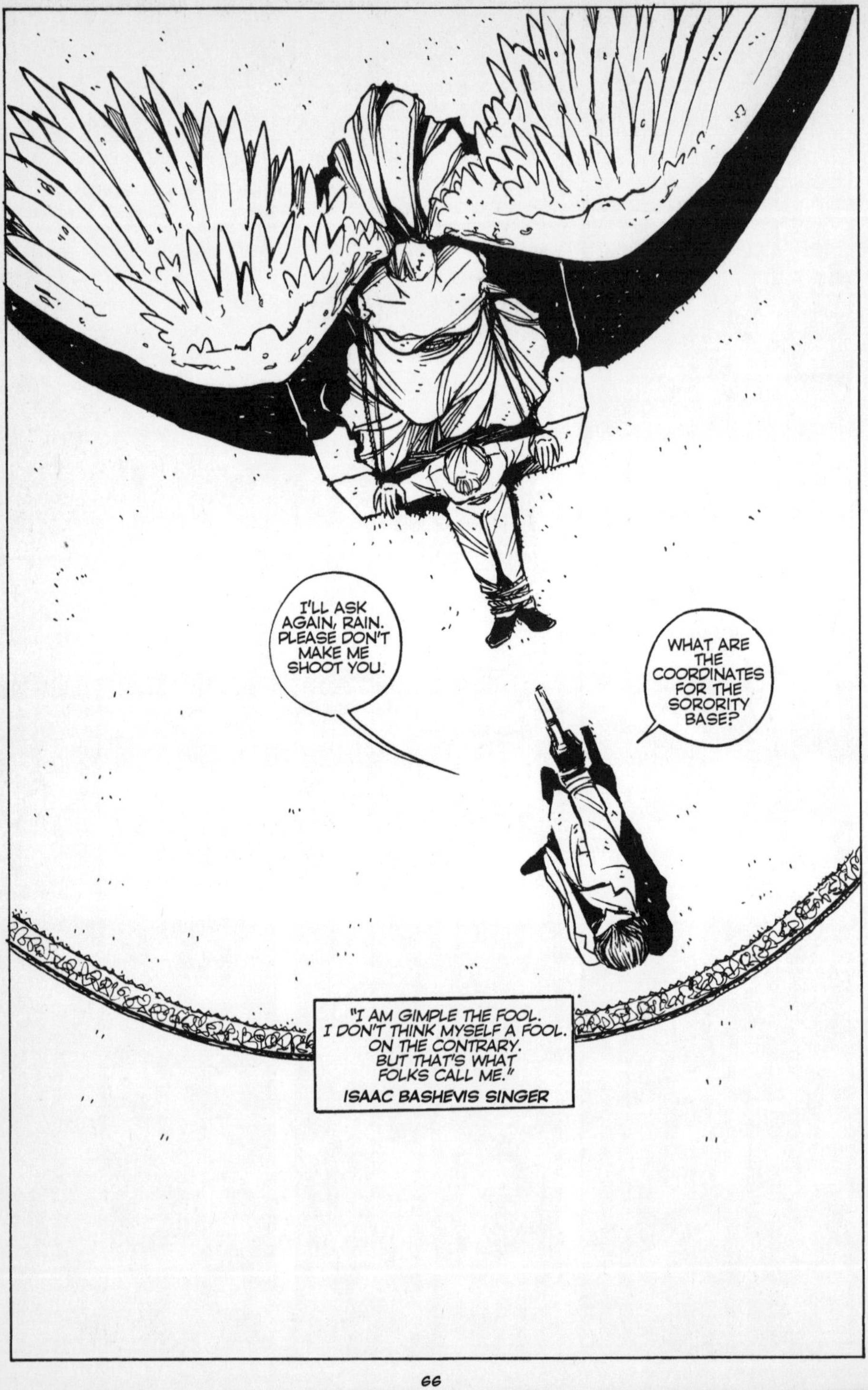

WHAT ARE THE COORDINATES FOR THE SORORITY BASE?
I'LL ASK AGAIN, RAIN. PLEASE DON'T MAKE ME SHOOT YOU.
"I AM GIMPLE THE FOOL. I DON'T THINK MYSELF A FOOL. ON THE CONTRARY. BUT THAT'S WHAT FOLKS CALL ME."
ISAAC BASHEVIS SINGER

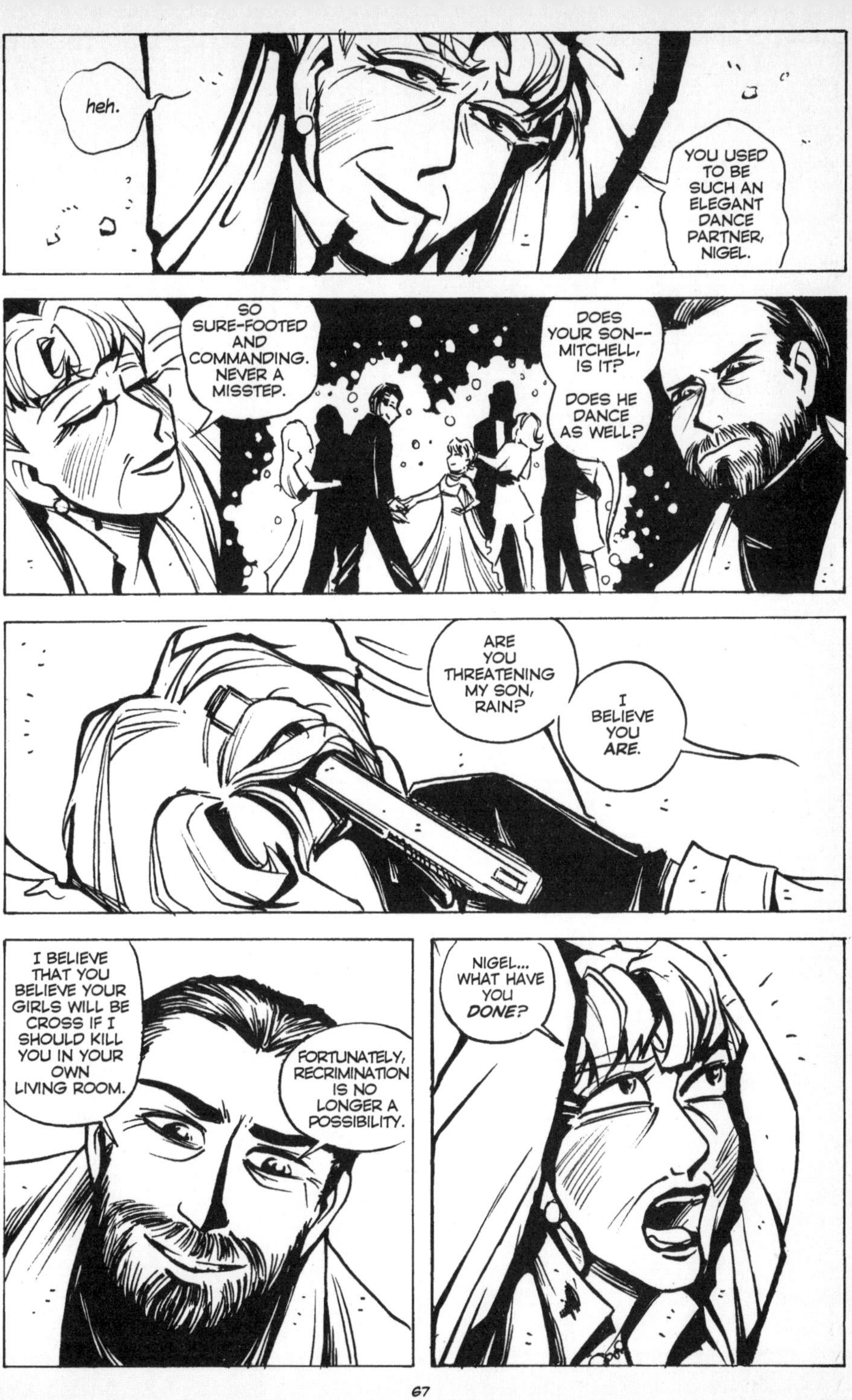
heh.
YOU USED TO BE SUCH AN ELEGANT DANCE PARTNER, NIGEL.
SO SURE-FOOTED AND COMMANDING. NEVER A MISSTEP.
DOES YOUR SON-- MITCHELL, IS IT?
DOES HE DANCE AS WELL?
ARE YOU THREATENING MY SON, RAIN?
I BELIEVE YOU ARE.
I BELIEVE THAT YOU BELIEVE YOUR GIRLS WILL BE CROSS IF I SHOULD KILL YOU IN YOUR OWN LIVING ROOM.
FORTUNATELY, RECRIMINATION IS NO LONGER A POSSIBILITY.
NIGEL... WHAT HAVE YOU DONE?

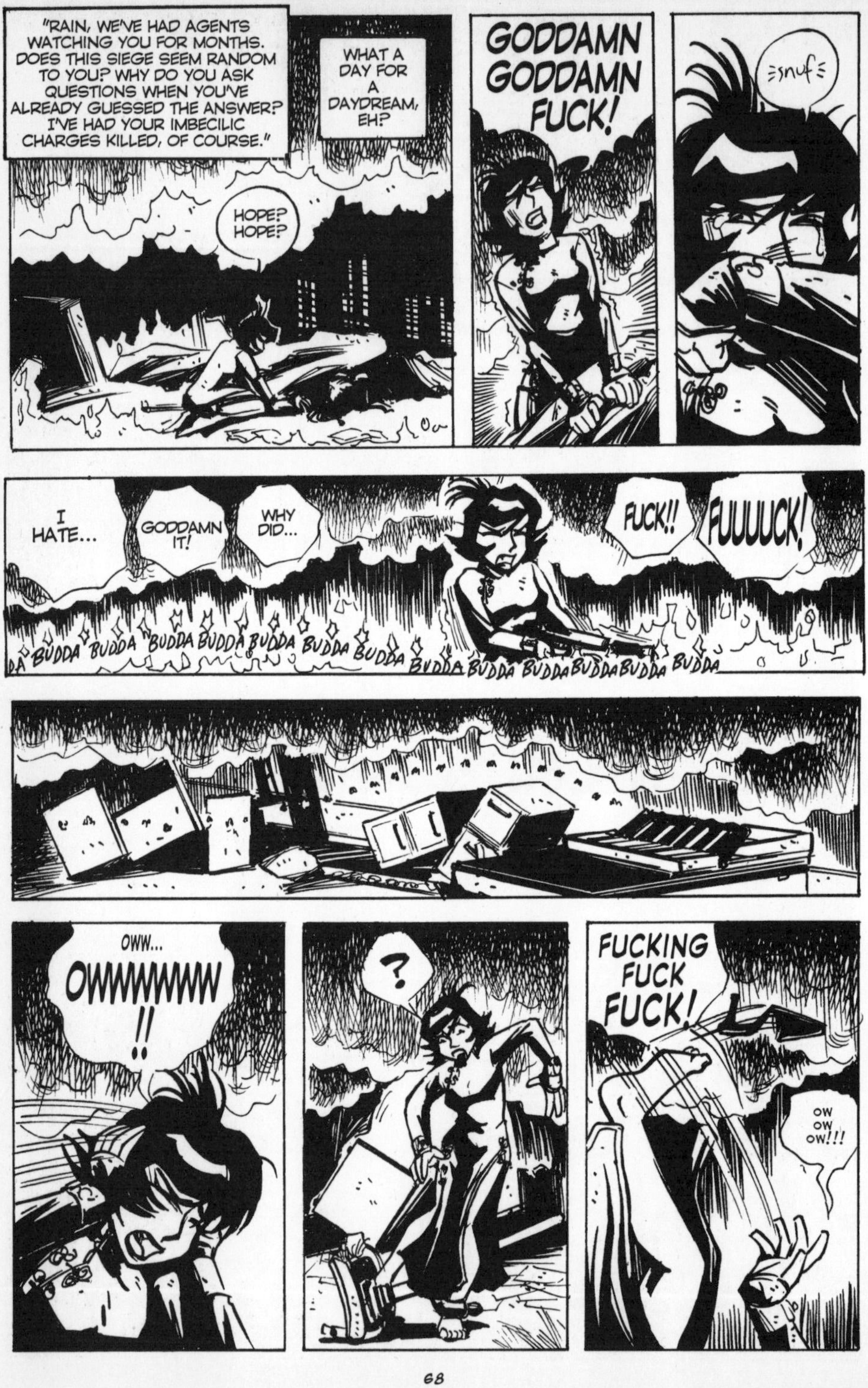
"RAIN, WE'VE HAD AGENTS WATCHING YOU FOR MONTHS. DOES THIS SIEGE SEEM RANDOM TO YOU? WHY DO YOU ASK QUESTIONS WHEN YOU'VE ALREADY GUESSED THE ANSWER? I'VE HAD YOUR IMBECILIC CHARGES KILLED, OF COURSE."
WHAT A DAY FOR A DAYDREAM, EH?
HOPE? HOPE?
GODDAMN GODDAMN FUCK!
snuf
I HATE...
GODDAMN IT!
WHY DID...
FUCK!!
FUUUUCK!
BUDDA BUDDA BUDDA BUDDA BUDDA BUDDA BUDDA BUDDA BUDDA BUDDA BUDDA BUDDA BUDDA
OWW...
OWWWWWW!!
?
FUCKING FUCK FUCK!
OW OW OW!!!

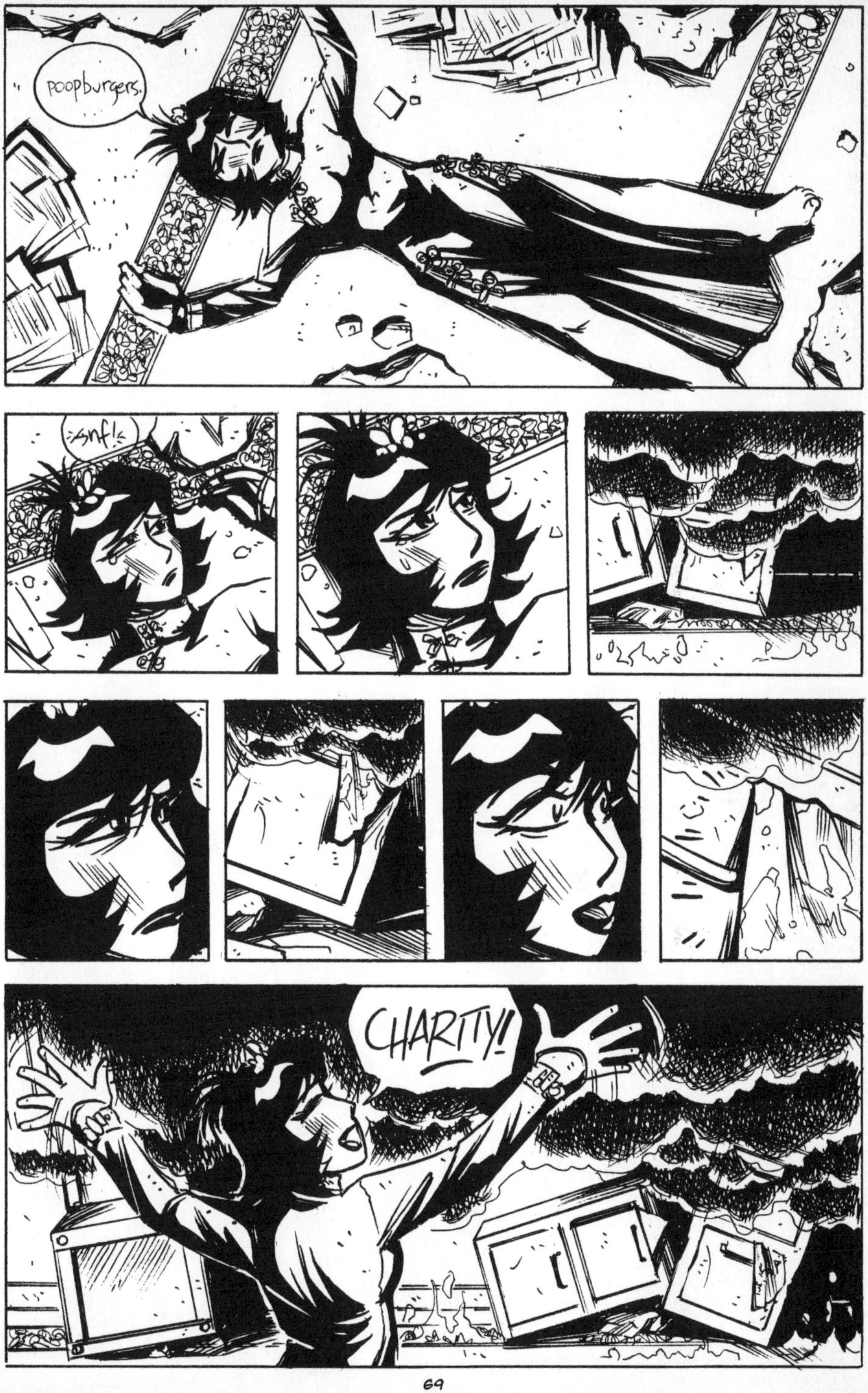
poopburgers.
snf!
CHARITY!

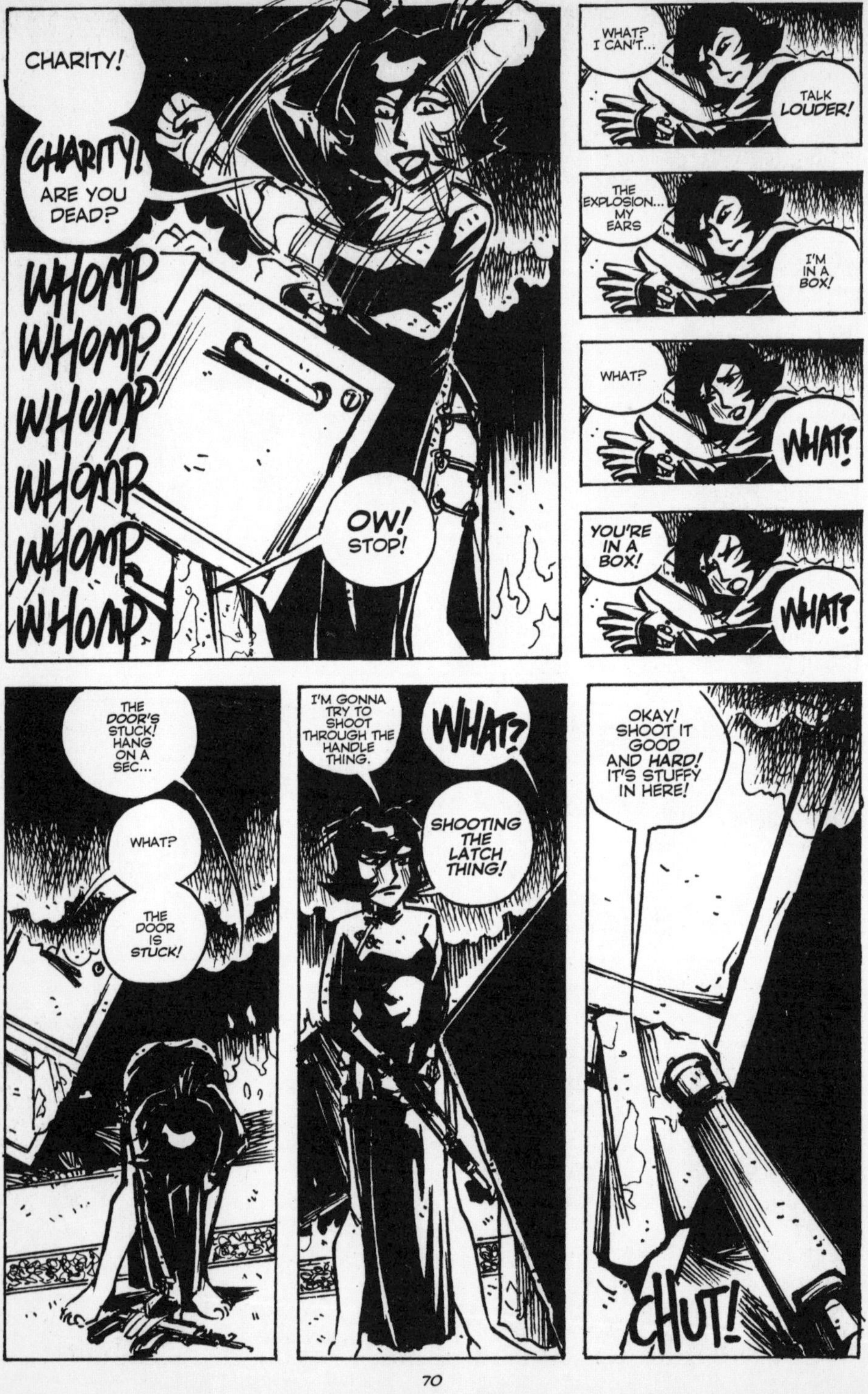
CHARITY!
CHARITY! ARE YOU DEAD?
WHOMP WHOMP WHOMP WHOMP WHOMP WHOMP
OW! STOP!
WHAT? I CAN'T...
TALK LOUDER!
THE EXPLOSION... MY EARS
I'M IN A BOX!
WHAT?
WHAT?
YOU'RE IN A BOX!
WHAT?
THE DOOR'S STUCK! HANG ON A SEC...
WHAT?
THE DOOR IS STUCK!
I'M GONNA TRY TO SHOOT THROUGH THE HANDLE THING.
WHAT?
SHOOTING THE LATCH THING!
OKAY! SHOOT IT GOOD AND HARD! IT'S STUFFY IN HERE!
CHUT!

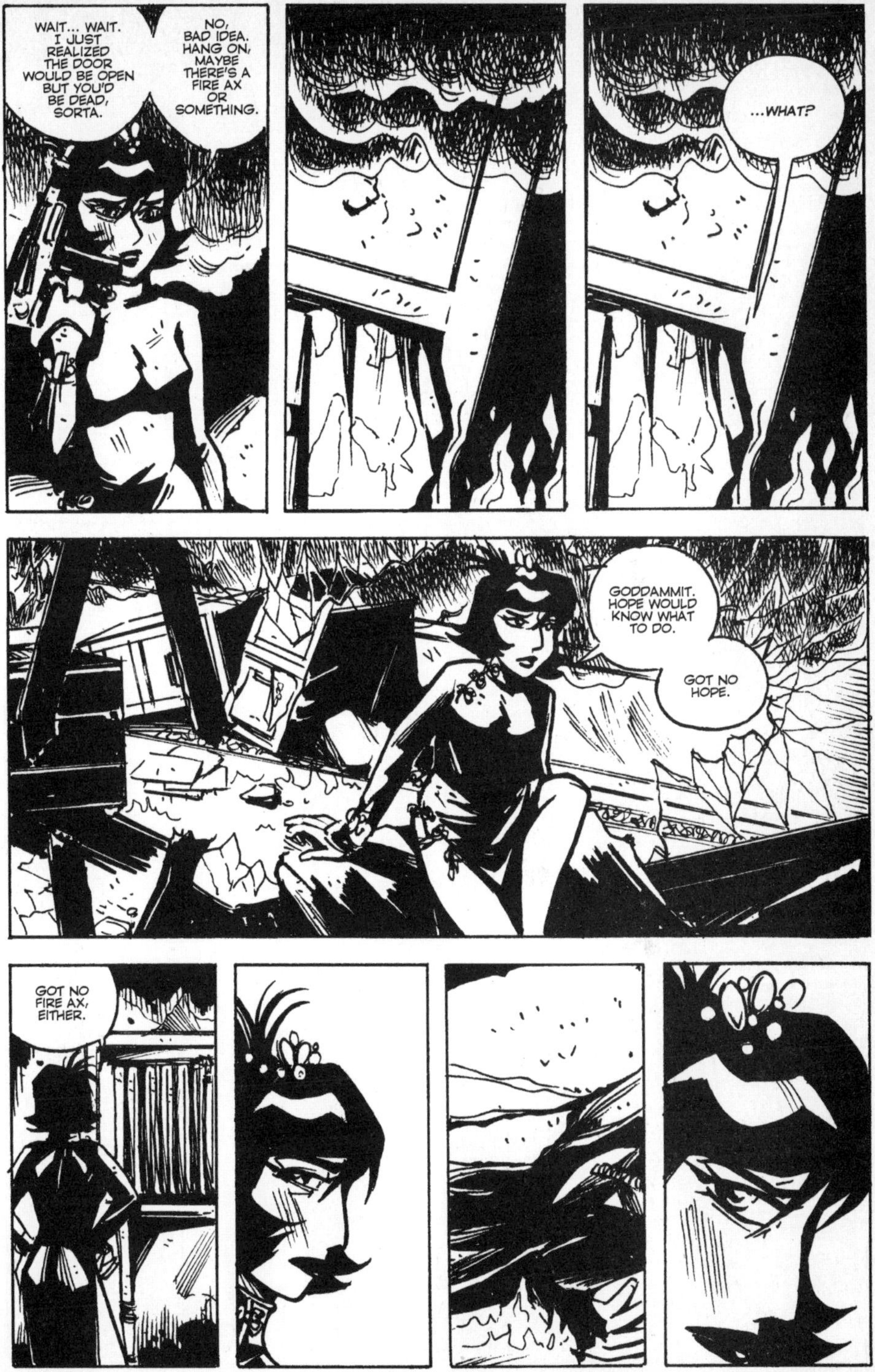
WAIT... WAIT. I JUST REALIZED THE DOOR WOULD BE OPEN BUT YOU'D BE DEAD, SORTA.
NO, BAD IDEA. HANG ON, MAYBE THERE'S A FIRE AX OR SOMETHING.
...WHAT?
GODDAMMIT. HOPE WOULD KNOW WHAT TO DO.
GOT NO HOPE.
GOT NO FIRE AX, EITHER.

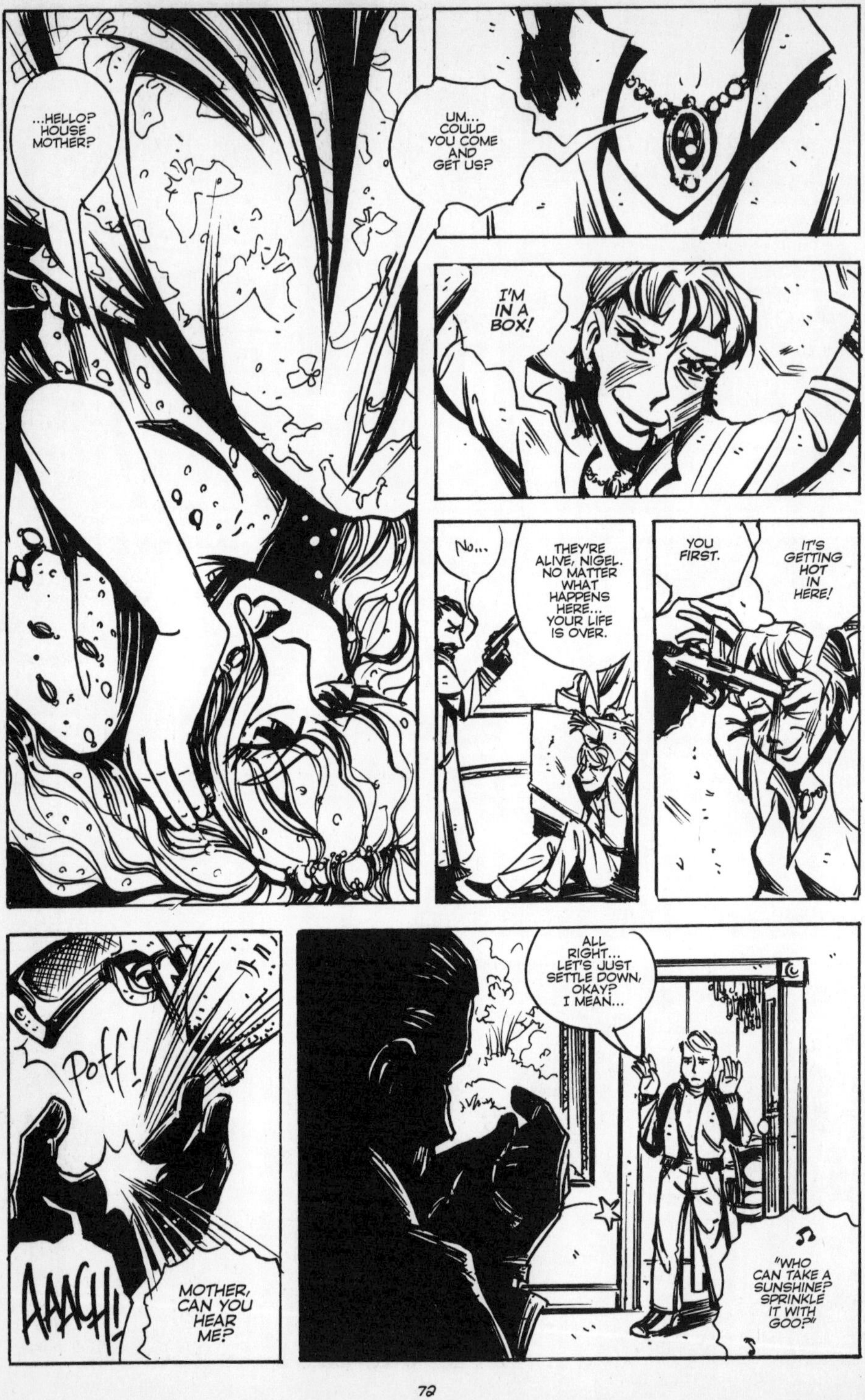
...HELLO? HOUSE MOTHER?
UM... COULD YOU COME AND GET US?
I'M IN A BOX!
No...
THEY'RE ALIVE, NIGEL. NO MATTER WHAT HAPPENS HERE... YOUR LIFE IS OVER.
YOU FIRST.
IT'S GETTING HOT IN HERE!
Poff!
AAACH!
MOTHER, CAN YOU HEAR ME?
ALL RIGHT... LET'S JUST SETTLE DOWN, OKAY? I MEAN...
"WHO CAN TAKE A SUNSHINE? SPRINKLE IT WITH GOO?"

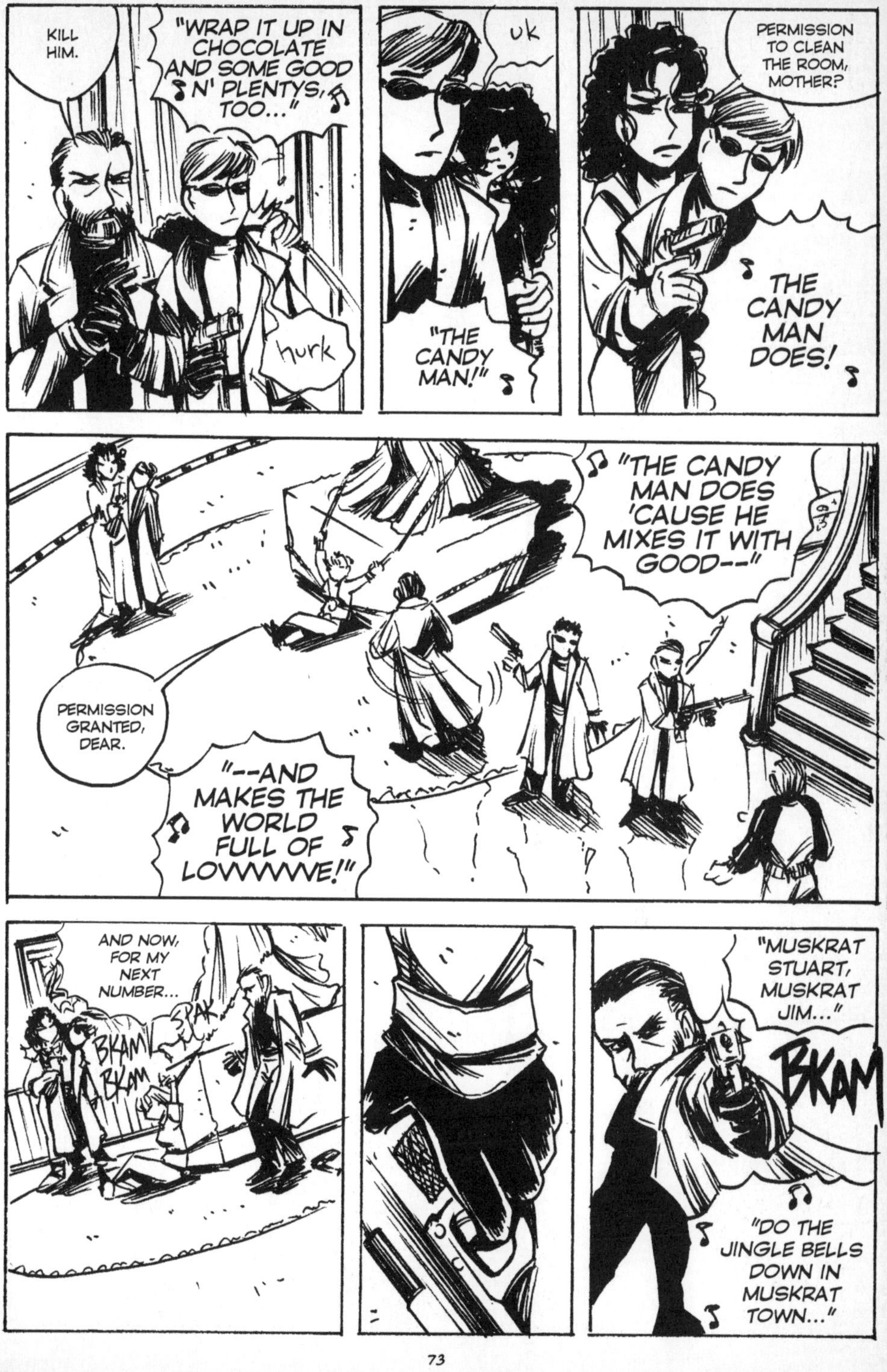
KILL HIM.
"WRAP IT UP IN CHOCOLATE AND SOME GOOD N' PLENTYS, TOO..."
hurk
uk
"THE CANDY MAN!"
PERMISSION TO CLEAN THE ROOM, MOTHER?
THE CANDY MAN DOES!
"THE CANDY MAN DOES 'CAUSE HE MIXES IT WITH GOOD--"
PERMISSION GRANTED, DEAR.
"--AND MAKES THE WORLD FULL OF LOVVVVVVE!"
AND NOW, FOR MY NEXT NUMBER...
BKAM
BKAM
SPAK
"MUSKRAT STUART, MUSKRAT JIM..."
BKAM
"DO THE JINGLE BELLS DOWN IN MUSKRAT TOWN..."

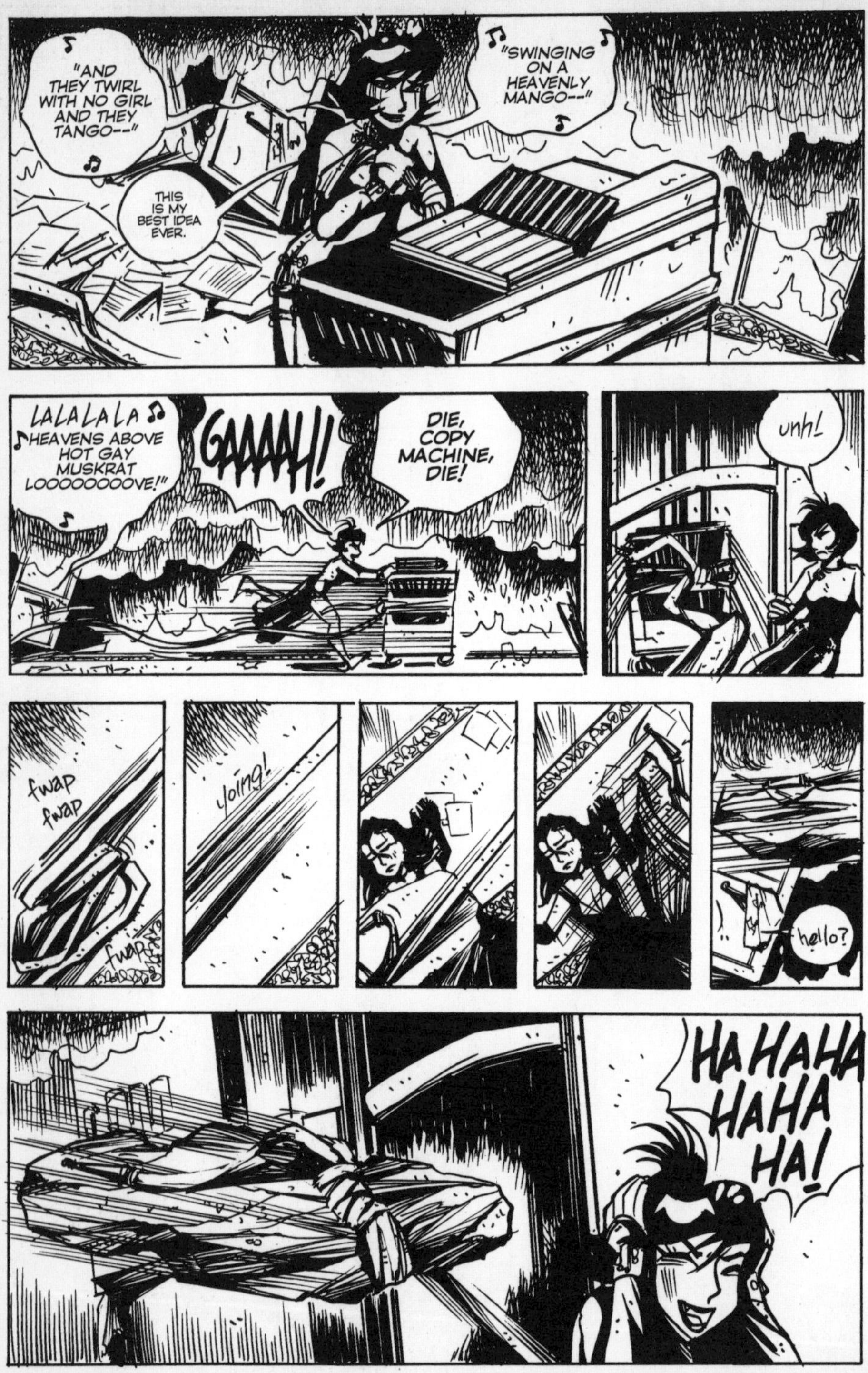

"AND THEY TWIRL WITH NO GIRL AND THEY TANGO--"
"SWINGING ON A HEAVENLY MANGO--"
THIS IS MY BEST IDEA EVER.
LALALALA HEAVENS ABOVE HOT GAY MUSKRAT LOOOOOOOOVE!"
GAAAAH!
DIE, COPY MACHINE, DIE!
unh!
fwap fwap
fwap
yoing!
hello?
HAHAHA HAHAHA HA!

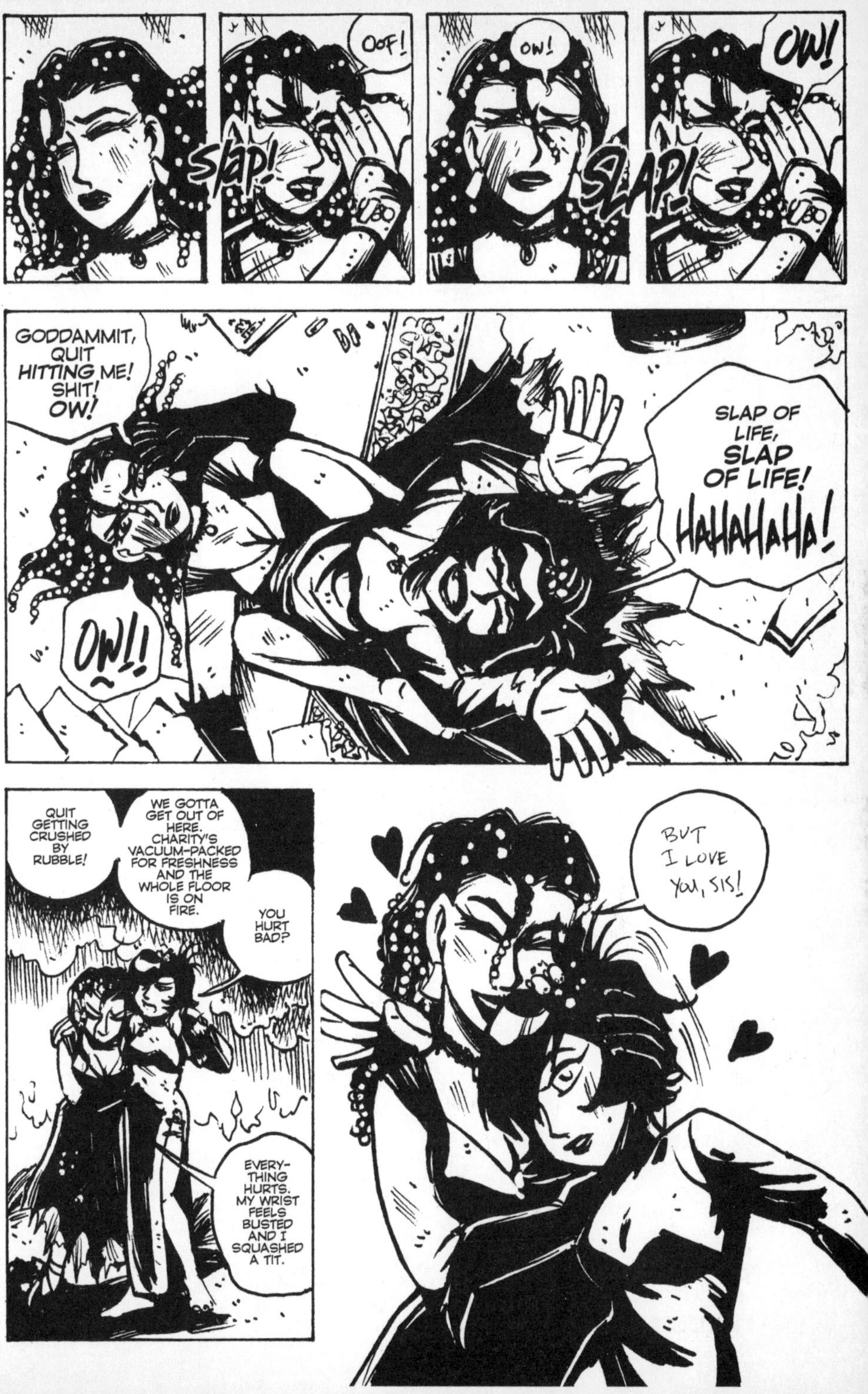

OOF!
SLAP!
OW!
SLAP!
OW!
GODDAMMIT, QUIT HITTING ME! SHIT! OW!
SLAP OF LIFE, SLAP OF LIFE! HAHAHAHA!
OW!!
QUIT GETTING CRUSHED BY RUBBLE!
WE GOTTA GET OUT OF HERE. CHARITY'S VACUUM-PACKED FOR FRESHNESS AND THE WHOLE FLOOR IS ON FIRE.
YOU HURT BAD?
EVERY-THING HURTS. MY WRIST FEELS BUSTED AND I SQUASHED A TIT.
BUT I LOVE YOU, SIS!

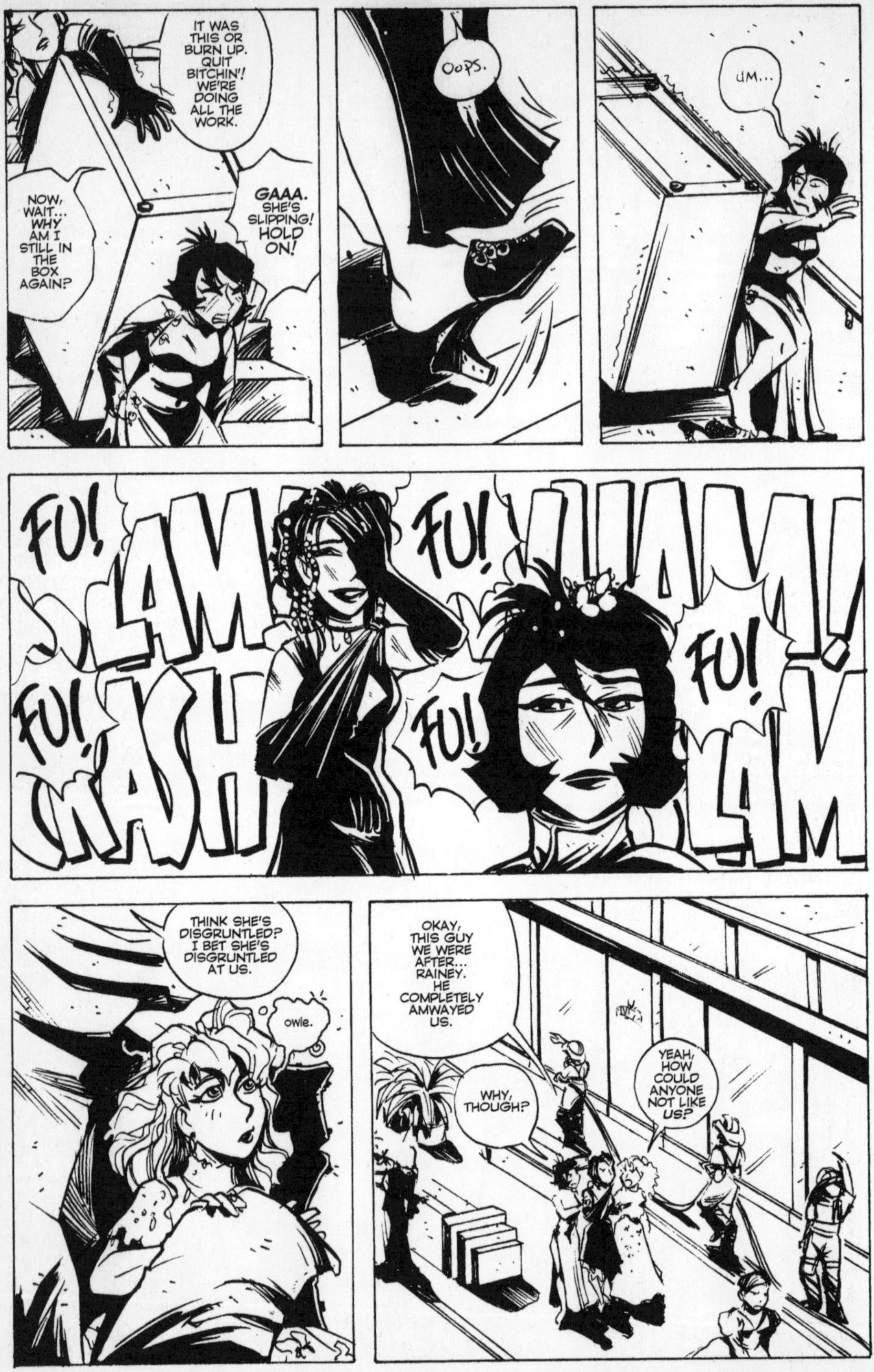
IT WAS THIS OR BURN UP. QUIT BITCHIN'! WE'RE DOING ALL THE WORK.
NOW, WAIT... WHY AM I STILL IN THE BOX AGAIN?
GAAA. SHE'S SLIPPING! HOLD ON!
OOPS.
UM...
FU!
LAM
FU!
RASH
FU!
FU!
FU!
LAM
THINK SHE'S DISGRUNTLED? I BET SHE'S DISGRUNTLED AT US.
owie.
OKAY, THIS GUY WE WERE AFTER... RAINEY. HE COMPLETELY AMWAYED US.
WHY, THOUGH?
YEAH, HOW COULD ANYONE NOT LIKE US?

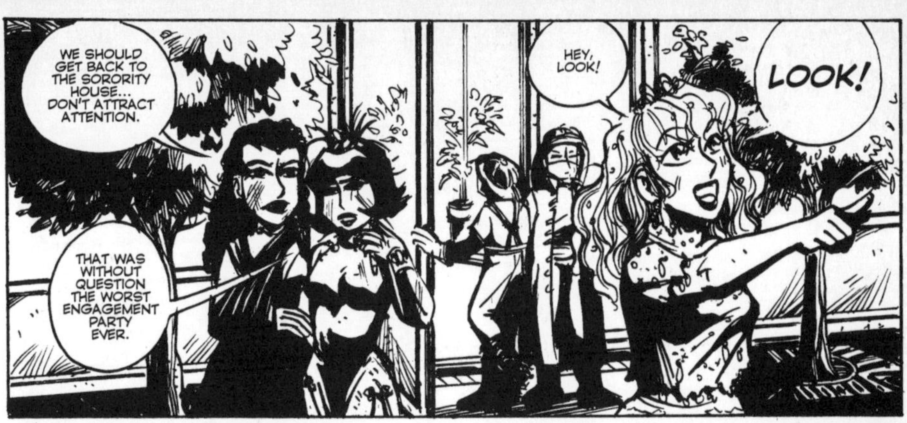
WE SHOULD GET BACK TO THE SORORITY HOUSE... DON'T ATTRACT ATTENTION.
THAT WAS WITHOUT QUESTION THE WORST ENGAGEMENT PARTY EVER.
HEY, LOOK!
LOOK!

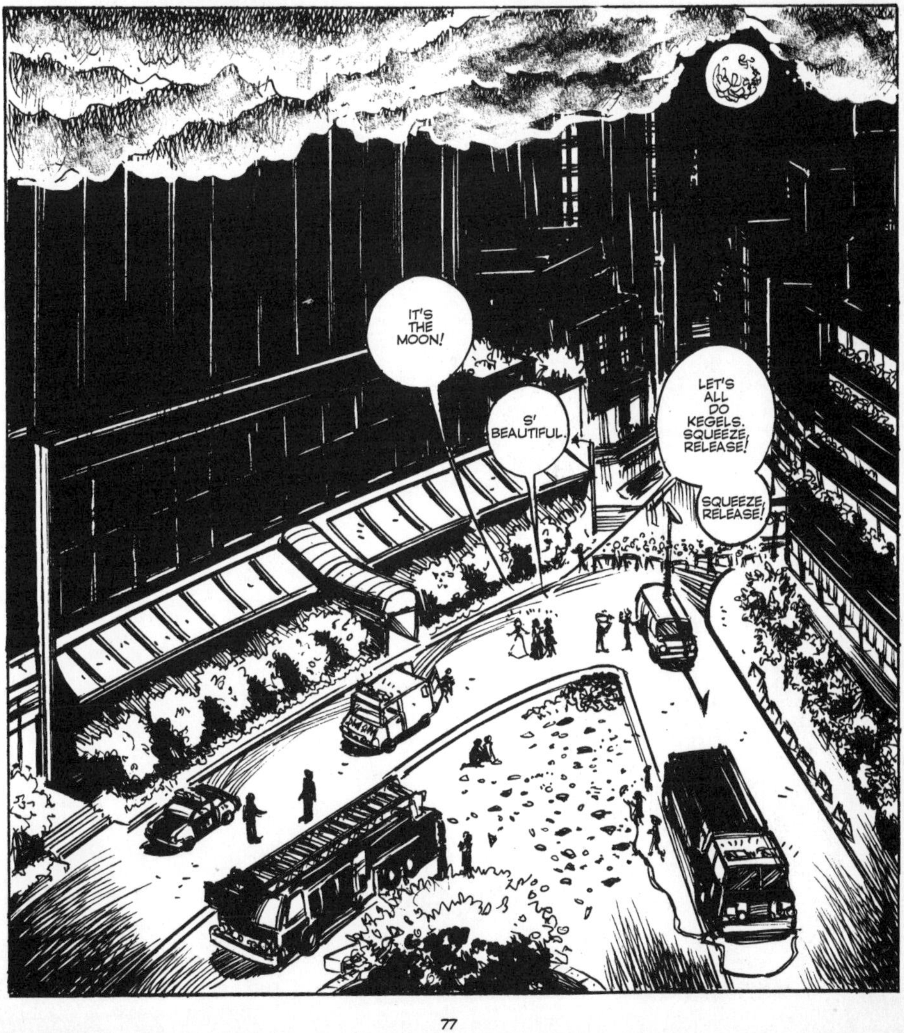
IT'S THE MOON!
S' BEAUTIFUL.
LET'S ALL DO KEGELS. SQUEEZE, RELEASE!
SQUEEZE, RELEASE!

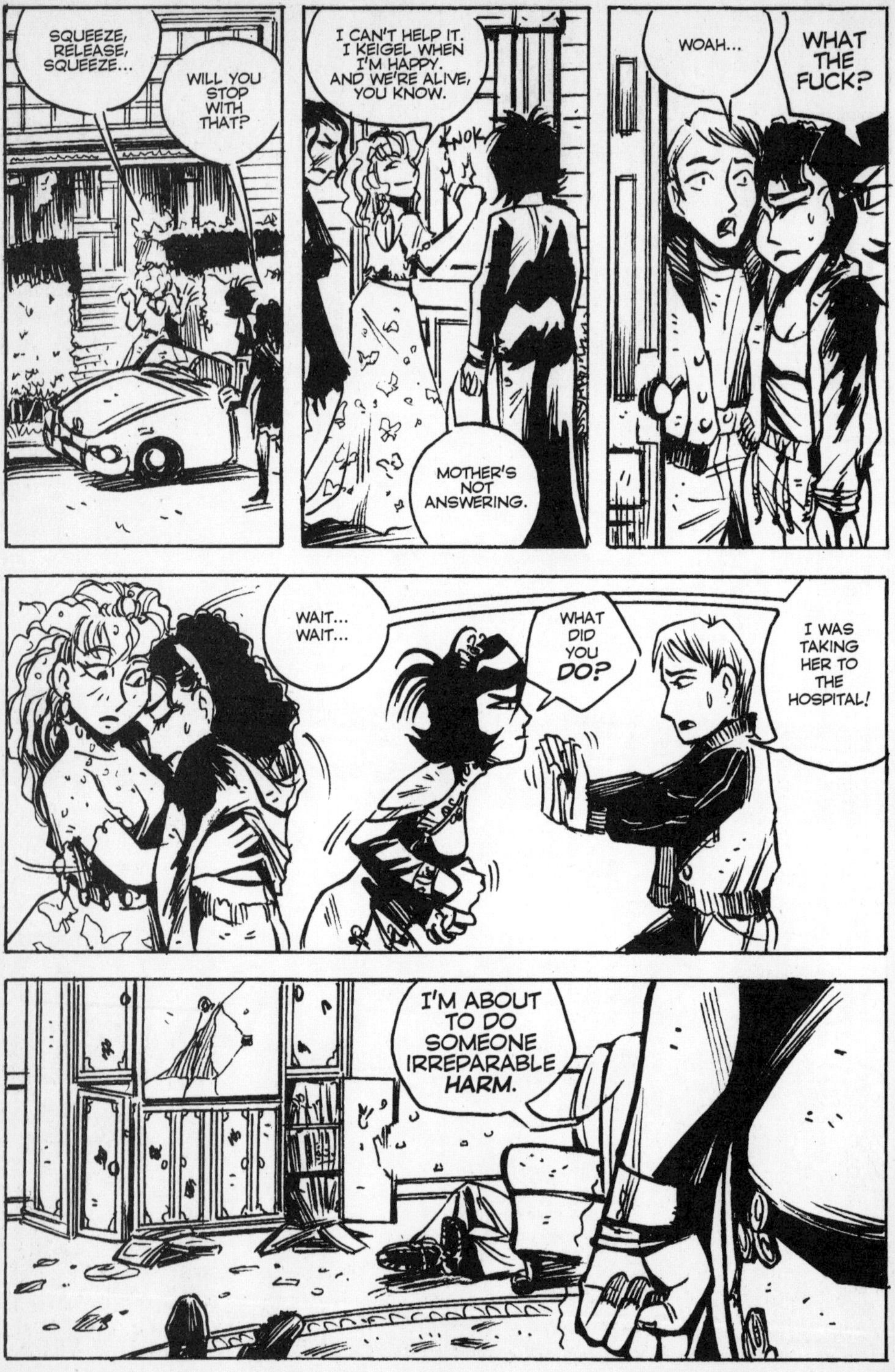
SQUEEZE, RELEASE, SQUEEZE...
WILL YOU STOP WITH THAT?
I CAN'T HELP IT. I KEIGEL WHEN I'M HAPPY. AND WE'RE ALIVE, YOU KNOW.
KNOK
MOTHER'S NOT ANSWERING.
WOAH...
WHAT THE FUCK?
WAIT... WAIT...
WHAT DID YOU DO?
I WAS TAKING HER TO THE HOSPITAL!
I'M ABOUT TO DO SOMEONE IRREPARABLE HARM.

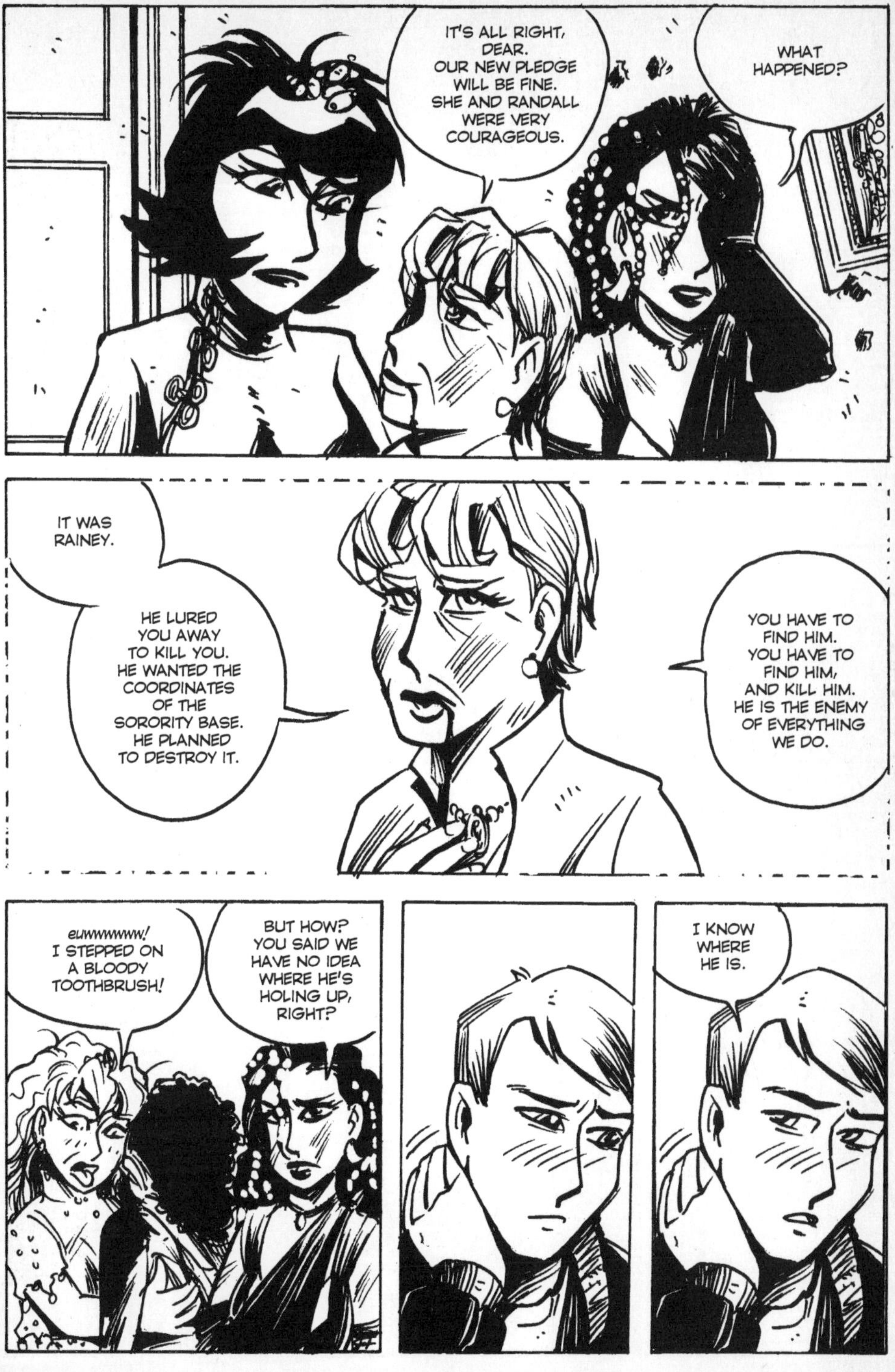
IT'S ALL RIGHT, DEAR. OUR NEW PLEDGE WILL BE FINE. SHE AND RANDALL WERE VERY COURAGEOUS.
WHAT HAPPENED?
IT WAS RAINEY.
HE LURED YOU AWAY TO KILL YOU. HE WANTED THE COORDINATES OF THE SORORITY BASE. HE PLANNED TO DESTROY IT.
YOU HAVE TO FIND HIM. YOU HAVE TO FIND HIM, AND KILL HIM. HE IS THE ENEMY OF EVERYTHING WE DO.
euwwwwww! I STEPPED ON A BLOODY TOOTHBRUSH!
BUT HOW? YOU SAID WE HAVE NO IDEA WHERE HE'S HOLING UP, RIGHT?
I KNOW WHERE HE IS.

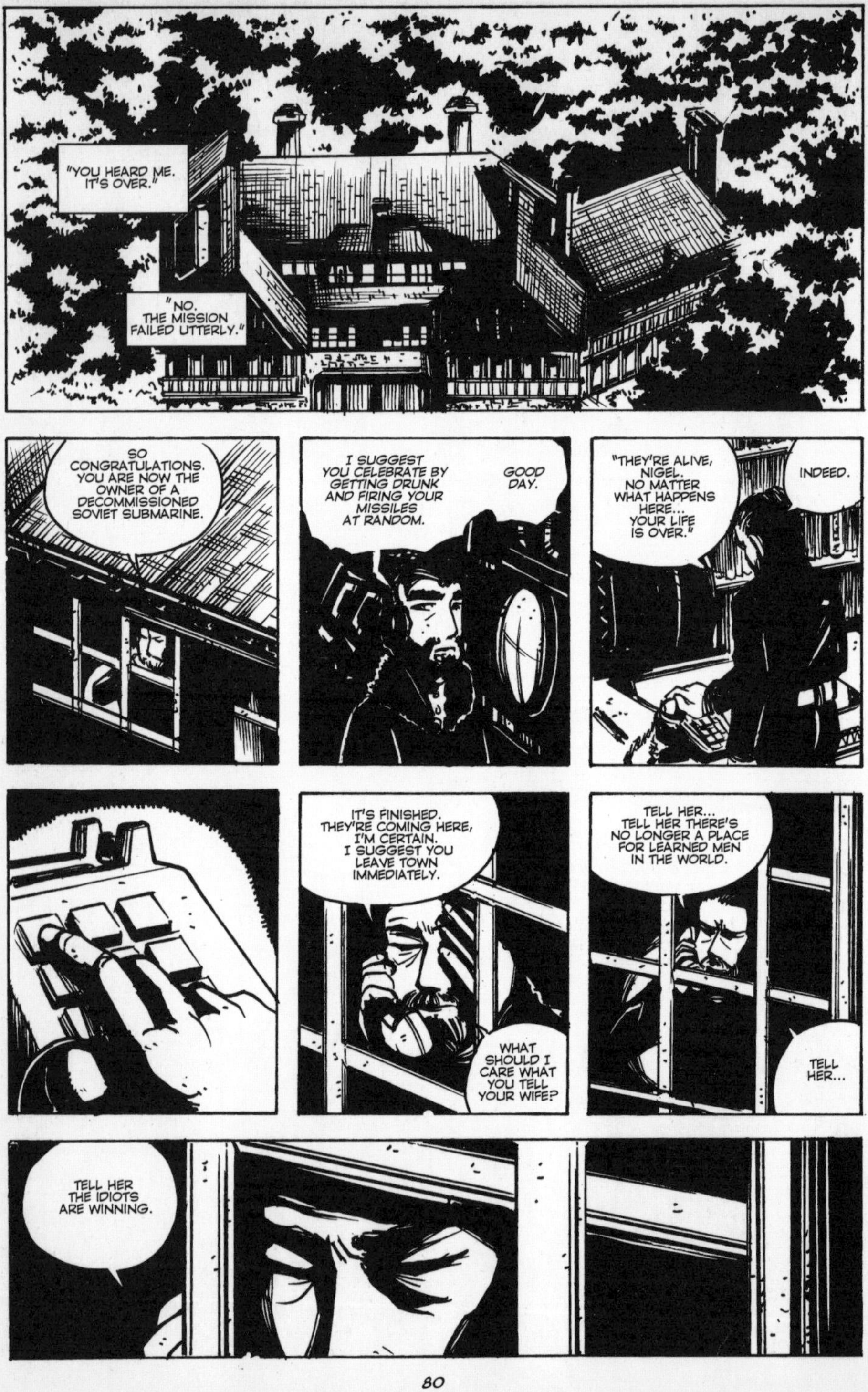
"YOU HEARD ME. IT'S OVER."
"NO. THE MISSION FAILED UTTERLY."
SO CONGRATULATIONS. YOU ARE NOW THE OWNER OF A DECOMMISSIONED SOVIET SUBMARINE.
I SUGGEST YOU CELEBRATE BY GETTING DRUNK AND FIRING YOUR MISSILES AT RANDOM.
GOOD DAY.
"THEY'RE ALIVE, NIGEL. NO MATTER WHAT HAPPENS HERE... YOUR LIFE IS OVER."
INDEED.
IT'S FINISHED. THEY'RE COMING HERE, I'M CERTAIN. I SUGGEST YOU LEAVE TOWN IMMEDIATELY.
WHAT SHOULD I CARE WHAT YOU TELL YOUR WIFE?
TELL HER... TELL HER THERE'S NO LONGER A PLACE FOR LEARNED MEN IN THE WORLD.
TELL HER...
TELL HER THE IDIOTS ARE WINNING.

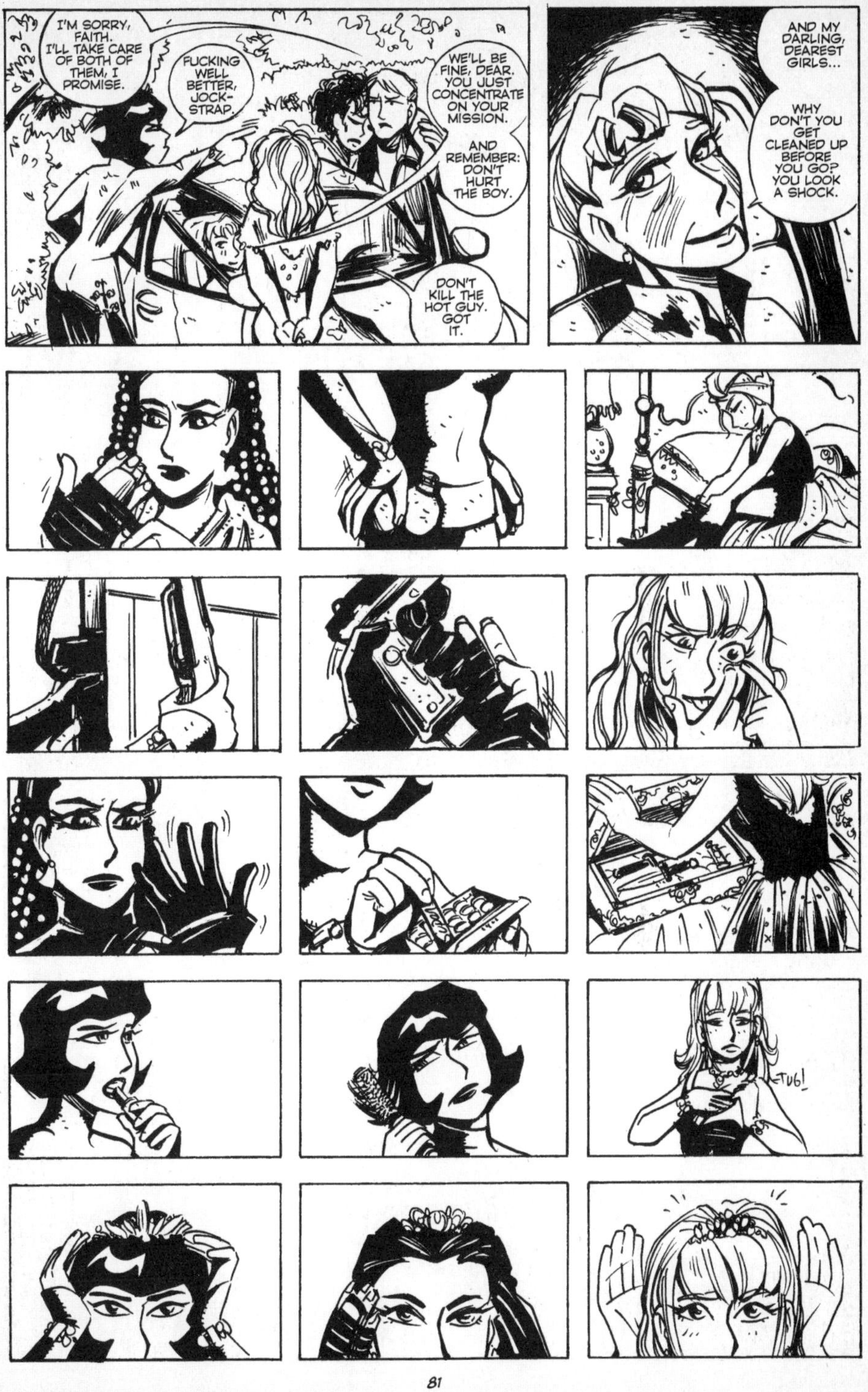
I'M SORRY, FAITH. I'LL TAKE CARE OF BOTH OF THEM, I PROMISE.
FUCKING WELL BETTER, JOCK-STRAP.
WE'LL BE FINE, DEAR. YOU JUST CONCENTRATE ON YOUR MISSION.
AND REMEMBER: DON'T HURT THE BOY.
DON'T KILL THE HOT GUY. GOT IT.
AND MY DARLING, DEAREST GIRLS...
WHY DON'T YOU GET CLEANED UP BEFORE YOU GO? YOU LOOK A SHOCK.
TUG!

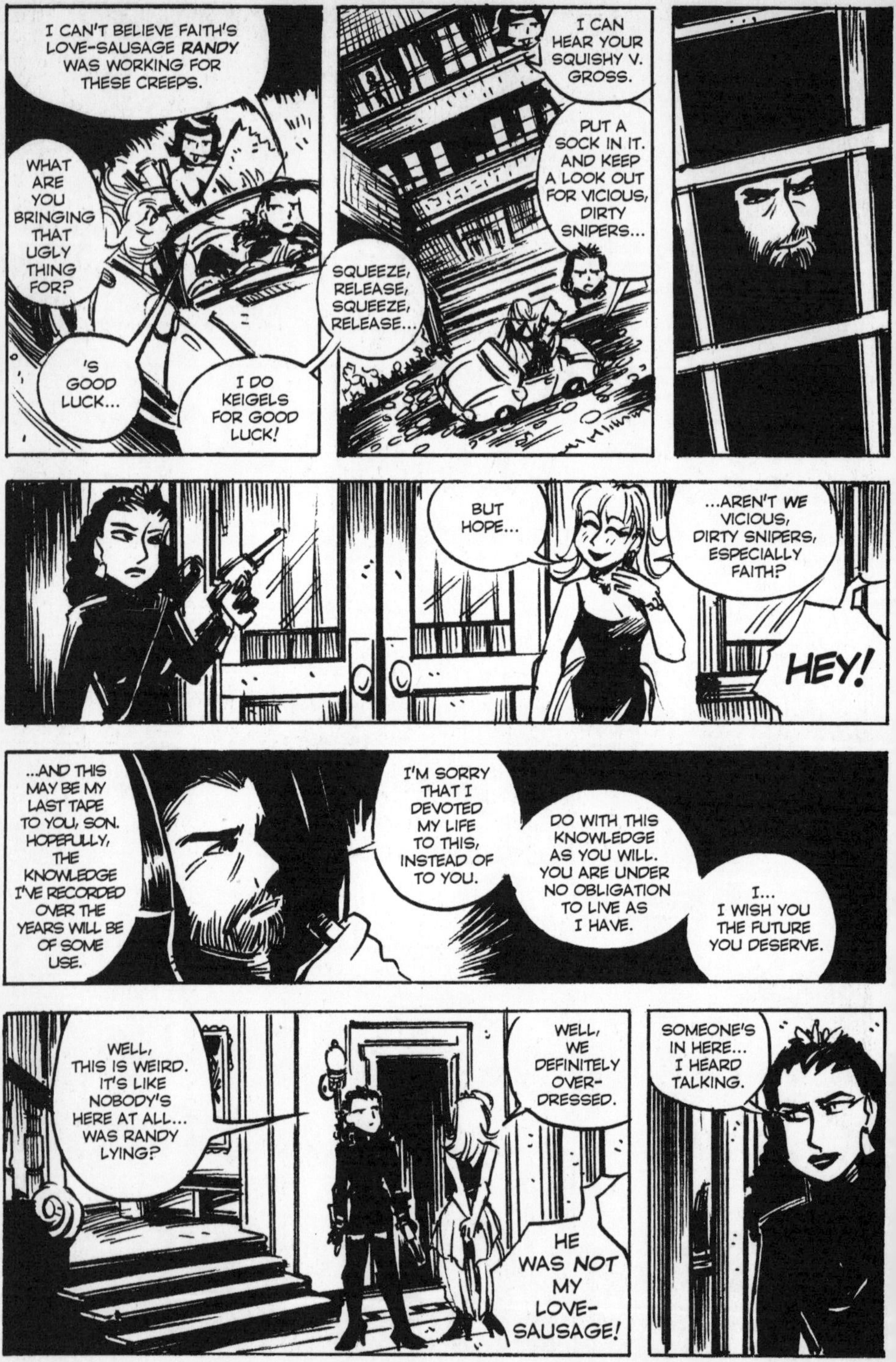

I CAN'T BELIEVE FAITH'S LOVE-SAUSAGE RANDY WAS WORKING FOR THESE CREEPS.
WHAT ARE YOU BRINGING THAT UGLY THING FOR?
'S GOOD LUCK...
I DO KEIGELS FOR GOOD LUCK!
SQUEEZE, RELEASE, SQUEEZE, RELEASE...
I CAN HEAR YOUR SQUISHY V. GROSS.
PUT A SOCK IN IT. AND KEEP A LOOK OUT FOR VICIOUS, DIRTY SNIPERS...
BUT HOPE...
...AREN'T WE VICIOUS, DIRTY SNIPERS, ESPECIALLY FAITH?
HEY!
...AND THIS MAY BE MY LAST TAPE TO YOU, SON. HOPEFULLY, THE KNOWLEDGE I'VE RECORDED OVER THE YEARS WILL BE OF SOME USE.
I'M SORRY THAT I DEVOTED MY LIFE TO THIS, INSTEAD OF TO YOU.
DO WITH THIS KNOWLEDGE AS YOU WILL. YOU ARE UNDER NO OBLIGATION TO LIVE AS I HAVE.
I... I WISH YOU THE FUTURE YOU DESERVE.
WELL, THIS IS WEIRD. IT'S LIKE NOBODY'S HERE AT ALL... WAS RANDY LYING?
WELL, WE DEFINITELY OVER-DRESSED.
HE WAS NOT MY LOVE-SAUSAGE!
SOMEONE'S IN HERE... I HEARD TALKING.

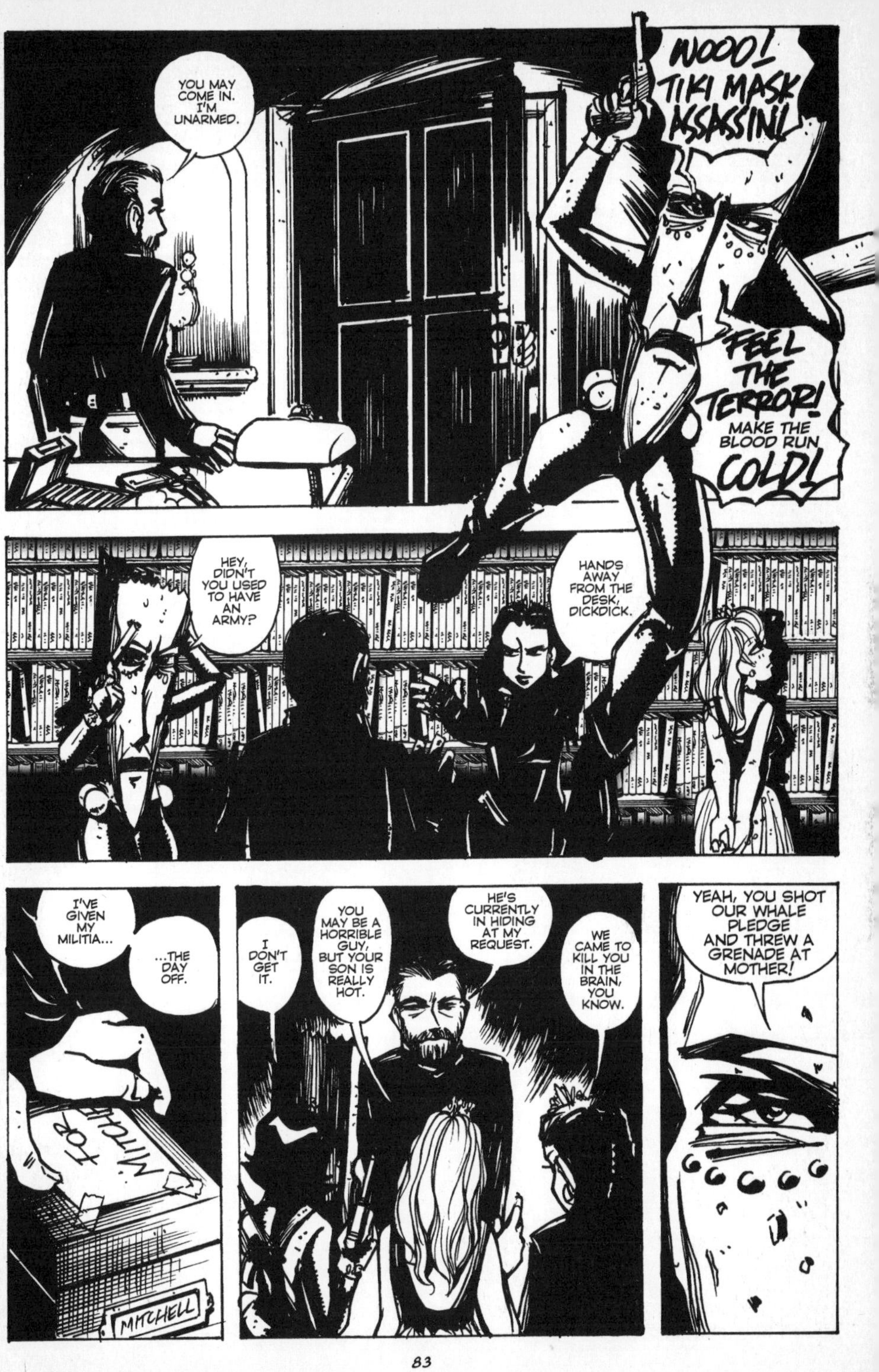

YOU MAY COME IN. I'M UNARMED.
WOOO! TIKI MASK ASSASSIN!
FEEL THE TERROR! MAKE THE BLOOD RUN COLD!
HEY, DIDN'T YOU USED TO HAVE AN ARMY?
HANDS AWAY FROM THE DESK, DICKDICK.
I'VE GIVEN MY MILITIA...
...THE DAY OFF.
FOR MITCHELL
MITCHELL
I DON'T GET IT.
YOU MAY BE A HORRIBLE GUY, BUT YOUR SON IS REALLY HOT.
HE'S CURRENTLY IN HIDING AT MY REQUEST.
WE CAME TO KILL YOU IN THE BRAIN, YOU KNOW.
YEAH, YOU SHOT OUR WHALE PLEDGE AND THREW A GRENADE AT MOTHER!

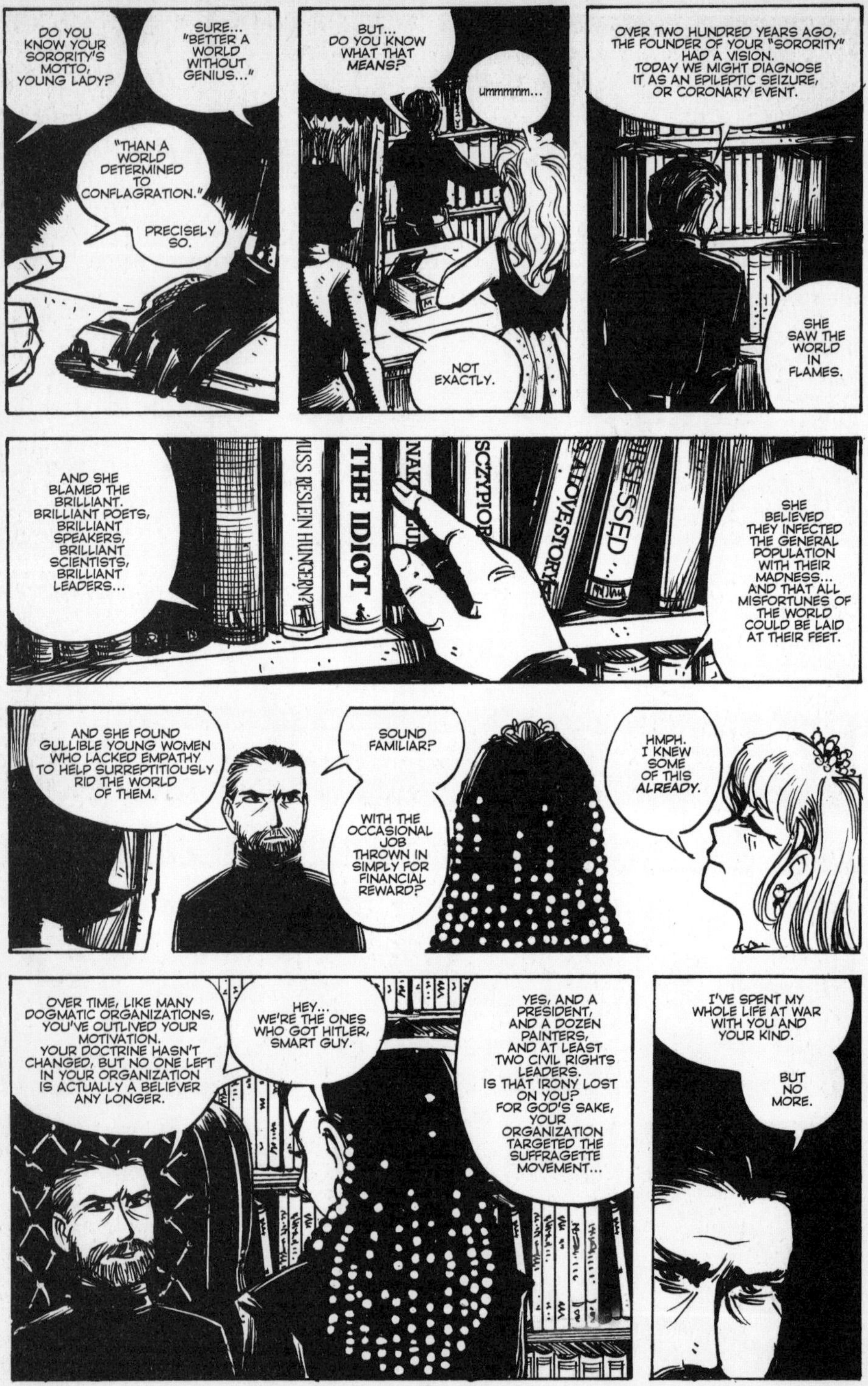

DO YOU KNOW YOUR SORORITY'S MOTTO, YOUNG LADY?
SURE... "BETTER A WORLD WITHOUT GENIUS..."
"THAN A WORLD DETERMINED TO CONFLAGRATION."
PRECISELY SO.
BUT... DO YOU KNOW WHAT THAT *MEANS?*
ummmmm...
NOT EXACTLY.
OVER TWO HUNDRED YEARS AGO, THE FOUNDER OF YOUR "SORORITY" HAD A VISION. TODAY WE MIGHT DIAGNOSE IT AS AN EPILEPTIC SEIZURE, OR CORONARY EVENT.
SHE SAW THE WORLD IN FLAMES.
AND SHE BLAMED THE BRILLIANT. BRILLIANT POETS, BRILLIANT SPEAKERS, BRILLIANT SCIENTISTS, BRILLIANT LEADERS...
MUSS RESLEIN HUNGERN?
THE IDIOT
SCZYPIOR
OBSESSED
SHE BELIEVED THEY INFECTED THE GENERAL POPULATION WITH THEIR MADNESS... AND THAT ALL MISFORTUNES OF THE WORLD COULD BE LAID AT THEIR FEET.
AND SHE FOUND GULLIBLE YOUNG WOMEN WHO LACKED EMPATHY TO HELP SURREPTITIOUSLY RID THE WORLD OF THEM.
SOUND FAMILIAR?
WITH THE OCCASIONAL JOB THROWN IN SIMPLY FOR FINANCIAL REWARD?
HMPH. I KNEW SOME OF THIS **ALREADY**.
OVER TIME, LIKE MANY DOGMATIC ORGANIZATIONS, YOU'VE OUTLIVED YOUR MOTIVATION. YOUR DOCTRINE HASN'T CHANGED, BUT NO ONE LEFT IN YOUR ORGANIZATION IS ACTUALLY A BELIEVER ANY LONGER.
HEY... WE'RE THE ONES WHO GOT HITLER, SMART GUY.
YES, AND A PRESIDENT, AND A DOZEN PAINTERS, AND AT LEAST TWO CIVIL RIGHTS LEADERS. IS THAT IRONY LOST ON YOU? FOR GOD'S SAKE, YOUR ORGANIZATION TARGETED THE SUFFRAGETTE MOVEMENT...
I'VE SPENT MY WHOLE LIFE AT WAR WITH YOU AND YOUR KIND.
BUT NO MORE.

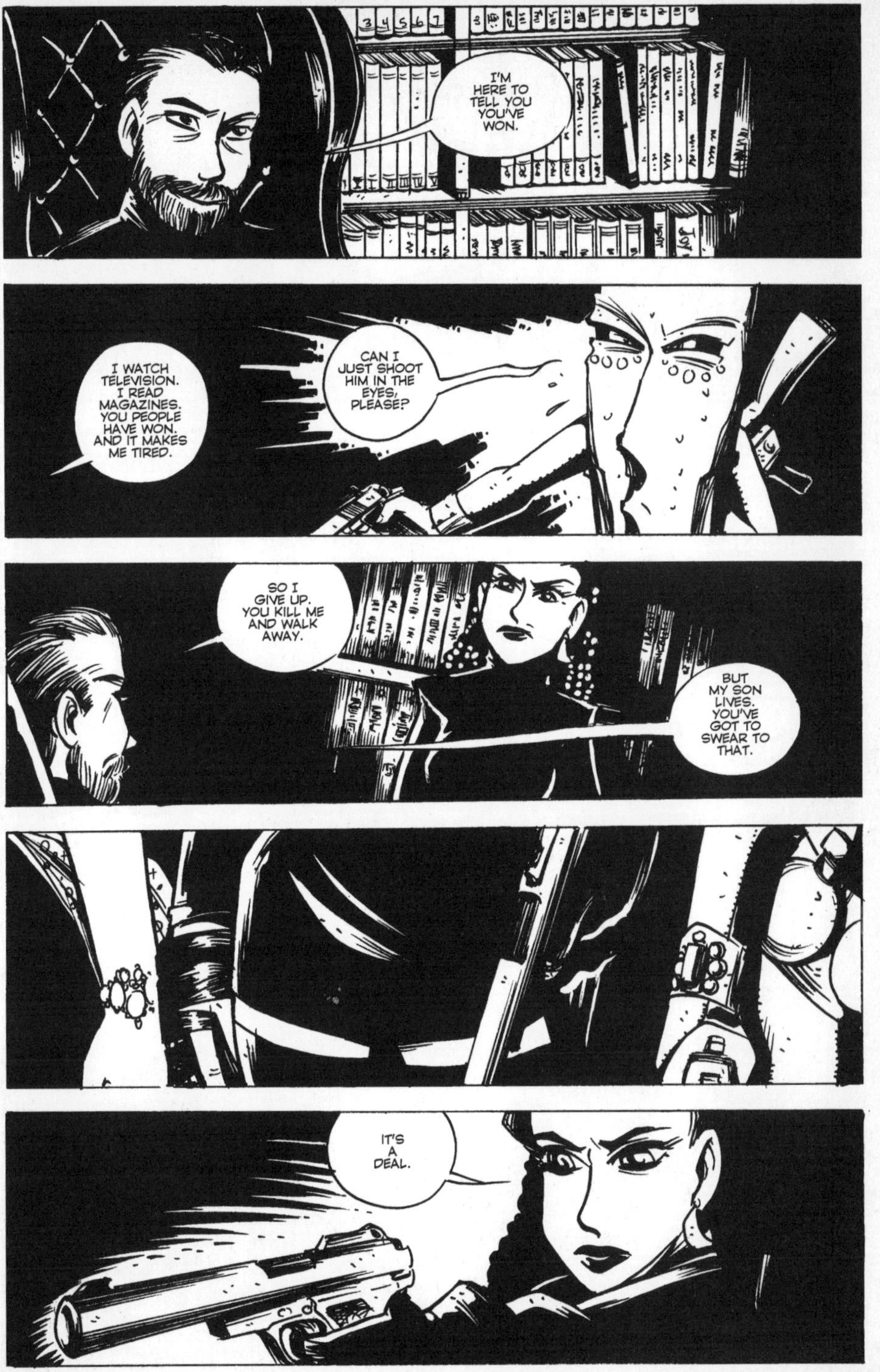
I'M HERE TO TELL YOU YOU'VE WON.
I WATCH TELEVISION. I READ MAGAZINES. YOU PEOPLE HAVE WON. AND IT MAKES ME TIRED.
CAN I JUST SHOOT HIM IN THE EYES, PLEASE?
SO I GIVE UP. YOU KILL ME AND WALK AWAY.
BUT MY SON LIVES. YOU'VE GOT TO SWEAR TO THAT.
IT'S A DEAL.

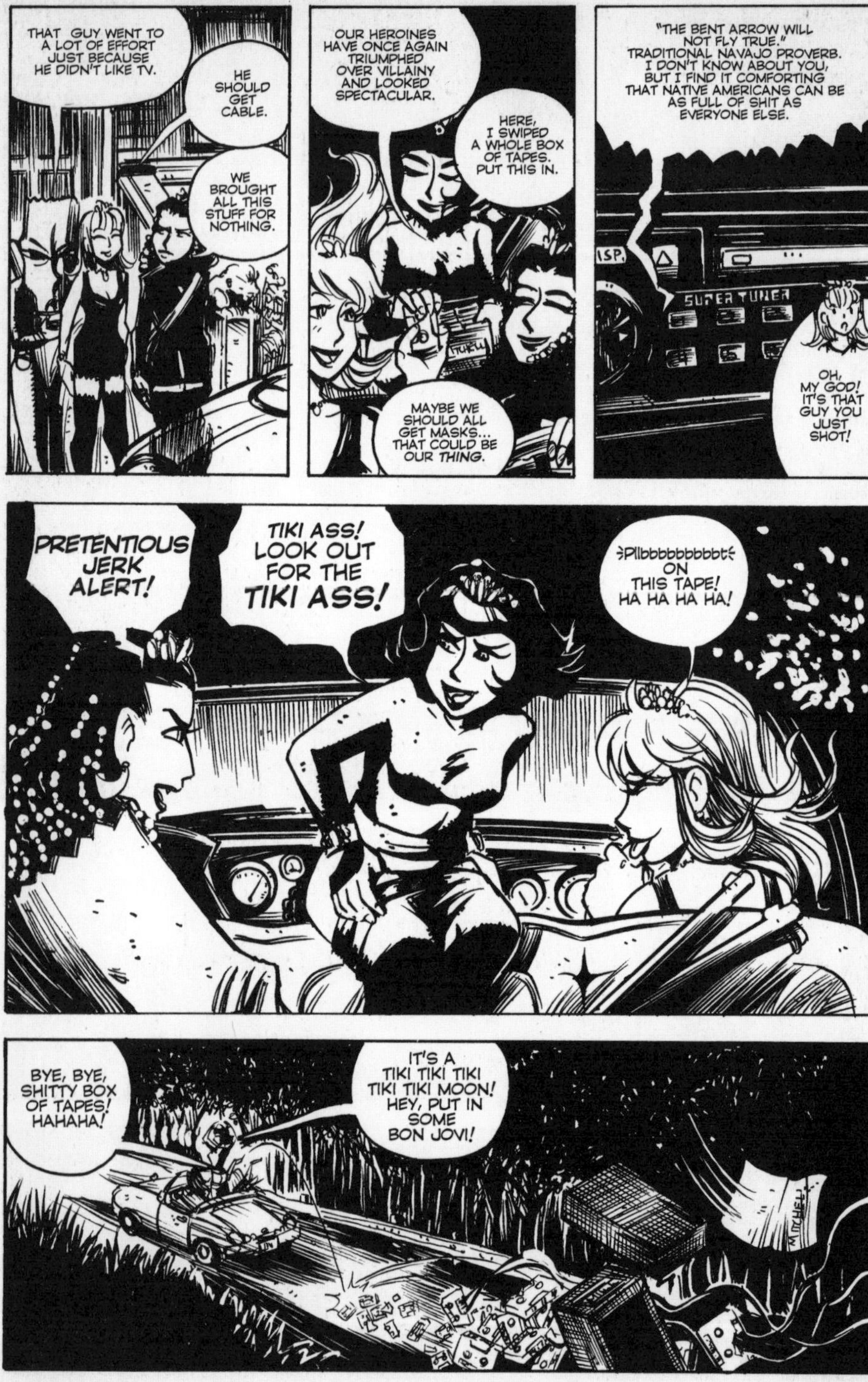
THAT GUY WENT TO A LOT OF EFFORT JUST BECAUSE HE DIDN'T LIKE TV.
HE SHOULD GET CABLE.
WE BROUGHT ALL THIS STUFF FOR NOTHING.
OUR HEROINES HAVE ONCE AGAIN TRIUMPHED OVER VILLAINY AND LOOKED SPECTACULAR.
HERE, I SWIPED A WHOLE BOX OF TAPES. PUT THIS IN.
MAYBE WE SHOULD ALL GET MASKS... THAT COULD BE OUR *THING*.
"THE BENT ARROW WILL NOT FLY TRUE." TRADITIONAL NAVAJO PROVERB. I DON'T KNOW ABOUT YOU, BUT I FIND IT COMFORTING THAT NATIVE AMERICANS CAN BE AS FULL OF SHIT AS EVERYONE ELSE.
SUPER TUNER
OH, MY GOD! IT'S THAT GUY YOU JUST SHOT!
PRETENTIOUS JERK ALERT!
TIKI ASS! LOOK OUT FOR THE TIKI ASS!
Pllbbbbbbbbbt ON THIS TAPE! HA HA HA HA!
BYE, BYE, SHITTY BOX OF TAPES! HAHAHA!
IT'S A TIKI TIKI TIKI TIKI TIKI MOON! HEY, PUT IN SOME BON JOVI!
MITCHELL

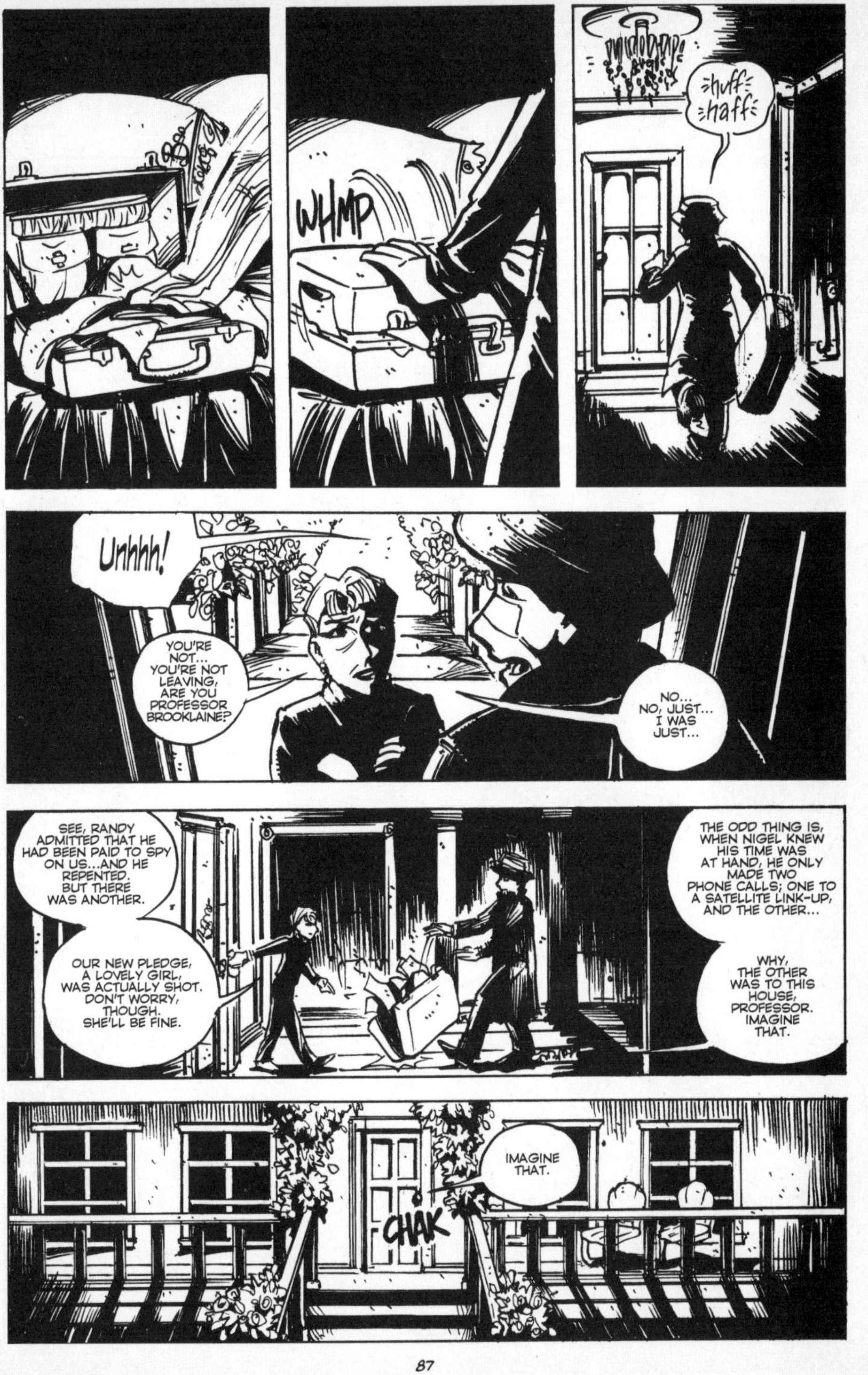
WHMP
huff haff
Unhhh!
YOU'RE NOT... YOU'RE NOT LEAVING, ARE YOU PROFESSOR BROOKLAINE?
NO... NO, JUST... I WAS JUST...
SEE, RANDY ADMITTED THAT HE HAD BEEN PAID TO SPY ON US...AND HE REPENTED. BUT THERE WAS ANOTHER.
OUR NEW PLEDGE, A LOVELY GIRL, WAS ACTUALLY SHOT. DON'T WORRY, THOUGH. SHE'LL BE FINE.
THE ODD THING IS, WHEN NIGEL KNEW HIS TIME WAS AT HAND, HE ONLY MADE TWO PHONE CALLS; ONE TO A SATELLITE LINK-UP, AND THE OTHER...
WHY, THE OTHER WAS TO THIS HOUSE, PROFESSOR. IMAGINE THAT.
IMAGINE THAT.
CHAK

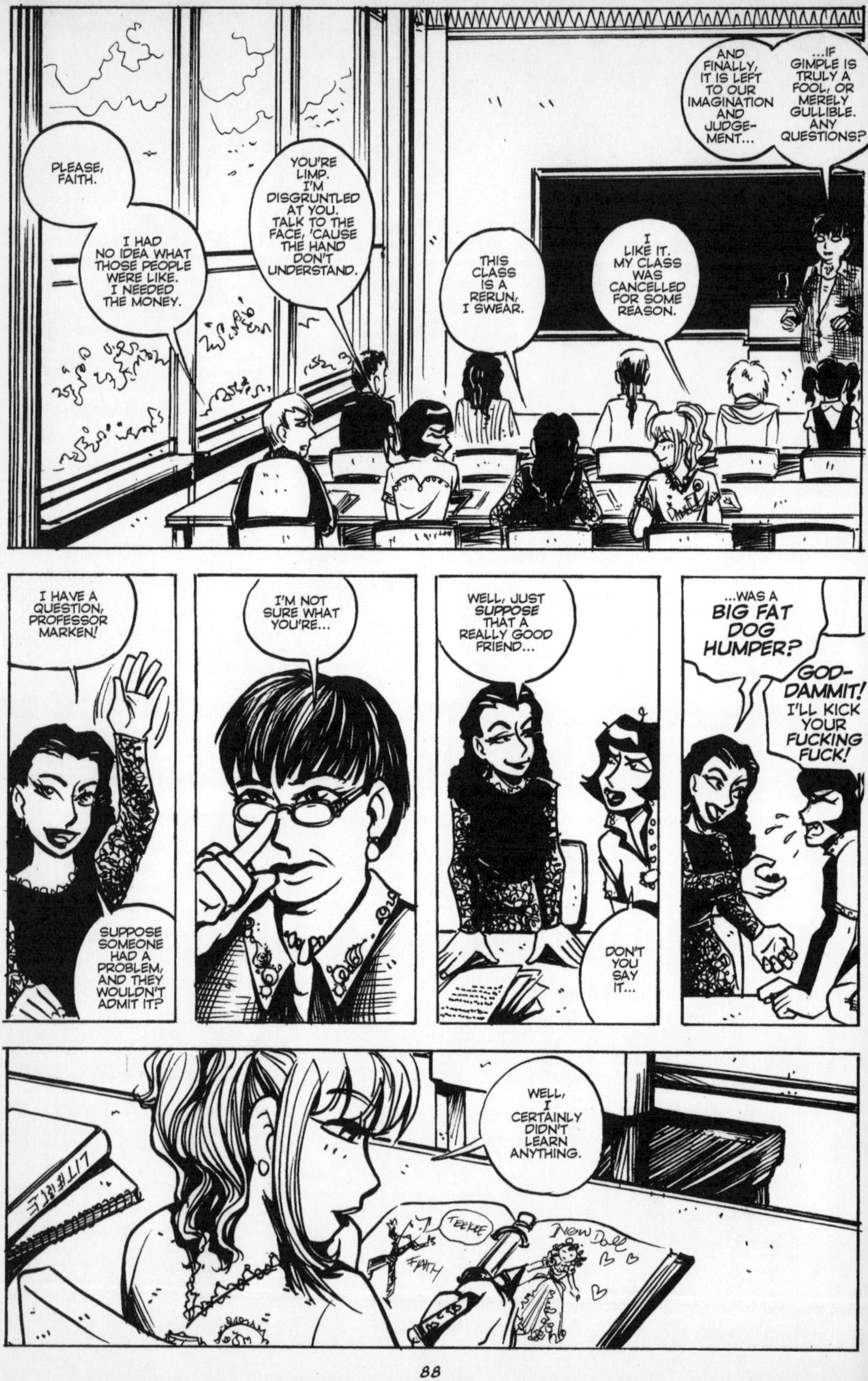
AND FINALLY, IT IS LEFT TO OUR IMAGINATION AND JUDGE-MENT...
...IF GIMPLE IS TRULY A FOOL, OR MERELY GULLIBLE. ANY QUESTIONS?
PLEASE, FAITH.
I HAD NO IDEA WHAT THOSE PEOPLE WERE LIKE. I NEEDED THE MONEY.
YOU'RE LIMP. I'M DISGRUNTLED AT YOU. TALK TO THE FACE, 'CAUSE THE HAND DON'T UNDERSTAND.
THIS CLASS IS A RERUN, I SWEAR.
I LIKE IT. MY CLASS WAS CANCELLED FOR SOME REASON.
I HAVE A QUESTION, PROFESSOR MARKEN!
SUPPOSE SOMEONE HAD A PROBLEM, AND THEY WOULDN'T ADMIT IT?
I'M NOT SURE WHAT YOU'RE...
WELL, JUST SUPPOSE THAT A REALLY GOOD FRIEND...
DON'T YOU SAY IT...
...WAS A BIG FAT DOG HUMPER?
GOD-DAMMIT! I'LL KICK YOUR FUCKING FUCK!
WELL, I CERTAINLY DIDN'T LEARN ANYTHING.
TEEHEE
NEW DOLL

XO XO XO

Pledge Charity's

Application Essay

by

Charity

Hello!

I HOPE WHOEVER GRADES MY TEST WILL TAKE INTO ACCOUNT THAT I'M NOT GOOD AT ESSAY QUESTIONS OR MULTIPLE CHOICE OR THOSE MAGIC EYE THINGS EITHER BUT I DO LIKE GOOD HISTORY WHEN IT'S NOT ABOUT EVENTS AND THINGS. HISTORY WOULD TOTALLY RULE IF THERE WERE NO EVENTS.

ANYWAY, THE TOPIC OF MY ESSAY IS "THE HISTORY OF THE SORORITY AND WHY I WANT TO BE A SORORITY ARROW AGENT". IT TOOK AN HOUR TO THINK OF THAT SO ALSO TAKE THAT INTO ACCOUNT ALSO, PRETTY PLEASE.

I WILL SAVE THE SECOND HALF FOR THE SECOND HALF WHICH I WILL CALL HALF B. THIS HALF IS HALF A. I WILL NOT HAVE FOOTNOTES OR FOOT ANYTHING. I DON'T LIKE FEET.

FIRST, IT'S IMPORTANT TO SAY RIGHT OUT THAT HISTORY IS REAL REAL IMPORTANT FOR IS IT NOT HISTORY WHICH IS OUR PAST? YES, IT IS. I AGREE WITH MY ASSERTION.

SO IN CONCLUSION, THE HISTORY OF THE SORORITY STARTED IN MIDEVIL TIMES OR SOMETHING AND THERE WERE PROBABLY COWBOYS, ALSO, BUT NOT AT THE SAME EPOX.

OUR FOUNDER WAS THIS LADY WHO THOUGHT THE WORLD WAS DOOMED TO CONFLAGRATION (FIRE) IF GENIUSES WERE ALLOWED TO BE THE BOSS OF PEOPLE SO SHE DID SOME STUFF AND GOT SOME GIRLS TO HELP, WHICH WAS AWESOME. IT SEEMS LIKE SHE MUSTA BEEN KINDA A GENIUS HERSELF TO COME UP WITH SUCH A GREAT IDEA, BUT MAYBE SHE WAS JUST DUMB ENOUGH TO SCOOT IN UNDER THE IQ ROOF WITHOUT HITTING HER NOGGIN, WHICH MAKES HER REMARKABLENESS EVEN MORE OR LESS REMARKABLE...

Randall had an impatient, ill-at-ease quality, as if his own skin suited him poorly, and gravity had a lesser impact upon his person than the rest of the gallery's pale occupants. Of all my admirers and suitors, I blush to say that Randall encouraged the strongest reaction in areas I shall not mention in this journal.

"A most disagreeable place to meet a lady, Katherine," he said. His disgust fascinated me on a level I did not full comprehend. The pursing of his lips, and the revulsion in his eyes intrigued and pleased me. Randall would not have understood this, I was certain, and so I made no effort to broach the topic.

"I have asked that you refer to me as Meadow, now, Randall..." I reminded him, hoping for a glimpse of anger and contempt.

He did not disappoint.

"You may continue to ask, Katherine, but I regret I shall not be able to accommodate your wishes in this matter, regardless of your absurd membership in that wretched organization."

I knew his air was sheer affectation. Randall was of poor stock, and his attendance at Medical College was predicated on the thinnest of confluent family devices. It appeared that snobbery could be a learned contagion. I must insist here that it was his intelligence that placed us in proximity, as he certainly was not particularly lovely to the eye.

"Surely, a future man of medicine cannot be shocked by the exposures of this meager collection?" I asked.

"A patient's nakedness is not immodesty. This 'art' is simply hedonistic shamelessness. I am shocked that seem unable to grasp the difference."

I gazed impertinently at a full-sized male nude study in marble, far longer than I should have. "Oh, I am able to grasp all manner of things, though they may be hard. Difficult, I mean."

SHE TRAINED HER GIRLS TO BE THE ARROWS IN HER ENEMIES' HEARTS, WHICH WAS GROSS BUT COOL. IN RETURN, THE GIRLS WERE GIVEN PRETTY MUCH ANYTHING THEY WANTED WHICH YOU HAVE TO ADMIT IS THE BEST PART. CARS, TOO, AND GREAT SNACKS!

PLUS YOU GET TO HANG OUT WITH THE OTHER AGENTS, LIKE THIS GIRL I MET TODAY, NAMED HOPE. SHE HIT ME IN THE FACE REALLY HARD AND PULLED MY HAIR. I CAN'T TELL IF SHE LIKES ME. I'M SORT OF AVOIDING HER, TO BE FRANK.

BUT IT'LL ALL BE WORTH IT, CAUSE IT'S LIKE THE SORORITY PLEDGE SAYS:

YOU WILL COME TO UNDERSTANDING THROUGH FORGETFULNESS, AND IN FORGETTING, YOUR LONELINESS WILL BE BRIEF. ONCE GONE, IT WILL NEVER RETURN.

YOU WILL WANT FOR NOTHING. NO WHIM SHALL GO UNEXAMINED, NO WISH SHALL GO UNFULFILLED.

THAT'S FOR ME, ALL RIGHT!   WOO, WOO, CHARITY RULES!

"Katherine, I'm reduced to begging. I'll not have my future bride concert with these...these 'artists,' with their diseased appetites. They seek not to uplift, but to degrade the human spirit, and while they may be powerfully told, they are too painful of a kind."

"Is that all you see here, Randall?" I asked, patiently.

He reddened. "They have thrown morality in the rubbish and asked the public to pay to watch. I find I am incapable of further expressing my distaste."

"The Royal Academy is full of nudes, I'm told. I shudder at the scandal." I sighed, more for his benefit than my own. "Randall, would you kiss me, this very moment? Would you lay your hands on me, in this very gallery, with strangers watching?"

"I will not, and for the sake of all decency, will you avert your gaze from that region of the statue?"

"I'm sorry. A very little thing may distract me, I confess. I am like the girl in the painting, watching a tortoise, I turned more fully towards him. Randall, tell me of your work, please. You know how I enjoy hearing of your work."

He lit up at that, as all men do. It is perhaps instinctual that they chuff themselves and the 'importance' of their pitiful efforts. "You needn't worry about our future," he replied, enthusiastically. "I am making fantastic progress, in point of fact. My surgical studies will change the practice of medicine throughout the world, doubtless. It is not boastful to say that my technique for relieving pressure on the brain will save..."

"Forgive me, but would these techniques qualify as works of genius, Randall?"

"By any standard, Katherine."

"Pity," I sighed, but this time, my pained expression was sincere, indeed.

Later that night I killed him with a garrote as he lay sleeping.

HALF B! (YAY!)

I'LL ADMIT THAT I MIGHT NOT UNDERSTAND EVERYTHING OUR SORORITY DOES. I ASKED MOTHER ONCE TO EXPLAIN IT TO ME, BUT WHEN I STARTED TO NOD OFF, SHE JUST SMILED AND BROUGHT THIS HOT CHOCOLATE WITH CINNAMON IN IT. I SPILLED A BUNCH ON THE CARPET BECAUSE I FORGOT IT WAS HOT, BUT SHE DIDN'T ACT MAD AT ALL. I LOVE HER A LOT ALREADY. THE POINT IS, SOMEONE THAT NICE MUST BE SMART. BUT NOT TOO SMART.

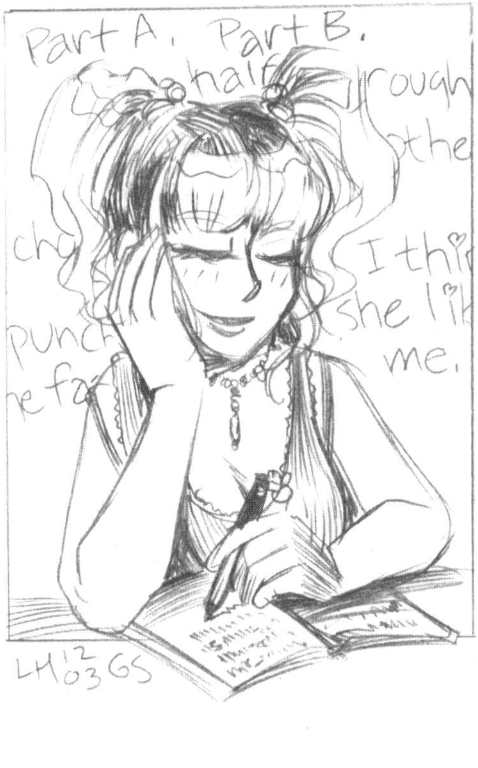
Part A. Part B.
half
me.
LH 12 03 GS

BECAUSE ONE THING I DO AGREE WITH IS THAT SMART PEOPLE ARE A BIG PAIN IN THE ASS NO MATTER HOW YOU SLICE IT. THE PAIN, I MEAN, NOT THE ASS.

SO FUCK 'EM. SERVES 'EM RIGHT FOR BEING SO SNOOTY. THEY'RE SNOOTY IN THE BOOTIE.

WHY DO I WANT TO BE AN ARROW AGENT, A SORORITY PRINCESS?

BECAUSE I THINK I CAN MAKE A REAL DIFFERENCE IN THE WORLD. THIS MAY SOUND STUPID, BUT I WANT TO LEAVE SOME-THING BEHIND, YOU KNOW?

I HAVE TO STOP NOW. I'M SUPPOSED TO GO TRAIN WITH THIS PRINCESS NAMED FAITH. IT SHOULD BE FUN.

SHE SEEMS REAL NICE.

KILLER Princesses

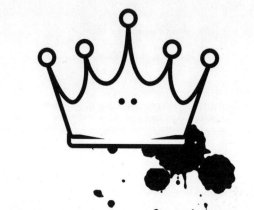

The Authors on Themselves

LEA HERNANDEZ BY GAIL SIMONE

DOG-HUMPER SUPREME

ONE OF THE GREAT THINGS ABOUT LEA IS THAT SHE HAS TEN GREAT IDEAS A MINUTE. UNFORTUNATELY, SHE TRIES TO TELL YOU ALL TEN AT THE SAME TIME, WHICH CAN BE A BIT CONFUSING FOR THOSE WHO ENJOY COHERENCE.

SHE HAS AWARD NOMINATIONS OUT THE WAZOO, AND I'M SURE, FOR THAT, HER WAZOO IS GRATEFUL. SHE RESIDES IN TEXAS BUT SEEMS TO WANT TO CONTINUE LIVING JUST THE SAME. AND A FEW YEARS AGO, WE ADOPTED EACH OTHER AS SISTERS, SO SHUT UP.

I LOVE LEA'S ART. I LOVE THE WAY SHE DESIGNS CHARACTERS, WITH UNAPOLOGETIC ELEGANCE AND CHARM. I LOVE HOW SHE CAN DELIBERATELY MAKE A BRUTAL ACTION SCENE CUTE. MOSTLY, I LOVE THE WAY SHE DRAWS HANDS.

I LOVE LEA'S WRITING, WHICH IS ALWAYS COMPLEX AND EMOTIONALLY TRUE. HIGHLY RECOMMENDED ARE HER STEAMPUNK GNS, *CATHEDRAL CHILD*, *CLOCKWORK ANGELS*, AND *RUMBLE GIRLS*. LEA ALSO DID THE ART FOR *MARVEL MANGA: PUNISHER*, SOME *TRANSMETROPOLITAN*, *DISNEY ADVENTURES*, AND MANY OTHERS, ALL WITH PERFECT LITTLE HANDS.

AFTER READING SOME WEIRDO COLUMN BY A COMPLETE NUT JOB, SHE ASKED SAID WEIRDO TO CO-CREATE A BOOK WITH HER, AND *KILLER PRINCESSES* WAS BORN, ONE OF THE MOST DEEPLY MESSED-UP COMICS IN YEARS, A FRIEND OF MINE ONCE CALLED IT.

I THINK HE NAILED IT EXACTLY.

LOVE YA, LEA. I DON'T DO HAIR IN SAN DIEGO HOTEL BATHROOMS FOR JUST **ANYONE**, YOU KNOW.

GAIL SIMONE BY LEA HERNANDEZ

DOES NOT HAVE MY PILLOWY BREASTS. I HAVE **WAY** BIGGER BOOBS. I'M SAYING THAT BECAUSE SHE'S GOING TO CALL ME A DOG-HUMPER. AGAIN.SHE KNOWS A LOT ABOUT DOG-HUMPING BECAUSE SHE HAS TO USE A DOGSLED AND TEAM TO GET FROM HER PALACE IN HER TEENSY OREGON KINGDOM TO THE NEAREST WAL-MART.

GAIL STARTED IN COMICS WRITING *SIMPSONS* FOR BONGO. SHE GOT THAT WORK BECAUSE SHE WROTE A COLUMN CALLED "YOU'LL ALL BE SORRY" FOR COMICBOOKRESOURCES.COM. (INCIDENTALLY, ONLY GAIL AND LISA JONTE CAN WRITE SATIRE IN VERSE THAT SCANS CORRECTLY, SO THE REST OF YOU DOING IT CAN JUST FUCKING STOP PUNISHING US WITH YOUR LUMPEN RHYMES NOW.) THIS COLUMN WAS SO FUNNY SOMEONE READING IT ON THEIR PALM LAUGHED SO HARD THEY DROPPED THEIR PALM IN THE POTTY. YABS GOT HER A LOT OF JOB OFFERS, INCLUDING FROM ME, ASKING IF SHE'D MAKE A FUNNY COMIC WITH ME FOR ONI PRESS. SHE SAID YES, WHICH MADE ME HAPPY.

WE DECIDED TO CALL IT *KILLER PRINCESSES*, IN MEMORY OF ALL THE EVIL AND MEAN BEAUTIFUL GIRLS WE KNEW IN HIGH SCHOOL. THERE IS NO PRODUCTION ART FROM *KP* BECAUSE GAIL WROTE IT SO GREAT I JUST DREW STRAIGHT FROM SCRIPTS, KNOWING EXACTLY WHAT EVERYTHING LOOKED LIKE.

GAIL ALSO STARTED WORKING FOR MARVEL, WRITING A BOOK THAT WAS ALMOST TITS-UP, *DEADPOOL*. SHE AND UDON PEOPLE MADE IT GREAT. *DEADPOOL* TURNED INTO *AGENT X*, AND GAIL AND UDON MADE THAT GREAT, TOO. ALSO AT MARVEL, SHE CREATED *GUZ BEEZER*, WHICH IS A COMIC FOR EVERY SINGLE ONE OF US WHO, AS A KID, TIED A TOWEL AROUND THEIR NECK AND JUMPED OFF THE ROOF. GAIL THEN WENT TO WORK FOR DC COMICS, TAKING OVER *BIRDS OF PREY*. LIKE *DEADAGENTXPOOL*, THE SALES ON BIRDS WENT UP WHEN GAIL TOOK OVER. THEN SHE GOT FREAKIN' *JLA*, TOO!

Other great books available from Oni Press:

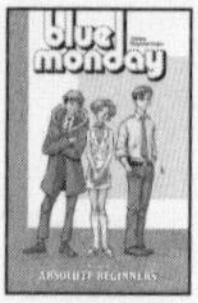
blue monday
ABSOLUTE BEGINNERS

BLUE MONDAY™, VOLUME 1: THE KIDS ARE ALRIGHT
by Chynna Clugston-Major
136 pages
black-and-white interiors
$10.95 US
ISBN 1-929998-62-7

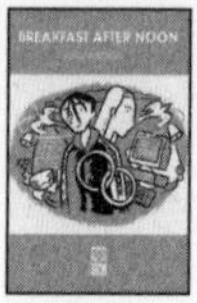
BREAKFAST AFTER NOON

BREAKFAST AFTER NOON™
by Andi Watson
208 pages
black-and-white interiors
$19.95 US
ISBN 1-929998-14-7

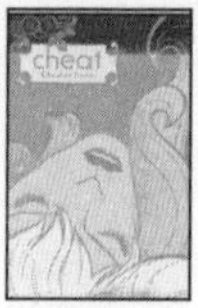
cheat

CHEAT™
by Christine Norrie
72 pages
black-and-white interiors
$5.95 US
ISBN 1-929998-47-3

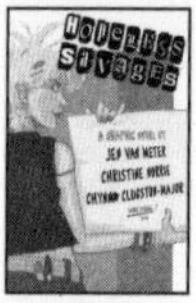
HOPELESS SAVAGES
JEN VAN METER
CHRISTINE NORRIE
CHYNNA CLUGSTON-MAJOR

HOPELESS SAVAGES™, VOLUME 1
by Jen Van Meter, Christine Norrie, & Chynna Clugston-Major
136 pages
black-and-white interiors
$11.95 US
ISBN 1-929998-60-0

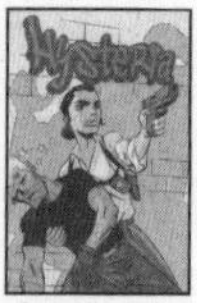
hysteria

HYSTERIA™
by Mike Hawthorne
104 pages
black-and-white interiors
$9.95 US
ISBN 1-929998-90-2

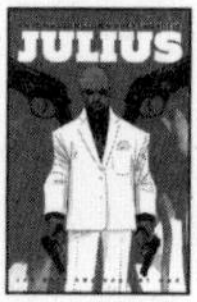
JULIUS

JULIUS™
by Antony Johnston & Brett Weldele
160 pages
black-and-white interiors
$14.95 US
ISBN 1-929998-80-5

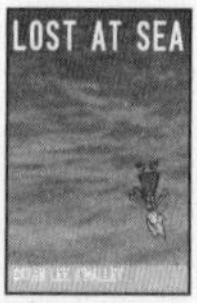
LOST AT SEA
BRYAN LEE O'MALLEY

LOST AT SEA™
by Bryan Lee O'Malley
168 pages
black-and-white interiors
$11.95 US
ISBN 1-929998-71-6

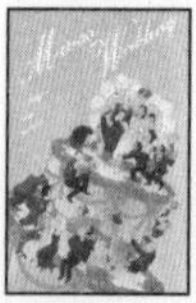

MARIA'S WEDDING™
by Nunzio DeFilippis, Christina Weir, & Jose Garibaldi
88 pages
black-and-white interiors
$10.95 US
ISBN 1-929998-57-0

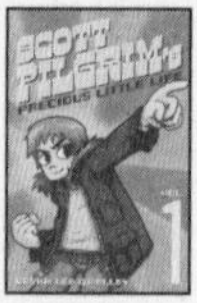
SCOTT PILGRIM'S
PRECIOUS LITTLE LIFE
1

SCOTT PILGRIM™, VOL. 1: SCOTT PILRGIM'S PRECIOUS LITTLE LIFE
by Bryan Lee O'Malley
168 pages
black-and-white interiors
$11.95 US
ISBN 1-932664-08-4

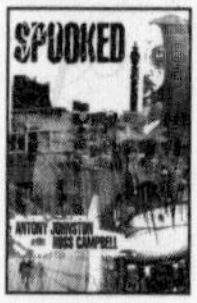
SPOOKED
ANTONY JOHNSTON
ROSS CAMPBELL

SPOOKED™ VOL. 1: THE TRANSFER STUDENT
by Antony Johnston & Ross Campbell
160 pages
black-and-white interiors
$14.95 US
ISBN 1-929998-79-1

AVAILABLE AT FINER COMICS SHOPS EVERYWHERE. FOR A COMICS STORE NEAR YOU, CALL 1-888-COMIC-BOOK OR VISIT WWW.THE-MASTER-LIST.COM.
FOR ADDITIONAL ONI PRESS BOOKS AND INFORMATION VISIT WWW.ONIPRESS.COM.